The end of the 20th century was marked by the spectacular whittling away of the milestones gained by the left in the decades earlier. The triumphant neoliberalism was not content to lay to waste the policies and institutions built from our collective struggles; it went further and smashed the bonds of human connection within the left, and battered us with the weapon of isolation. Through the beauty of words, music and colors, the contributors to this volume are reaching out to comfort us and tell us that we are not alone. Their creativity and reflection remind us that to admit defeat, is an act of courage, and to admit our loneliness, invites comfort. I invite readers to partake of this gift of beauty, care and solidarity which the contributors have generously shared with us.

– **Wandia Njoya**, scholar and public intellectual, Kenya

The contemporary left talks of solidarity, but all too often parcels itself out into bubbles and cliques, communicating in caricatures or simply not communicating at all. The effect of this is everywhere obvious – a deep disconnection. These writings against loneliness register that lack, and show some of the ways we can transcend it, together.

– **Owen Hatherley**, writer and editor

Left Alone offers extraordinary ways to reflect on the meaning of loneliness. As illuminated by the book's contributors, loneliness evokes the political possibility of thinking ahead in time and fighting for a better condition for human beings in the world, even when the world is not prepared to hear our voices.

– **Rosemere Ferreira da Silva**, Titular Professor at the State University of Bahia (Universidade do Estado da Bahia/UNEB) and author of the forthcoming *Black Intellectual Experiences: Fourteen Conversations*

Left Alone:

On Solitude and Loneliness Amid Collective Struggle

Hjalmar Jorge Joffre-Eichhorn
editor

Patrick Anderson
language editor

Daraja Press

KICKASS B O O K S

Published by Daraja Press
https://darajapress.com
Wakefield, Québec, Canada
and KickAss Books

Left Alone: On Solitude and Loneliness amid Collective Struggle

ISBN: 978-1-990263-7-05

Edited by Hjalmar Jorge Joffre-Eichhorn
Language Editing by Patrick Anderson
Cover Design by Johann Salazar
Cover Image by Sula Gordon
Typesetting by Kate McDonnell

Library and Archives Canada Cataloguing in Publication

Title: Left alone : on solitude and loneliness amid collective struggle / edited by
    Hjalmar Jorge Joffre-Eichhorn and Patrick Anderson.
Other titles: Left alone (2023)
Names: Joffre-Eichhorn, Hjalmar Jorge, 1977- editor. | Anderson, Patrick, 1970- editor.
Description: Includes bibliographical references.
Identifiers: Canadiana 20230169538 | ISBN 9781990263705 (softcover)
Subjects: LCSH: Political activists—Mental health. | LCSH: Political participation—
    Psychological aspects. | LCSH: Social justice—Psychological aspects. | LCSH:
    Political participation. | LCSH: Social justice. | LCSH: Loneliness.
Classification: LCC JF799 .L44 2023 | DDC 323/.042—dc23

Lena Grace Anyuolo – **alejandra** ciriza – **Richard** Gilman-Opalsky
Nina Bagdasarova – **İsmail** Beşikçi – **Sevgi** Doğan – **James** Martel
Jane Anna Gordon – **Derefe** Kimarley Chevannes
Lena Stoehrfaktor – **Georgy** Mamedov – **Giulia** Longoni – **Leo** Zeilig
Hjalmar Jorge Joffre-Eichhorn (ed.) – **Patrick** Anderson (language ed.)
Johann Salazar (visual ed.) – **Sula** Gordon – **Tate** Quesada
Mohira Suyarkulova – **Marcello** Sessa – **Meghan** Markin
Kimberly Chiimba – **Daria** Davitti – **Anastasiya** Kotova

The being alone is better. That is what one has to learn ultimately.
It really is better to be alone; it is horrible – but it is better.

– Lorraine Hansberry

Whatever else we were or were not as Communists, we were not
lonely. This disease that's slowly killing off everybody today,
that's killing *me*, this disease was unknown to us as Communists.

– Selma Gardinsky

You go off between two goddesses, they reassure you, they lead you
away, consoling you: solitude, friendship.

– Victor Serge

CONTENTS

Prologue 1:
Spelling Out Left Loneliness

Hjalmar Jorge Joffre-Eichhorn

Left Loneliness
Easing the Pain
Freeing the Mind
Tempering the Self

Left Loneliness
Oppressing the Soul
Negating Joy
Eliminating Hope
Losing Control
Injuring Potential
Numbing Belief
Eroding Self-Worth
Stifling Enthusiasm
Sapping Power

•

Left Loneliness
Erasing Trust
Fracturing Comradeship
Tarnishing Dreams

Left Loneliness
Organising Exhaustion
Nourishing Desire
Encouraging Solidarity
Liberating Action
Incubating Community
Nudging Resolve
Energising Will
Surmounting Impotence
Sparking Revolution

•

Ease, Erase
Free, Fracture
Toughen, Tarnish

Loneliness
Oppress, Organise
Negate, Nourish
Eliminate, Encourage
Lose, Liberate
Injure, Incubate
Numb, Nudge
Erode, Encourage
Stifle, Surmount
Sap, Spark

•

Left
Alone and Together
Alone Together[1]

1 *Merci/спасибо*, Victor Serge, who uses the expression "*seuls ensemble*/alone together" in his 1947 French-language poem "*Mains*/Hands." See Victor Serge (2017), *A Blaze in the Desert* (translated and edited by James Brook. Afterword by Richard Greeman). Oakland: PM Press.

Prologue 2:
An Etymological Uprising

Patrick Anderson

Alone
A word derived from 'all' and 'one'

Solitude
from *'solus'*
and ultimately from 'self'

The one in relation to all
the self in relation to world
the self in relation to other selves

The awful, paradoxical aloneness one can feel
when striving to create a world that

remembers

that we are all one

every 'living' and 'non-living' thing
(believe me, a rock is alive, pulsing with life in fact, with the lived
memory of ages)
constructed from the same universal molecules

Isn't that
on a 'soul' level at least
(and here we can wonder at the homophony of sole and soul)
what the Left project is really about?
A project that has as its starting point
a view of the world
as something we experience, receive, have, hold, share in common?

But we live (apparently)
in a world predicated on
division
I versus you
we versus them
we humans versus everything else

A division held so sacred
that there is (apparently)
no cruelty or stupidity not condoned in its name

A division that thrives on
loneliness
that revels in
despair
as the very fuels that feed it

.

But
what if... we could cheat the system?
what if... we could be Left Alone together?

Could we forge from our (in-common) aloneness
from our hopeless desire to make a world in which no-one is ever
truly alone

a force

capable of subsuming division
of grasping and transcending the hand that created and creates it?

Might this book
be a first step toward such a surreptitious uprising
(of soul soles)?

Artist: Sula Gordon

Introduction:
Alone Together – The Singing Veins of Left Loneliness

Hjalmar Jorge Joffre-Eichhorn

0. About this book: Left Loneliness born in Struggle

The zero point of this book is my ongoing battle with Left Loneliness and my utter incapacity to deal with it in a way that I can continue to contribute my skills, passions and, yes, (more than) occasional flaws, to our larger, collective Left struggles against all forms of oppression, and for the creation of new, radically better worlds for us to live in, enjoy each other's company, and whenever needed, relish the occasional period of sweet solitude and idle isolation. No kidding, I am just so flat-out exhausted, overwhelmed, hopeless and discouraged right now, so disillusioned and unhappy – and no matter how I try to mend it, it's just not getting any better. No snapping out of it. Fuck me.

What are we hoping for? What are we waiting for? We're crazy with resignation!
Our resignation is driving us crazy! Impossible to live this way.
I tell you it's impossible, comrades!
Impossible to die this way, unless they kill us.
Nothing to expect, except from ourselves.[1]

Impossible to live this way indeed. Dismal, disgusting and more than a little sickening. I am breathing defeat and resignation, have been for many years now, and it is literally driving me crazy. All the while, THEY continue to kill us. Heartbreakdown. No life force left, only a great deal of anger and hatred for the world. I just don't know what to do anymore. And yet, giving up is a not an option. What is to be done? And perhaps more importantly, why should anybody care? Good question. I guess I am going with Richard Wright here: "If you possess enough courage to speak out what you are, you will find that you are not alone."[2] Nothing to expect, except from ourselves. Condemned to wager on each other and continue to resist. "As we have always done."[3] So here is my speaking out: I am left and I am lonely, and this book is another attempt at engaging with this loneliness, this time round in comradely company.

1 Serge 2014: 179.
2 Wright in Crossman 1963: 118.
3 See Simpson 2017.

Says feminist writer Sara Ahmed: "Loneliness might be what we are threatened with if we persist in being or doing what we are being or doing."[4] In this sense, Left Loneliness is neither a metaphor nor a secondary contradiction, and definitely not some type of petty-bourgeois 'personalism.' No more (neo-)Stalinist character assassination, please. Rather, it is a loneliness born in and of struggle[5] and as such it may just be one of the rank-and-file psycho-affective elements that both shapes and results from our myriad, intersecting, unremitting, yet always fragile and potentially shattering political attempts to revolutionise our inner and outer worlds. Recognising its (growing?) existence in our everyday left subjectivities, this book argues that Left Loneliness and related states of solitude, isolation and alienation, among others, have both debilitating and productive (epistemic) dimensions, an "inner fecundity,"[6] with very concrete psycho-somatic repercussions for Left Mental and Physical Health and hence our capacity to persist, "to organize a duration,"[7] and to build on "being or doing what we are being or doing."

Given that this continuing and deepening of our multiple ongoing struggles for liberation will depend heavily on our constant ability to (re-)create, sustain and care for both our individual selves and the communities that we are a part of and to which we are accountable, the aim of Left Alone is to contribute to the strengthening of these personal collectivities in action in-against-and-beyond capitalism, colonialism and heteropatriarchy by inviting you, comrade-readers, into what we hope will be a stimulating and enabling engagement with experiences of Left Loneliness from Argentina, Kenya, Kyrgyzstan, Kurdistan/Turkey, Jamaica, Italy, Australia, the UK, Germany and the USA. No rest for the weary.

–1. Left Loneliness: The End of Comradeship is the End of the World

Says our *Genossin* Rosa Luxemburg, "The most revolutionary act is and will always be to say the truth out loud," or, to say what is, in the original German. She also said: "Oh how I dread meeting people. I wish I lived among animals."[8] Well, as touched on above, on a personal-

4 Ahmed 2017: 82.
5 See Santos 2018 for his theorisation of "knowledge born in struggle."
6 Benjamin 1994: 527.
7 See Fernández-Savater 2022 (my translation).
8 Luxemburg 1982: 85 (my translation).

political level the truth is that I have been feeling pretty damaged and depleted lately, lately meaning the past 1,2,3,4,5,6,7 years, a fucking long time, I tell you. Not pretty. Not good for the morale at all. Some of you will know what I am talking about. And yes, as much as it hurts me to admit it, one outcome of this rather nasty, still ongoing period of solitary left zombification – this disgusting, seemingly never-ending dialectical process of falling apart every day only to be reborn shortly after in an even more monstrous version of yourself – has indeed been that I have come to increasingly dread meeting people, even friends and comrades, though I have not yet felt a strong desire to live among animals. As such, Left Loneliness could be described as a kind of exhaustion of (being in the company of) others, or rather of one's relation to others, or perhaps of oneself in relation to others, or perhaps just of oneself, or all of the above, among many other possible forms of engaged dis-engagement.

In the same vein, I also wanna say out loud that I am struggling mightily with what Doris Lessing in her 1962 *The Golden Notebook* described as "the thinning of language against the density of our experience."[9] Fuck yeah. Echoing Pat Parker in a letter to Audre Lorde, "I feel so betrayed by words right now; there is nothing I can say that says what I feel."[10] In this regard, Left Loneliness is a dense physical silence that betrays one's very capacity to be in verbal communion with others. It's a type of neural and somatic fatigue with and alienation from language itself, to make sense of things – for oneself and for others, especially for others. It literally hurts to speak, and as a result not speaking becomes a form of self-protection, to avoid yet another 'misunderstanding,' all the while deepening the abyss inside and between yourself and everyone around you. A dirty vicious cycle. Clearly, and thanks to the work of Bifo Berardi and others, we know that one reason for this self-gagging is semiocapitalism's constant exploitation of mental energy, "the exploitation of the soul as a productive force," in the form of ever more precarious cognitive labour.[11] One is so tired of non-stop producing meaning for the (financial) benefit of others, one stops trusting one's very own means of production – heart, mind and body – to give expression to the inevitable implosion in face of this merciless onslaught. Or in the words of bell hooks,

9 Lessing 1981: 302.
10 Enszer 2018: 104.
11 Berardi 2014: 160.

Rest in Power: "Isolation and loneliness are central causes of depression and despair. Yet they are the outcome of life in a culture where things matter more than people."[12]

Then again, and here I am indebted to Elizabeth McKenzie's introduction to Guido Morselli's 1967 novel *The Communist*, a perhaps even more distressing reason for this thinning of language may have to do with the sobering possibility that – contrary to our ever solidaristic self-image – our very own everyday left beliefs, convictions, ideals and actions, that is to say, our left projects as such, give us no language with which to understand and articulate our loneliness,[13] as well as other related "potentially damaging implications of political struggles,"[14] as Larne Abse Gogarty and Hannah Proctor so aptly called it. Asks the latter in another text on the Left and mental illness:

> If orthodox Marxism-Leninism envisioned the ideal revolutionary vanguard as organized, disciplined and committed, marching in step from spontaneity to consciousness, then how to deal with people who experienced reality as bewildering or fragmentary, who broke down or cracked up, who hallucinated or dissociated, who were mistrustful, exhausted, frenzied or withdrawn?[15]

From all I know the number of lefties openly embracing "orthodox Marxism-Leninism" has dwindled considerably since the end of the USSR, but growing commitment to the importance of "affect, emotional labor, and relational organizing"[16] inside left activism notwithstanding, the question of how we deal with those of us struggling inside the struggle, up to the point of withering away and comradely collapse, remains as pertinent as ever. Here I fully back Gogarty and Proctor's call to urgently analyse "marginalised emotional histories, too often dismissed as negligible or considered as phenomena outside the realm of political struggle proper."[17]

Now this is where it gets really uncomfortable and complicated, because apart from finally giving long overdue attention to the variety of really existing individual and collective psycho-affective

---

12 hooks 2001: 105.
13 See McKenzie in Morselli 2017: vii-xv.
14 See Gogarty & Proctor 2019.
15 Proctor 2016: 36.
16 See Battistoni 2020.
17 See Gogarty & Proctor 2019.

damages resulting from our everyday struggles against oppression, Left Loneliness being one of them, another part of this analysis should naturally include determining who is doing the marginalising and dismissing, and surely the one place to look for an answer is in our very own left communities of fellow strugglers, and our seemingly quite well-developed capacity for wilful ignorance and sometimes straight-out abuse in response to our comrade's alleged acts of 'whining' or 'self-pity.' In comes Sara Ahmed once more: "To be heard as complaining is not to be heard."[18] Does this resonate with anyone? Ouch. I thought so. Why are we doing this to each other? It's heart-blowing.

> The first time the community failed you,
> what did you tell yourself to get up the next morning?[19]

Thanks for asking, Eric. The response is simple: I was in total shock and didn't want to believe it. Call me an idealist, but I was sure that no matter what, I could always rely on 'my people.' So when this turned out not be the case, not just once, but several times, something really broke inside of me, and I haven't been able to put the pieces back together. It was a type of death; and I can't stop mourning. No bitterness here, it's just that my trust in others has been severely undermined. One result: Left Disillusionment-cum-Loneliness, to the point of what Luxemburg only half-jokingly called "opting out of humanity."[20] Now, let me be as precise as possible here. My problem is not actually with the fact that as a 'community' we sometimes fail one another, that we don't always manage to practise what we preach – care, solidarity, etc. – and/or that in the contradictory reality of our everyday struggles we may occasionally feel obliged to prioritise having our own backs over those of our comrades. Never believed in left angelhood. Shit happens and it's ok, let's have a drink and move on. What is not ok, what really produces this visceral need to withdraw up to the point of breaking ties, to execute the "leftist snap,"[21] with what just a minute ago seemed to be a real, rock-solid collective, is all the left bullshit and self-left-eousness in regard to our fuck-ups, i.e. our predilection to not only not hold ourselves accountable, but to deny, excuse, minimise, rationalise,

....

18 Ahmed 2021: 1.
19 Hadikwa Mwaluko 2019: 109.
20 Luxemburg 1987: 7 (my translation).
21 I am inspired here by what Sara Ahmed calls the "Feminist Snap": "What I call feminist snap is about how we collectively acquire tendencies that can allow us to break ties that are damaging as well as to invest in new possibilities" (Ahmed 2017: 162).

condescend or nowadays, just ghost or block each other. It's just so dispiriting and unnecessary. What the fuck? We can and must do better than this, otherwise the only thing we will ever successfully abolish are our own chances of winning. More kaya, less running away.

As Jodi Dean reminds us in a reading of Lessing's aforementioned novel:

> The end of comradeship is the end of the world: non-meaning, incoherence, madness, and the pointless, disorienting, insistence on the I. [...] Worries about the end foreclose possibilities of beginning. Relationships end. Failures happen. But failure is nothing to fear – it's something to learn from, a next step. We lose our comrades. The fact of an end should not forestall beginning.[22]

In dialectical contrast to Dean's encouraging call for an eternal wager on comradeship, Vivian Gornick, in her biography of Elizabeth Cady Stanton and her description of the latter's struggles with loneliness as part of the early women's rights movement in the United States, warns us:

> [Stanton] had always known that the bonds of human connection are fragile, subject to time, circumstance, and the mystery of slowly altering sympathies, but she had never before doubted that connection was the norm; it represented a defining trait: the need for intimacy [...] Now, suddenly, it flashed on her that loneliness was the norm. Connection was an ideal; the exception, not the rule, in the human condition.[23]

Listening to Jodi and Vivian from inside my lonely rabbit hole, both of their sentences ring true – one in the head, the other in the heart – though at the time of writing, I cannot say for certain which one goes with which. What I do know is that faith in the possibility of concrete collectivity to take on the world is not a type of false consciousness and that, historically, we on the political left have been very reluctant to accept any so-called "human condition" that further cements the violent status quo. We have also been pretty good at abusing, policing and excommunicating each other,[24] thereby, on occasion, making the

22 Dean 2019: 155.
23 Gornick 2005: 6.
24 See Fischer 2013.

retreat into solitude or even loneliness the potentially healthier option to continue the struggle...

+1. We are Legion – Toward Tidalectical Left Choralities

In the absence of each other, we need each other. Sometimes near, sometimes far, but always each other. Despite ourselves and because of ourselves. No matter what. Withness and withoutness necessarily go together. Comradery and loneliness nourish and condition one another, and as such, they are tidalectical, marked by the ebbs and flows of the really existing desires, demands and deflations of collective struggle waged by individuals, with our multiplicity of quality qualities and despairing defects.[25] Let's not take each other for granted. Without each and every one of us, our communities and struggles are incomplete,[26] our chances of creating beautiful worlds without oppression much diminished. In this sense, Left Loneliness and what we do with it dialogues deeply with what Mecca Jamilah Sullivan has called "battling tenderly with and for community,"[27] though I get the impression that many of us still have a bit of self-tenderising to do before/while continuing the battle. I know I do, and it's fucking hard. This calls to mind Che Guevara's unforgettable *"hay que endurecerse, pero sin perder la ternura jamás!"* ("one has to grow hard but without ever losing tenderness!"). Given the fucked-upness of the world and the psychosomatic consequences involved in constantly trying to revolutionise it, alone and together, gradually growing hard towards ourselves and others may just be one of the ultimate default options available to us when growing despair beats tired hope, in turn leading to new, arguably even more devastating bouts of loneliness, impotence and heartbreakdown, among so many other related madnesses. Then again, "what's wrong with living emotionally from hand-to-mouth,"[28] with being "slightly mad out of sheer exhaustion,"[29] with (hopefully just) temporarily having to say out loud *I can't do it anymore*, or *I am breaking down*, or *I am sad, discouraged and lonely and can't seem to find the strength to re-connect with myself and with others?*

25 With thanks and respect to Caribbean poet and scholar Kamau Brathwaite (1930-2020), whose genius for words gave birth to the expression 'tidalectics,' though I am giving it a different use in the context of this book. For more on the tidalectics of Left Loneliness and comradeship, see Joffre-Eichhorn 2021: 1-7.
26 My 'spasibo' goes out to Soviet writer Andrei Platonov whose 1940 short story "The Engine Driver's Wife" inspired this particular sentence.
27 Sullivan in Enszer 2018: 23.
28 Lessing 1981: 10.
29 Ibid: 92.

There is of course nothing wrong whatsoever with any of these lived, solitary experiences, nothing wrong with those of us who go through them, except that they fucking hurt and that we gotta make sure that none of them leave us and our personal-political commitments and besieged psychic economies permanently weakened.

Needless to say, this is not in any way a call for a type of Leninist toughening up, left self-disciplining and -optimisation and/or neoliberal self-care, though I do continue to subscribe to Audre Lorde's 1980s womanist version of the latter: "Caring for myself is not self-indulgence, it is self-preservation, and that is an act of political warfare."[30] Rather, in the first instance this may have something to do with learning how to caringly "break down into each other,"[31] with quite literally having each other's backs, in ways that allow for another day of life, another day of struggle to be/come possible again, or in the words of Lorraine Hansberry, "to become – an insurgent again! [...] throwing [ourselves] back into the movement."[32] It may also be about individually and collectively developing ways not just of coping, though cope we must, but of relating in novel, comradely manners to our own recurring left fragilities and shatterings. One, because they are real and in a sense here to stay and must therefore be taken seriously, and two, because taking them seriously, honouring them for what they are – i.e. but one (important) aspect of the struggle for justice we have committed ourselves to wage – we are likely to discover in them much-needed productive, that is, enabling psycho-epistemic use-value capable of informing present and future collective actions. Citing and re-applying Sara Ahmed once more, "the task is to stay with the difficulty, to keep exploring and exposing [it],"[33] and who knows, if and when we do this, I am positive, something very bittersweet-cum-powerful may just come out of it, especially when done in "good company."[34]

It is hence this good company, this "strange and powerful plural-singular,"[35] based on the "forgotten reserves of warmth stored up for centuries,"[36] that we are asked to create, (at times) let go of and then re-create time and again, "despite all," as our forever

30 See Lorde 1988.
31 Lessing 1981: vii.
32 Hansberry 2011: 183 & 257.
33 Ahmed 2017: 12.
34 Ibid: 17.
35 See Connor 2015.
36 For a version of this sentence, see Platonov 1978: 199.

comrade-teachers Rosa Luxemburg and Karl Liebknecht, themselves often "lone voice[s] in the wilderness,"[37] would say. And yes, this is likely going to be a very ambivalent, emotionally draining process of what Robin D.G. Kelley has recently described as "communing," because willing and wilful romanticisation of "good company" aside, chances are that in this world-building process of "dancing together, singing together, meditating, worshiping and studying together by sharing, by making [ourselves] vulnerable to one another [...],"[38] it is precisely this latter element, this mutual opening up to our profound vulnerabilities, which will lay bare some of our equally profound intersectional differences and needs, and the very multiplicity of left lonelinesses that materialise from these, thus making this exercise in communing a very delicate matter indeed. Our differences do matter. And so do our similarities. In this sense, I feel that Audre Lorde speaks a beautiful truth when, in a depiction of her relationship with her then-partner Muriel, she affirms that "[f]or every secret hurt of Muriel's, there was one of mine to match, and the similarities of our lonelinesses, as well as of our dreams, convinced us that we were made for each other."[39]

Taking Lorde's truth-telling beyond the interpersonal level, I cannot be sure that a collective being made for each other is possible or even always desirable, let alone sustainable in time and space, but, clearly, some form of convincing matching of hurts, lonelinesses and dreams will have to happen if we are to finally abolish the deeply traumatising, totally unacceptable, fucking unbearable everyday capitalist, colonial-racist, ableist and heteropatriarchal, civilisational status quo. It is about time.

> Why should it be my loneliness,
> Why should it be my song,
> Why should it be my dream deferred overlong?
> (Langston Hughes)[40]

No doubt, for way too many of us the realisation of our dreams, even in the tiniest of doses, the most fleeting of moments, has been one (life-) long, often inter-generational journey of (deadly) deferral, in spite of our combined superhuman-like efforts to dance and sing and [... please choose your own verb] them into being. One result of this is that "most

37 Brie & Schütrumpf 2021: 231.
38 Kelley in Maynard & Simpson 2022: 269.
39 Lorde 1993: 195.
40 Hughes 1995: 396.

of us are at the limit of our emotional capacity to struggle."[41] Or in fact long beyond, but somehow still putting on a brave face, a forced smile and of course miraculously managing to get up every damn day, making things happen – especially for others, we are givers – because if not, well, if not, then, "anticipating the butcher,"[42] literally "opting out" of life may just be all that's left for a left with nothing left to give.[43] That, or we self-hermitise, we "crawl even more into [our] solitary shell[s],"[44] as Compagno Gramsci felt forced to do on so many occasions, including before he was put away for good by the fascists. As Belén Gopegui asks in her gut-wrenching novel *Existiríamos el Mar:* "[There are] so many lonely people who from their corners keep saying 'I can't do it anymore,' but never at the same time, why can't we all say it at the same time?"[45]

I hear you, Belén, I hear you. Adrienne Rich calls it the "hermit's scream"[46] and "the dream of a common language":

> No one who survives to speak
> new language has avoided this:
> the cutting-away of an old force that held her
> rooted to an old ground
> the pitch of utter loneliness
> where she herself and all creation
> seem equally dispersed, weightless, her being a cry
> to which no echo comes[47]

The hermit's scream is "Love should be put into action!" and Rich asks for "it to become a general cry," because we are legion.[48] That's right. We gotta remember this. We are legion. We are fucking legion, everyone. Even if we are at times fragmented and disconnected and tired and depressed and lonely, colonising our little corners, our muchneeded sanctuaries, which we shall have to find ways to connect with each other so that our echoes can finally reach.

41 Simpson 2017: 246.
42 After the 1940 suicide of Walter Benjamin, Bertolt Brecht wrote: "I am told that you raised your hand against yourself. Anticipating the butcher. After eight years of exile, observing the rise of the enemy. Then at last, brought up against an impassable frontier, you passed, they say, a passable one [...]" (See Brecht 2015).
43 For a recent engagement with personal-political suicides in the former USSR, see Fitzpatrick's 2011 insightful review of Kenneth Pinnow's *Lost to the Collective: Suicide and the Promise of Soviet Socialism, 1921-29.*
44 Gramsci 1979: 194.
45 Gopegui 2021: 130 (my translation).
46 See Rich 1993: 54-71.
47 Fragment from "Transcendental Étude", see Rich 1978.
48 Rich 1993: 57 & 56.

Am I alone, deaf as I am and so far removed from you,
so detached as I am from myself,
am I alone in knowing how alone you are,
I so alone at this moment and reaching out to you
through time?
Or are we alone together
with all those who in the course of time are alone with us,
forming the unique chorus that murmurs in our shared veins, our singing veins?
(Victor Serge)[49]

We are and will always be legion, but in order to be able to keep composing these old ground-breaking screams at the same time, to keep forming the "organic, messy, bottom-up choralit[ies],"[50] composed of unique sonic warriors and their/our revolutionary singing veins (and more), I am asking myself how we can begin to know and understand how alone many of us really are and then reach out to one another, and become alone together so that we can keep up the good fight, "wage love,"[51] wage power, wage ourselves, and change everything...

With this lofty goal in mind – yes, sometimes loneliness can be a lofty place – Left Alone brings together 15 authors and 7 visual artists from across the globe to individually and collectively explore their personal and/or vicariously lived experiences of Left Loneliness, Soledad de Izquierdas or Linke Einsamkeit, from a variety of genres and left political currents: Marxist, Feminist, Anti-/De-Colonial, Anti-Racist, Queer, Anarchist, Post-Soviet, Anti-Ableist... Admittedly, there are some important absences of perspective, but alas it just could not be otherwise in an unfunded, precariously produced publication such as ours. Yet what a beautiful group of amazing people we were able to gather. I am so grateful to everyone who contributed to this hard-fought-for endeavour in what I know were in many cases very difficult life situations indeed. THANK YOU. *La lucha continúa!*

To finish, an imaginary dialogue between Queer Communist Bini Adamczak and Afro-Feminist artist Simone Dede Ayivi: "With whom to share [our] loneliness? At least that."[52] – "So many things can only be endured in community. Many are suffering, but many also find ways to each other. Because the opposite of (being in the) shit is being (in the shit) together."[53]

49 Serge 2017: 131.
50 Engelhardt, Bancroft, Rule & Wang 2022: 76.
51 Kelley in Maynard & Simpson 2022: 266.
52 See Adamczak 2021.
53 See Ayivi 2019 (Translation: P. Anderson).

References

Adamczak, Bini (2021), *Yesterday's Tomorrow: On the Loneliness of Communist Specters and the Reconstruction of the Future*. Cambridge: MIT Press.

Ahmed, Sara (2017), *Living a Feminist Life*. Durham: Duke University Press.

Ahmed, Sara (2021), *Complaint*. Durham: Duke University Press.

Ayivi, Simone Dede (2019), "Zusammen," *in* Fatma Aydemir & Hengameh Yaghoobifarah (eds.) *Eure Heimat ist Unser Albtraum*. Berlin: Ullstein.

Battistoni, Alyssa (2020), "Bad Romance," *Dissent*. Available at: https://www.dissentmagazine.org/article/bad-romance.

bell hooks (2001), *All About Love. New Visions*. New York: Perennial.

Benjamin, Walter (1994), *The Correspondence of Walter Benjamin. 1910-1940*. (Translated by Manfred R. Jacobson & Evelyn M. Jacobson). Chicago: University of Chicago Press.

Berardi, Franco (2014), *And. Phenomenology of the End*. Helsinki: Aalto University.

Brecht, Bertolt (2015), "On the Suicide of the Refugee W.B." *Red Wedge*. Available at https://www.redwedgemagazine.com/online-issue/suicide-wb.

Brie, Michael & Schütrumpf, Jörn (2021), *Rosa Luxemburg: A Revolutionary Marxist at the Limits of Marxism*. Cham: Palgrave Macmillan.

Connor, Stephen (2015), "Choralities." Available at: http://stevenconnor.com/choralities.html.

Crossman, Richard (1963), *The God that Failed*. New York: Harper and Brothers.

Dean, Jodi (2019), "Capitalism is the End of the World," *Meditations*, 33.1-2, 149-158. Available at https://www.mediationsjournal.org/articles/end-of-world.

Engelhardt, Jeffers; Bancroft, Kate; Rule, Alex & Charlotte Wang (2022), "Chorality's Sonic-Social Relationships," *Resonance: The Journal of Sound and Culture*, Vol. 3, Number 1, 76–97. Available at: https://online.ucpress.edu/res/article/3/1/76/122332/Chorality-s-Sonic-Social-Relationships1.

Enszer, Julie R. (ed.) (2018), *Sister Love: The Letters of Audre Lorde and Pat Parker. 1974-1989*. Dover: A Midsummer Nights Press.

Fernández-Savater, Amador (2021), *La Fuerza de los Débiles*. Madrid: Akal.

Fisher, Mark (2013), "Exiting the Vampire Castle," *openDemocracy*. Available at https://www.opendemocracy.net/en/opendemocracyuk/exiting-vampire-castle/.

Fitzpatrick, Sheila (2011), "Deaths at Two O'Clock," *London Review of Books*. Available at https://lrb.co.uk/site/the-paper/v33/n04/sheila-fitzpatrick/deaths-at-two-o-clock.

Gogarty, Larne Abse & Proctor, Hannah (2019), "Communist Feelings," *New Socialist*. Available at: https://newsocialist.org.uk/communist-feelings-lessing-gornick/.

Gopegui, Belén (2021), *Existiríamos el Mar*. Barcelona: Penguin Random House.

Gornick, Vivian (2005), *The Solitude of Self – Thinking about Elizabeth Cady Stanton*. New York: Farrar, Straus and Giroux.

Gramsci, Antonio (1979), *Letters from Prison* (Translated by Lynne Lawner). London: Quartet Books.

Hadikwa Mwaluko, Nick (2019), "A Love Letter to Andre Lancaster," *in* Dale Holmes & Sharon Kivland (eds.) *The Graveside Orations of Carl Einstein*. London: MA BIBLIOTHÈQUE.

Hughes, Langston (1995), *The Collected Poems of Langston Hughes.* New York: Vintage Classics.

Joffre-Eichhorn, Hjalmar Jorge (ed.) (2021), *Post Rosa: Letters against Barbarism.* New York: Rosa Luxemburg Stiftung.

Kelley, Robin D.G. (2022), "An Afterwor(l)d," *in* Robyn Maynard and Leanne Betasamosake Simpson *Rehearsals for Living.* Canada: Alfred A. Knopf, 265-274.

Lessing, Doris (1981), *The Golden Notebook.* New York: Bantam Books.

Lorde, Audre (1988), *A Burst of Light and other Essays.* Ithaca: Firebrand Books.

Lorde, Audre (1993), *Zami. Sister Outsider. Undersong.* New York: Quality Paperbook Club.

Luxemburg, Rosa (1982), *Gesammelte Briefe. Band 3.* Institut für Marxismus-Leninismus beim ZK der SED. Berlin: Dietz Verlag.

Luxemburg, Rosa (1987), *Gesammelte Briefe. Band 5.* Institut für Marxismus-Leninismus beim ZK der SED. Berlin: Dietz Verlag.

McKenzie, Elizabeth (2017), "Introduction," *in* Guido Morselli *The Communist.* New York: New York Review Books.

Platonov, Andrei (1978), *Chevengur* (Translated by Anthony Olcott). Ann Arbor: Ardis.

Proctor, Hannah (2016), "Lost minds Sedgwick, Laing and the Politics of Mental Illness," *Radical Philosophy,* 197, 36-48.

Rich, Adrienne (1978), *The Dream of a Common Language. Poems 1974-1977.* New York: W.W. Norton & Company.

Rich, Adrienne (1993), *What is Found There. Notebooks on Poetry and Politics.* New York: W.W. Norton & Company.

Santos, Boaventura de Sousa (2018), *The End of the Cognitive Empire.* Durham: Duke University Press.

Serge, Victor (2014), *Midnight in the Century* (Translated by Richard Greeman). New York: New York Review Books.

Serge, Victor (2017), *A Blaze in a Desert: Selected Poems* (Translated by James Brook). Oakland: PM Press.

Simpson, Leanne Betasamosake (2017), *As We Have Always Done. Indigenous Freedom Through Radical Resistance.* Minneapolis: University of Minnesota Press.

Sullivan, Mecca Jamilah (2018), "Introduction," *in* Julie R. Enszer (ed.) *Sister Love: The Letters of Audre Lorde and Pat Parker. 1974-1989.* Dover: A Midsummer Nights Press, 11-24.

Artist: Sula Gordon

How the world works

Lena Grace Anyuolo

It's a lonely house in here.
I'm cold, anxious and disillusioned.
I am empty and passionless.
It was better when I had no clue about how the world works.

•

How to talk to my comrades about this?
Because the despair feels more ancient,
it is deep and runs through all that I am.

•

Pill bottles and meditation journals litter my bedroom.
A drag of the reefer and a quick shag keeps the boredom away.
At least with the boredom gone I am less depressed.
Less prone to giving up and taking my life.

•

I wonder why I fought so hard.
Choking on tear gas smoke in hiding from the police
underneath a grocery stand.
In the end the police caught us anyway
and threatened to kill us.

•

I was ready to die that day
if it meant standing up for justice.
Now I'd rather watch reality shows and fornicate.
I don't give a damn which way it goes.
We will all die anyway.

•

Left Alone

I am traumatised by the struggle.
Do you see how I duck when I see my comrades?

•

Lacerations in my stomach like I'd swallowed cut glass.
The pain emanating from my womb
because I cannot believe what I am hearing.
That we are toxic,

•

That we are broken pieces of wood
Alone.

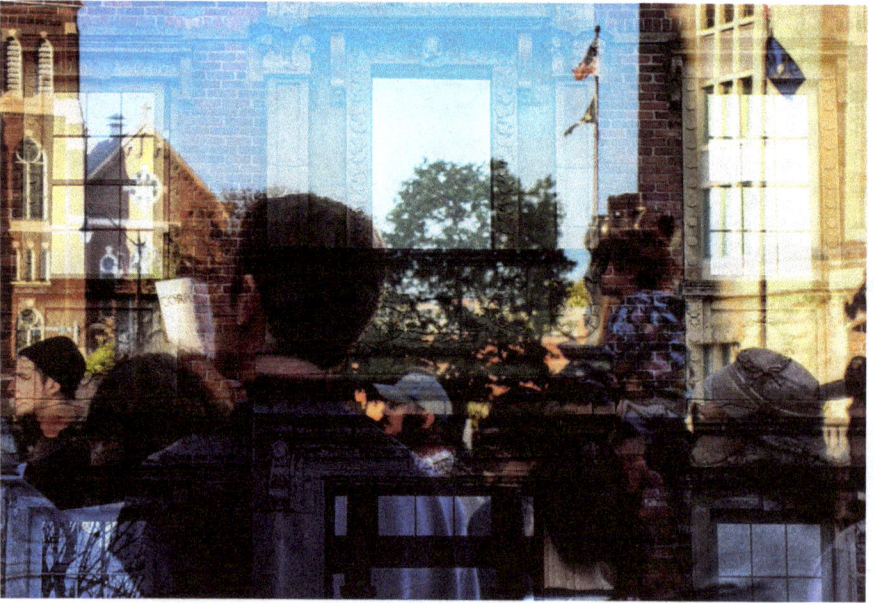

Photos: Richard Gilman-Opalsky / Visual Editing: Johann Salazar

The Practicality of Utopianism: Capitalist and Communist Forms of Life and Loneliness

Richard Gilman-Opalsky

1: Introduction to Forms of Life and Loneliness

Let us consider capitalism and communism as forms of life, and not as is usually the case, as forms of government, or as opposing systems of political economy. Of course, we can also imagine and talk about capitalist and communist logics of governmentality and economy, and these are ultimately always implicated in any discussion of capitalism and communism. However, we do not have to begin with statecraft and modes of production. We may take a different starting position and doing so is necessary if we want to focus on forms of life and experiences of loneliness. That is the overarching aim of the present essay.

I shall argue that we cannot be abolitionists of loneliness. Loneliness cannot be abolished. First, loneliness will have to be defined and distinguished from solitude. Also, loneliness lies within the manifold experiences of a lifetime, and no matter the form of society, it will most certainly recur throughout the course of a human life, often without warning. Still, some forms of loneliness are dangerous. As Hannah Arendt understood with penetrating insight, loneliness can be preyed upon by fascists who offer to bring an end to loneliness in the solidarity of chauvinistic patriotism and nationalist togetherness. But we who prefer the *Gemeinwesen* of anti-fascist internationalism can also be stricken with the pain of loneliness.[1] There is, as David Riesman studied, loneliness inside the crowd, as well as loneliness outside the crowd.[2] The question, then, is to consider different forms of loneliness, and to try to understand what or how forms of loneliness emanate from different forms of life. In this short essay, I can only offer a sketch of an answer, a preliminary theorisation that can hopefully clarify certain problems, as well as key terms and concepts. In so doing, I hope to make a small contribution to our understanding of forms of life and loneliness.

---

1 *Gemeinwesen* is a German word that means community, both that which actually exists and an aspirational community, or communal sensibility. For example, we may juxtapose the existing *Gemeinwesen* to the community we desire. The word and concept were of great concern to German philosophy, most notably, to G.W.F. Hegel and Karl Marx.

2 See Riesman 1961.

To begin, let us define a capitalist form of life. This is one that is more or less governed by capital, which is to say, a life ruled by concerns about money. In capitalist societies, money (which is not itself capital) circulates as a power of acquisition, and most things necessary and useful to life depend upon it. I say "most things" because in a capitalist form of life, not every single aspect of life is governed by money. I studied communist relations in capitalist societies in my book, *The Communism of Love: An Inquiry into the Poverty of Exchange Value* (2020). Despite the existence of non-monetary and even communist social relations inside of capitalism, the basic orientations of a capitalist form of life are acculturated from early childhood education. Early education and upbringing prepare young children for life experiences in a world where what they can or must do will largely be decided by the logic of capital, and they soon learn that most of their life choices will be governed by money. In short, a capitalist form of life is one where what we do with our lives is centrally concerned with or determined by the logic of capital, which organises so much of the world.

Now, a communist form of life is a very different idea. This is a form of life which is more or less governed by a concept of the healthy community, the common *wealth*, or even by the ideal of a commune, a life ruled by an overarching concern about communal life with others. To avoid any misunderstanding, however, in a communist form of life one would also be free to seek solitude and to be alone as often as one wished. The difference is that no one is acculturated or compelled to be alone, or to consider 'competitive individualism' as any kind of virtue. A communist form of life follows a very different logic and organisation than the capitalist form, which can be seen in its attitude toward the acquisition of things that are necessary and useful to life. Necessary and useful things, including care of others, educational opportunities, access to healthcare and well-being, recreational options, mobility, and support for human flourishing are regarded not as commodities, but as features of a decent society available to all. A capitalist declares this 'utopian.' Indeed, that is exactly what it is within the parameters of the capitalist form of life. In a communist form of life, not every aspect of life would be governed by the concept of community; communism is not about having dinner parties or abandoning the peace of solitude. Rather, the basic orientations of a life, which would begin in childhood education and stretch through a lifetime of experiencing the world, would be determined by the logic of common *wealth*, which is to say, by a belief in sharing the common wealth of the world. And so, a communist form of life – what capitalists call utopian, and therefore impossible – is one where what we do with our lives is centrally concerned with or determined by a deep and abiding regard for common sociality.

It is worth emphasising that these forms of life can mingle to a certain extent, which can be seen in real experiences of love, kindness, the voluntary sharing of burdens, and other forms of solidarity inside of a lifeworld of the capitalist kind. Therefore, just as we can speak of certain experiences of communism within capitalist societies, if we had communist societies, we would likely have experiences of capitalism there as well. Rosa Luxemburg explored this latter possibility in her essay, "The Dissolution of Primitive Communism," which presented her study of communist forms of life in ancient tribal community – or what she referred to as the "mark" communities – of Germany, Greece, the Americas, India, South Africa, and Russia. There, Luxemburg observed that even in early communist forms of life, certain tendencies toward the subjugation of others or for the consolidation of power and resources were already present. However, such tendencies were only exacerbated to the point of the extinction of primitive communism by the spread of European capitalism and slavery. According to Luxemburg, primitive communism, for all its violence and shortcomings, "endures for centuries the strains of every form of conquest, foreign rule, despotism, and exploitation. There is only one contact that it cannot tolerate or overcome; this is the contact with European civilisation, i.e. with capitalism."[3] The common *wealth* and primitive communist *Gemeinwesen* of ancient mark societies, tribes and villages, was essentially privatised, the shared overtaken as private, human life converted by force to a source of free labour for capitalists. As Luxemburg put it, "Slavery accelerates the dissolution of the communist association and goes hand in hand with the rise of private property."[4]

This will have to suffice, for our present purposes, to distinguish between capitalist and communist forms of life. That is because I want to shift our attention to a consideration of the status of loneliness, which is not solitude, in different social settings. What is the basic

---

3 Luxemburg 2004a: 103.
4 Luxemburg 2004b: 114.

position of loneliness in a capitalist society, and would loneliness take a different shape in a communist form of life?

But what is meant by this *thing* called 'loneliness'? One could forgive, to some extent, the confusion of loneliness with solitude since, going back to the sixteenth century, loneliness referred to a condition of being solitary. We must be careful not to confuse loneliness with solitude. People deliberately carve out space and time for being alone. Loneliness, on the other hand, may follow you into solitude even if you do not want it to come. There is a difference between being happily in solitude and being lonely in solitude. Also, while one does not expect to find solitude in family gatherings, at meetings of friends and comrades, or even at parties or festivals, loneliness may be pervasive in such spaces. I therefore prefer a more recent meaning of loneliness stemming from the nineteenth century, which is about a feeling one may have whether they are alone on a train or deep in a crowd. This feeling is not a good one. It is a feeling of being dejected, deprived of companionship, without sympathy or human solidarity. This definition can therefore explain the lonely child or husband or wife who suffers this feeling even when sharing their bed with their nearest and dearest. This definition can also help us to appreciate the fact that fellow fighters and activists who join us in rallies or meet us in the streets as participants in shared movements may be suffering from loneliness despite such activity. Loneliness must be defined as something we can experience in a world of regular interactions with other human beings.

Hannah Arendt takes this further. In *The Origins of Totalitarianism*, Arendt writes: "Loneliness is not solitude. Solitude requires being alone whereas loneliness shows itself more sharply in company with others."[5] For Arendt, solitude was not a problem. A person seeks it out for good feeling, for the space and time to think about what one wishes to be or do, about life and society and tomorrow. Solitude, from its etymological roots in the fourteenth century, indicates a state of being alone. One can be alone without the feeling of loneliness. "What makes loneliness so unbearable is the loss of one's own self which can be realised in solitude, but confirmed in its identity only by the trusting and trustworthy company of my equals."[6] This means that the company of trusting and trustworthy equals is ready at hand, and one

5 Arendt 1968: 476.
6 Ibid: 477.

can therefore move in and out of solitude as they wish. One cannot move in and out of loneliness that way.

What is perhaps the most striking feature of Arendt's attention to loneliness is that it appears in the final pages of a 479-page study of twentieth century totalitarianism, and not as a fleeting observation. For Arendt, the predatory regimes of fascists, Nazis, and totalitarians seize upon the loneliness of society, packaging and presenting fatal antidotes as sweet relief. Why does Arendt end her famous study of totalitarianism with an extended deliberation on loneliness? "Loneliness, the common ground for terror, the essence of totalitarian government, and for ideology or logicality, the preparation of its executioners and victims, is closely connected with uprootedness and superfluousness which have been the curse of modern masses since the beginning of the industrial revolution and have become acute with the rise of imperialism at the end of the last century and the break-down of political institutions and social traditions in our own time."[7] There is a lot to unpack here, but essentially, Arendt is saying that widespread loneliness in the mass societies of the twentieth century is the groundwork of totalitarian government. When people feel uprooted, disconnected from purpose, dejected, cut off from human solidarity, totalitarian government presents itself as a rallying cry against that condition. Disconnected and dejected people are called to come together under the banner of the nation's great power. I would consider the phenomenon of Trumpist white nationalism in the US, widespread among the disaffected white working class, as a contemporary example of this. What is missing from the example, and from Arendt's analysis, is the extent to which not only fascism but capitalism preys upon loneliness.

Perhaps Max Horkheimer said it best in 1939 in "The Jews and Europe" when he declared, "whoever is not willing to talk about capitalism should also keep quiet about fascism."[8] While Arendt provides sustained class analysis throughout her major study of totalitarianism, Horkheimer clarifies the dialectical and causal relationship between capitalism and fascism. Nonetheless, we could not say about loneliness what Horkheimer says here about fascism. Not unless we want to say that loneliness can have no cause outside of capitalist society. But that

7 Ibid: 475.
8 See Horkheimer 1939/2015.

would be an absurd claim, so we must alter the question: What is the capitalist form of loneliness? Let us see if we can approach an answer to that question.

2: Loneliness of Capital

John Cacioppo was one of the foremost recent scholars of loneliness, who dedicated much of his life to understanding the human experience we are focused on here. He wrote in his book, *Loneliness*, that while money may motivate people to work their entire lives doing jobs they hate, money has "a negative impact on their behavior toward others. There are data to suggest that merely having money on the periphery of consciousness is sufficient to skew us away from prosocial behavior."[9] Prosocial behaviour counteracts loneliness, whereas antisocial behaviour exacerbates loneliness. Research shows that heightened money-consciousness tends toward the antisocial. Cacioppo's research is full of such data, supported variously by study after study. Loneliness is a major problem impacting not only psychological and social but also physical health and well-being. According to Cacioppo, one problem with loneliness is that "feelings of social isolation deprive us of vast reservoirs of creativity and energy."[10] Despite his ability to identify social causes of loneliness in an individualist society ruled by money, Cacioppo is no socialist or communist. He is no Marxist or anti-capitalist. He simply wants us to try as hard as we can to respond to loneliness as the very serious problem it is, but only by way of kindness and through an improved interpersonal comportment. He calls on us to make use of "individual actions, to continuously adjust the social environment towards something slightly better." As Director of the Centre for Cognitive Neuroscience at the University of Chicago, Cacioppo was not so unhappy with the existing capitalist reality. He was wholly uninterested in the social or political transformation of the world. We can appreciate him stopping where he did, but we cannot accept a program of minor individual adjustments aimed at making things slightly better.[11] Cacioppo's own research diagnosed loneliness as an urgent social catastrophe, so that his own recommendation appears as a mismatch for the scale of the emergency. Cacioppo tells us that there are political-economic and social causes of the present

9 Cacioppo & Patrick 2008: 264.
10 Ibid: 269.
11 Ibid: 266.

plague of loneliness, but we will have to make a more critical reading of such facts ourselves.

What I want to suggest is that, while loneliness cannot be abolished as a human experience, *and while I do not think we should want to abolish it altogether*, there is a capitalist form of loneliness that we must confront as such. Why should we do that? First, by considering the capitalist form of loneliness, we can learn something about the social tendencies of capital and their relation to human health and well-being. In fact, if we were lonely in a different world of our own making, then the same would presumably be true. We could use loneliness in that society, or in any society, to learn something about the health of human relations there too. We cannot suggest that a revolutionary transformation of society against capitalist social relations would solve every problem. It would not. The problems would only be different, and we would have to approach them with an appreciation of those distinctions.

Roland Barthes tried to think about forms of life too. He was interested in certain tensions and difficulties of capitalist society. Barthes's idea was that people variously want or need to live together with other people, and yet, at the same time, that they have no faith in other people and find grief and other torment in efforts to live with others. There is, then, a paradoxical pull both toward and away from others. This paradox could be explained by the presence of a social instinct on the one hand, broken apart by a culture of competitive individualism on the other. We become suspicious of and hostile to other people, and yet cannot easily overcome an urge to be with them. In *How to Live Together*, Barthes studied tendencies of living-alone in relation to tendencies of living-together. He wrote about "acedy," a word related to asceticism. This word indicates a form of life in which people place little faith in other people and therefore adopt a practice of avoiding the world. Barthes describes modern acedy as follows: "I can wake up in the morning, see the schedule for the week unfolding before my eyes, and feel hopeless. It's repetitive, it goes round and round: the same old tasks, the same old meetings, and yet there's no investment whatsoever... Acedy (modern acedy): no longer being capable of investing in other people, in Living-with-several-other-people and yet at the same time being incapable of investing in solitude."[12]

12 Barthes 2013: 22-23.

What is remarkable is that Barthes appears to have predicted phenomena like *otaku* and *hikikomori*, which I have discussed in several of my own books.[13] *Hikikomori* refers to those who have opted to remove themselves from the world of other people (well over a million people in Japan), those who only want to interact with other people through screens. *Otaku* is different. *Otaku* refers to people who prefer a world of video games and comic books to the actual world, and often, *otaku* become *hikikomori*. The difference is that Barthes's concept of acedy contains both sides – the side of not wanting to be with other people, but also the side of not wanting to live in total isolation either – whereas, *otaku* and *hikikomori* seem to have moved us, in the time since Barthes's study, closer to the possibility of being totally cut off from the world. One could argue that *otaku* and *hikikomori* are still within Barthes's model of acedy because these isolating and socially withdrawn people are still reaching out to others through screen-mediated relations and in imaginary worlds. But even that seems to move the situation beyond the scope of Barthes's imagination in the late 1970s.

Barthes also writes about "idiorrhythmy" and about "idiorrhythmic clusters, where each subject lives according to his own rhythm."[14] *Idios* means "particular" and *rhuthmos* means rhythm. So what we are talking about with idiorrhythmy is each person establishing their own particular rhythm of life. Living together is complicated, like musicians playing together according to peculiar rules; imagine musicians playing together but only following their own idiorrhythmic preferences. In such idiorrhythmic music, players would be both together and apart in the music. And this is how we are in life. Idiorrhythmic clusters do not make for a communist togetherness. The communist idea is to be responsive and attentive to the needs and abilities of the others. As Marx put it, a communist form of life would be guided by the motto, "from each according to their ability, to each according to their needs."[15] A capitalist form of life, however, encourages general indifference to the needs and abilities of others, unless or until the needs and abilities of other people obstruct one's own idiorrhythmic preferences.

But there are, as I have argued in *The Communism of Love*, irrepressibly communist tendencies of human beings, which can be

13 Most recently in my *The Communism of Love: An Inquiry into the Poverty of Exchange Value* (2020).
14 Barthes 2013: 6.
15 Marx 2002: 10.

disfigured and suppressed, but never totally extinguished. It is part of the reason why people who are traumatised by failures of friendship and love nonetheless seek out friendship and love: even though they have been hurt by bad experiences, they feel that they need them for their own human flourishing. This can also be seen in the direst and deepest traumas of family abuse, which nonetheless send victims off in search of healthy families of choice, which people sense that they need for their flourishing. But Barthes understood a great challenge facing the communist aspirations of everyday people. As he put it: "Living-Together, especially idiorrhythmic Living-Together, must incorporate the values of Living-Alone as its paradigmatic opposite."[16] This means that the challenge facing us today is to find ways of living together that do not threaten our dispositions of acedy. One wants to be reassured that they can be with others without having to give up any of their idiosyncratic rhythms. One wants to, in other words, ameliorate the dangers of loneliness without giving up the perks of being alone.

But this is only one aspect of loneliness in the capitalist form of life. We cannot possibly hope, or dare to pretend, that loneliness is some simple thing with singular causes and a fixed shape. It certainly is not. But at the same time, we mustn't pretend that loneliness in a capitalist society has nothing at all to do with the capitalist form of life that defines such a society. This would make us just as stupid as those economists – and there are too many of these – who want to analyse an economic crisis as if it has no relation to the economic system in which it occurs.

In *Powers of Horror*, Julia Kristeva introduces a third term to the usual subject/object dichotomy in philosophy. We know about the subjects who perceive, and the objects of their perception. But Kristeva writes about the abject, which is neither subject nor object. The abject is in the world, outside of one's self (like an object), but unlike an object, it is against one's self.[17] Abjection is an important concept because it captures the experience of feeling opposed, even detested, marked for exclusion, deportation, or death, by forces around you. When we think about abjection, we may think of an abject situation, a reality in which one is abandoned, degraded, cast out.

16 Barthes 2013: 84.
17 Kristeva 1982: 1.

Abjection has been the historical position of the marginalised and excluded peoples of the world, whether we are talking about early and out transgender people, gays and lesbians, or BIPOC (Black, Indigenous, People of Colour) sectors of society that have been vilified, despised, criminalised, and incarcerated. Abjection is the condition of a Black teenager in the United States who walks around in Middle School with a lopsided expectation that they – or someone they love – will be arrested, jailed, or killed by police. Abjection is a regular feature of the state of BIPOC life in a white supremacist society. According to Kristeva, abjection is the sphere of the worst horrors whereby some humans are confronted by other humans, for abjection is found in "a hatred that smiles, a passion that uses the body for barter instead of inflaming it, a debtor who sells you up, a friend who stabs you."[18] The sensibility of abjection is not simply that of loneliness, but of being unwanted in or by the world.

In later books like *Strangers to Ourselves*, Kristeva deals with the abjection of foreigners, immigrants, women in patriarchal societies, strangers, and aliens. Thinking about immigrant labour in a foreign land, Kristeva writes: "Since he has nothing, since he is nothing, he can sacrifice everything. And sacrifice begins with work: the only property that can be exported duty free, a universally tried and tested stock for the wanderer's use. What bitterness then, what disaster is it when one does not obtain one's green card."[19] What a sad description of abjection: the immigrant worker who is regarded as nothing or invisible, who sacrifices all of their time and life's energy for survival, who is then repaid with denial, detainment, or deportation.

Let us not proceed as if this abjection were not a feature of capitalism. It is only the logic of capital that can lead to such abjection as this, the abjection of giving everything in work, yet being regarded as nothing (or not even regarded at all), and then facing expulsion by the capitalist state at the very point of visibility. A communist form of life may appear as a utopian idea, but does it not offer a response to such abjection? A communist form of life would have to oppose itself to such abjection, would have to imagine an antithetical orientation, or else it could mean nothing at all. If we want to imagine, let alone to pursue, real alternatives to the capitalist form of life, we will have to

18 Ibid: 4.
19 Kristeva 1991: 19.

think about a social reality that pushes back against acedy and abjection, and thus, pushes back against forms of loneliness bred in and by the existing idiorrthythmic reality. We must not forget that the original definition of communism, provided by Marx in *The German Ideology*, called communism "the *real* movement which abolishes the present state of things."[20] Communists would have to be abolitionists, and that includes the abolition of the capitalist form of life. Such abolitionism does not mean the abolition of loneliness writ large, but certainly, of forms of loneliness bred by the existing society.

3: Toward an Antithetical Loneliness

I think that what we are talking about is the practicality of utopianism. This appears as a contradiction in terms. If it is utopian, then it is supposed to be impractical, impossible. But in fact, we cannot move toward a different reality unless we are willing to think about what is desirable and possible. The only other path would be a path of accidents, catastrophes, or coercion. We must allow ourselves the freedom to think about what is desirable and possible, and we must demand that freedom. We must stick to some concept of agency, and not simply accept that we will get where we're going like leaves in a stream.

In the world of science and technology, so many things were impossible, until they were done. So many things we now take for granted, from airplanes to smartphones, would have been declared impractical and unreal, until they were real and integrated into the practical activity of the world. Do not forget that a long time ago, people called the abolitionists who stood against chattel slavery, and the radical suffragettes, utopian. They were regarded as dreamers with nothing practical to advance. The truth is that naysayers of the utopian suffer from bad imaginations, poor understandings of history, or worse, are too favourably disposed towards the status quo. But with imagination, historical understanding, and a hatred of the status quo, the utopian appears as a kind of North Star. Who would dare tell a sailor of old that the North Star is impractical?

Erich Fromm, in *To Have or To Be?*, writes: "*If I am what I have and if what I have is lost, who then am I?* Nobody but a defeated, deflated, pathetic testimony to a wrong way of living."[21] Yes, we can speak of a

20 Marx 1983: 179.
21 Fromm 2013: 94.

wrong way of living. That does not mean there is only one right way. However, if a person is nobody beyond what they have, if their possessions define them, then people who own little are not very much. Fromm's critique of the "having mode" of life was, for him, a critique of the capitalist form of life. But is there not a certain wisdom among the impoverished peoples of the world that they are something even when they own little or nothing? Many impoverished people know that they are worth more than their possessions, which they express especially in moments of indignation and protest. We must not assume that the "having mode" of life has totally decided the question of the value of our being-in-the-world.

Axel Honneth, in *The I in We*, explains as the central claim of his argument that "the 'I' seeks the 'We' of shared group experience, because even after maturity, we are dependent on forms of social recognition imbued with direct encouragement and affirmation."[22] From a position of loneliness, we cry out for recognition, encouragement, and affirmation. These things are even necessary to our health and well-being when we are not feeling particularly lonely. For a child's sense of self-worth and human development, others must say to them, you are seen, you are good, you can be or become what you should be, what you desire to be. A child deprived of these things is not only lonely, they are subverted, undermined, their sense of self disfigured. One moment of recognition is not enough. Drawing on psychosocial research, Honneth says: "In order to maintain and perhaps even strengthen their self-confidence, subjects need to receive constant, reliable affection, which for the most part they encounter in relationships of friendship and love."[23]

We cannot speak of the 'I' all alone without some yearning for the recognition and affirmation of a 'We.' Deprived of such social recognition, one might diagnose that they are lonely. But that is a red herring. This is not simply loneliness, but a condition of life in a culture of social deprivation. Capitalists like to praise the heroic individual who needs nobody else. Capitalists chronically mistake interdependence as some despicable weakness they call dependency. However, their own lives, and the lives of their children or other beloveds, refute their point of view. No infant is independent, no child. A young child would

22 Honneth 2014: 214.
23 Ibid: 206.

not live long without a certain communism of care, a certain dependency that is natural and necessary. Indeed, without other people, there could be no human life at all. How can we call capitalist individualism, which forgets the child and ignores interdependency, anything but dehumanising? We dare not. There is nothing more humanising than being seen, heard, recognised, affirmed, and in regular receipt of the affection and care of others.

It is not impossible to move from the 'I' to the 'We,' even if it is utopian. Jean-Paul Sartre, who thought a lot about individuals and collectives, understood this well. When he considered the 'I' becoming 'We' in *Being and Nothingness,* he provided the following illustration:

> I am on the pavement in front of a café; I observe the other patrons and I know myself to be observed. We remain here in the most ordinary case of conflict with others (the Other's being-as-object for me, my being-as-object for the Other). But suddenly some incident occurs in the street; for example, a slight collision between a jeep and a taxi. Immediately at the very instant when I become a spectator of the incident, I experience myself non-thetically as engaged in 'we.' The earlier rivalries, the slight conflicts have disappeared... 'we' look at the event, 'we' take part.[24]

Here you have a case of seeing something together. The togetherness of the witnessing moves the 'I' to the 'We.' But in this case, an event, an incident, makes it happen: 'I' becomes 'We' in the face of a collision. Perhaps we will abandon our lonely individuation when we face an unexpected, jarring catastrophe. Are there not historical events that throw us together? Indeed, there are many. Here, we could imagine a crisis theory according to which the capitalist form of life meets its limitations in the face of catastrophe. It is possible to consider that, in the face of the COVID-19 catastrophe, for example, we tested some of the limits of the capitalist form of life. So many people asked the question, both practically and rather unexpectedly, could I live without work? Could I adapt to a different form of life? The pandemic form of life is not the one we would choose, but perhaps it reveals that other forms of life are more possible than we may have previously thought.

24 Sartre 1966: 505-506.

31

There are moments when loneliness is temporarily ameliorated in collective action, inside the living camaraderie and shared passions of a social movement or even a revolt. We can find many things, for example, in the George Floyd rebellion, such as anger, sadness, hope, cynicism, disagreement, and furious indignation. However, I wonder if, in the throes of the rebellion itself, participants would have said they felt lonely.[25] In *Revolt, She Said,* Kristeva assesses the health and well-being of contemporary capitalist societies, and what she diagnoses is a measurable mass depression, widespread anxiety, and a deep feeling of being alienated from other people. It is unlikely that people will gather and rise up together in such an affective state. She says that "incapacity to rebel is the sign of national depression."[26] However, Kristeva argues that such feelings do dissipate in the throes of revolt, that "people who rebel are malcontents with frustrated, but vigorous desires."[27] She worries more about the absence of revolt than about its presence, because, from a psychoanalytic perspective, a healthy society actively gathers to throw into question its own justice and reality. On the contrary, a profoundly lonely society is locked up inside, and individuals view the outside world more as a field of abjection. As a response to this, Kristeva argues for "the necessity of a culture of revolt."[28] That is something she thinks we must try to cultivate in art, writing, psychoanalysis, and social movements, for example.

Imagine that we could find our way to a new reality through a culture of revolt. Still, why would we want to confront a particular form of loneliness in the existing capitalist society only to discover a new form of loneliness on the horizon? I think that the answer is because utopians can and must be practical. We can say both that we want a totally different world, and that we expect there will be serious and intractable problems in that different world too. The first part would be utopian, the second part practical. The first part is on the side of desirability, whereas the second part is on the side of possibility.

However, is it worth the effort to aim at North Stars? Personally, I live in a world where it is not easy to find people who share my basic sensibilities about the world. I usually feel that I have to attend

---

25 It is worth noting here, especially, that the George Floyd rebellion broke out during the lockdowns of COVID-19, and so it likely even served as an "insurgent togetherness" in a time of great social isolation.

26 Kristeva 2002: 83.

27 Ibid: 84.

28 Kristeva 2000: 7.

a conference or align with or participate in social movements, just to ameliorate the loneliness of thinking against the grain of my own life-world. As a university professor and writer, there are those who are eager to ask for my perspective, but they are often interested only because they know I espouse a certain point of view that, behind their sociable outward kindnesses, they regard as utopian, unreasonable, or worse. Interest in my point of view does not indicate agreement with it, and I have never been unaware of the disregard that lurks behind the collegial veneer of so many people around me. We are surrounded by people – generally regarded as smart and sensible – who think that the only thing wrong with the capitalist reality is that some of the presidents and prime ministers could be better. The world, such as it is, is resolutely hostile to radical thinkers, revolutionaries, and people who live in the margins of society, not only because of what they think, but because of who they are. For many, there is nowhere to go. It can be a lonely place for those who are nonconforming, despised, or who think about the world from the far left of politics. After all, what does it mean to vacillate between being marginalised and tolerated? It is no kind thing or great gift to learn that you are merely tolerated. In a world such as this, I would welcome the opportunity to find out what kinds of loneliness we might find in a communist form of life. If that is utopian, it is a precarious utopianism at best.

One of the greatest defenders of the practicality of utopianism was Simone Weil. When Weil considered different possible forms of life from different revolutionary traditions, namely from Marxism and anarchism, she concluded: "No doubt all of this is purely utopian. But to give even a summary description of a state of things which would be better than what actually exists is always to build a utopia; yet nothing is more necessary to our life than such descriptions."[29] Indeed, loneliness is there in the manifold of human experience, and I think it always will be; but we can imagine and describe a world that would be better than this one. We may expect that the loneliness of a communist form of life would be better because, in a communist form of life, we would be oriented by a logic of interdependency, seen instead of disappeared by separation and abandoned by extreme acedy. I can imagine a world extrapolated from the best experiences of friendship and love, a world of being attentive to the principles of differential

29 Weil 2001: 100.

ability and needs. We have to fight for that world, as precarious, practical utopians, so that we might possibly move beyond the capitalist form of life, so that we may experience a different form of loneliness, the loneliness of an antithesis to everything awful in the present.

References

Arendt, Hannah (1968), *The Origins of Totalitarianism*. San Diego, New York, and London: Harcourt.

Barthes, Roland (2013), *How to Live Together: Novelistic Simulations of Some Everyday Spaces* (translated by Kate Briggs). New York: Columbia University Press.

Cacioppo, John T. & Patrick, William (2008), *Loneliness: Human Nature and the Need for Social Connection*. New York and London: W.W. Norton & Company.

Fromm, Erich (2013), *To Have or To Be?*. London and New York: Bloomsbury.

Gilman-Opalsky, Richard (2020), *The Communism of Love: An Inquiry into the Poverty of Exchange Value*. Chico and Edinburgh: AK Press.

Honneth, Alex (2014), *The I in We: Studies in the Theory of Recognition* (translated by Joseph Ganahl). Malden, MA: Polity Press.

Horkheimer, Max (1939/2015), "The Jews and Europe," *The Charnel House*. Cited at: https://thecharnelhouse.org/2015/03/20/the-jews-and-europe.

Luxemburg, Rosa (2004a), "The Dissolution of Primitive Communism: From the Ancient Germans and the Incas to India, Russia, and Southern Africa," *in* Peter Hudis & Kevin B. Anderson (eds.) *The Rosa Luxemburg Reader*, New York: Monthly Review Press, 71-110.

Luxemburg, Rosa (2004b), "Slavery," *in* Peter Hudis & Kevin B. Anderson (eds.) *The Rosa Luxemburg Reader*, New York: Monthly Review Press, 111-122.

Kristeva, Julia (1982), *Powers of Horror: An Essay on Abjection* (translated by Leon S. Roudiez). New York: Columbia University Press.

Kristeva, Julia (1991), *Strangers to Ourselves* (translated by Leon S. Roudiez). New York: Columbia University Press.

Kristeva, Julia (2000), *The Sense and Non-Sense of Revolt: The Powers and Limits of Psychoanalysis* (translated by Jeanine Herman). New York: Columbia University Press.

Kristeva, Julia (2002), *Revolt, She Said* (translated by Brian O'Keeffe). Los Angeles and New York: Semiotext(e).

Marx, Karl (1983), "The German Ideology," *in* Eugene Kamenka (ed.) *The Portable Marx*, New York: Penguin Books, 162-196.

Marx, Karl (2002), *Critique of the Gotha Programme*. New York: International Publishers.

Riesman, David (1961), *The Lonely Crowd*. New Haven and London: Yale University Press.

Sartre, Jean-Paul (1966), *Being and Nothingness* (translated by Hazel E. Barnes). New York: Washington Square Press.

Weil, Simone (2001), *Oppression and Liberty* (translated by Arthur Wills and John Petrie). London and New York: Routledge.

Artist: Tate Quesada

A Red Rooster Does Not Give Up —
Subjectivity and Politics. Notes on Defeat

alejandra ciriza

> How is it possible that dawn continues to break?
> We wondered when they didn't come back.
> In truth, it continued to break as if nothing had ever happened.
> People worried about their little quarrels,
> Checked that there were no holes in their pockets, nor open windows in their souls.
> But time, which is not a fool, taught us that it was the other way around;
> exactly the opposite of what we feared.
> It was for them, for those who did not return that dawn continued to break.
> And still breaks.[1]
> (Liliana Bodoc)

This brief text aims to reflect upon the complex relationship between the singular and the collective, based on my experience as part of a decimated generation, and informed by theoretical insights from the writings of Marx, Gramsci and Walter Benjamin, a trio of thinkers who, due to their strong interest in the fields of praxis, history and the political dimensions of singular and collective political experience, have accompanied me in the recurring attempt to find responses, even if transitory and often precarious, to the social and subjective impact of the brutal defeat suffered by my generation of leftist activists in Argentina in the wake of the military coup of March 1976.

The coup produced objective changes in the economic realm (in the distribution of wealth and in the productive structure for the benefit of selected companies); the political arena (in the organisational forms of the subaltern sectors and in their political horizons by tarnishing any reference to revolutionary transformations and making so-called democratic capitalism the *non plus ultra* of their aspirations)[2]; on the level of the State (due to the impact of neoliberal

---

1 See Bodoc 2019.
2 Atilio Borón analyses the processes of democratic transition in *Nuestra América* based on the idea that the dictatorships carried out a transformation of the state through indebtedness and neoliberal reforms, thereby converting hitherto guaranteed citizen rights into tradable goods. He further points out that the post-dictatorship democratisation processes are marked by the evolution of capitalism. The nodal point is found precisely there, in questioning the fact that they are *capitalist democracies*, which implies the displacement of capitalism to a more discrete position, behind the political scene. If we talk about capitalist democracy, capitalism becomes invisible despite being the structural foundation of contemporary society, the decisive factor in the processes of the concentration of wealth and impoverishment of the majority of the population. Hence, more than capitalist democracies, the current regimes are democratic capitalisms (Borón 2006).

policies on the form and function of state institutions); and in the cultural sphere (pushing back and trying to replace leftist, third-worldist and Latin American indigenous cultural manifestations with individualist/individualising visions of the world). It also deeply affected people's subjectivities, their/our structures of feeling, as well as the myriad ways of constructing '*lazos colectivos*', collective bonds.

Along similar lines, Perry Anderson points out that the South American dictatorships of the 1960s (Brazil) and 1970s (Bolivia, Uruguay, Chile, Argentina) brought about profound objective changes in our societies.[3] Various studies indicate that during the decade 1964-1974 Argentina registered a redistribution of income favourable to wage-earners, with very low unemployment[4] and poverty rates that reached a historical low in 1974: 4.6% of households.[5] Then came the coup and in 1977, Rodolfo Walsh described the situation of Argentine workers in the following way:

> In just one year you have reduced the real salary of workers to 40%, reduced their participation in the national income to 30%, raised from 6 to 18 hours the hours a worker needs to work daily to pay for the family basket, thus reviving forms of forced labour that do not persist even in the last colonial redoubts [...].[6]

What's more, the bloody dictatorships of the *Cono Sur* shared, in addition to an economic project characterised by the first experiments with neoliberalism, a project of extermination perpetrated with national particularities, but united under the common matrix of the systematic exercise of terror. The so-called *Plan Cóndor* had an international dimension of enormous importance to perpetrate dictatorial crimes and persecute left militants beyond national borders.[7]

In general terms, the 1960s and 1970s, the decades that shaped our subjectivities, were marked by a series of transformations in the field of the material conditions of existence. I am referring to the transformations in capitalism that promoted, along with the massive entry of women into the labour market, a vertiginous process of the commodification of the reproduction of life, and of the globalisation

3 See Anderson 1988.
4 See Basualdo 2008.
5 See Arakaki 2011.
6 See Walsh 1977.
7 See Calloni 2016.

of the production process through the increased centralisation, concentration, and hierarchisation of work.[8] These transformations not only sharpened the contradictions between imperial countries and former colonies, and between salaried workers and capitalists, but also led to transformations in family life that particularly affected proletarians, indigenous populations, women of all social classes, and young people.[9] Nonetheless, in a context in which the working class retained an enormous capacity for organisation and mobilisation, and in which new political subjects emerged from the critique of racism, imperialism, productivism and sexism, the responses would not take long to emerge. In those years, after the Battle of Dien Bien Phu in 1954, the triumph of the 1959 Cuban Revolution stimulated in many Latin American countries the expectation of impending socialist and anti-imperialist revolutions that would open up the possibility of finally inhabiting a better world.

There remain in those of us who were young at the time indelible marks of that revolutionary subjectivity, which comes back to life with particular vivacity in moments of remembrance: the collective joy, the trust we had in one another, the warmth of living life collectively, the knowledge and understanding that we were, even in moments of conflict, "many more than two" as Mario Benedetti once said.[10] The strength of friendships born and nourished in the heat of militant commitment and the expectation of future redemption, as Walter Benjamin and more than one of us so fervently desired, has forever remained embedded in our lives, perhaps because as Liliana Bodoc so poignantly says, we were and are still waiting and struggling for the return of *lxs nuestros*/our loved ones/those who disappeared every single night.

What is missing – the irreparable absence of our comrades and relatives, and the uncertain, but once palpably open horizon of taking heaven by storm present in the fierce debates, the doubts and tensions that Marta Vassallo so well illustrates in *La terrible esperanza/The terrible hope* – has somehow become a part of those of us who have been trying to keep alive those earlier utopias. The tension between who we used to be and who we are today looms everywhere like a heart-breaking

8 See Mandel 1979.
9 See Mandel 1979 & Larguía and Dumoulin 1976.
10 Editor's note: Fragment from the poem "*Te quiero*/I love you" by the great Uruguayan poet Mario Benedetti (1920-2009).

shadow, especially when dealt with alone. And yet the terrible hope continues to haunt us, notwithstanding the fierce rupture caused by defeat and the deep pain the absences have inflicted on us.

In reality, the dictatorship produced objective and subjective transformations that weigh not only on us, but on current generations. The unpayable debt; the devastation of nature – both our human nature and the natural environment in which we live and of which we are a part; the persecution of the indigenous peoples of *Nuestramérica*[11] whose territories have once again become the target of capitalist depredation; the terror that has been imprinted on/in/within the field of political relations, overdetermining them; the degradation of public institutions transformed into mere instruments for the arbitrary exercise of power by those Rodolfo Walsh called "the owners of all things;" rape as a form of terrorism and 'instruction' aimed at 'correcting' insurgent women, sexual dissidents, dissident bodies and emasculated and defeated men. It is worth quoting Walsh again because this particular text was written in a more hopeful time:

> Our ruling classes have always ensured that the workers have no history, no doctrine, no heroes or martyrs. Each struggle must start anew, separate from the previous ones. The collective experience is lost, lessons are forgotten. History thus appears as the private property of those who are already the owners of all things. This time, however, the [vicious] circle may be broken...[12]

In those days, Walsh, assassinated by the dictatorship the day after the publication of his 1977 "Open Letter to the Military Junta,"[13] concluded with cautious hope: "This time the [vicious] circle may be broken..." From our present perspective, we would not have ended the reflection in this way. On the contrary, almost every time Walsh's text is quoted today, the hopeful part is left out.

---

11 Editor's note: *Nuestra América,* Our America, is an important text written by Cuban poet and politician José Martí in 1891. His eloquent insistence on the need for a genuinely independent and sovereign Latin American subcontinent, free of colonial and imperialist interference, has since become a rallying call of the Latin American Left.
12 See Walsh 1969.
13 Editor's note: For an English-language version of Walsh's letter, see: https://www.inversejournal.com/ 2022/01/20/rodolfo-walshs-1977-open-letter-to-the-military-junta-in-argentina-introduced-and-trans-lated-by-arturo-desimone/.

Apparently, the revolutionary horizon is now closed once and for all and we find ourselves (once more/still) dispersed, ruminating in solitude and isolation, as if this erstwhile need-cum-ability to disperse has gradually sapped our propensities for association with others.[14]

To dream and exist in the open air of history

> "Wo/Men make their own history,
> but [...] they do not make it under self-selected circumstances."[15]
> (Karl Marx)

For many years these words of Marx have been reverberating inside me. The experiences that were most decisive for me in the field of the personal and the political took place in the early 1970s, in a climate defined by the rise of the masses and the peak of revolutionary expectations in territories located in the south of the globe. One element that many of us share(d) are the marks left by the experiences of colonialism and the hopes born of the Vietnamese triumph, the Cuban Revolution, the Algerian experience... Hence the precious presence of Fanon and Césaire among those who helped us to imagine the times to come, hidden in Césaire's *Cahier d'un retour au pays natal*, which brushes against the grain of the scourges of colonial Martinique towards the inaugural moment of the Haitian revolution.[16] Hence, the recurrence of the idea of a second independence, which this time round would finally include all of us: Afros, Indixs, Proletarians, Women...

Speaking of the latter, we, the *muchachas*, the young women, of that generation, opened the debate about different bodily experiences and sexualities in myriad ways in different parts of the globe. It was in those years that Margaret Randall published a book that had a wide impact on our continent: *Las Mujeres/Women*. In it she points out:

> Women, like Blacks, do not want equal rights, but are re-examining the world from the bottom up. Patriarchal culture has pitted women against each other. Now, women's liberation groups have managed to get women to talk to and discover

----

14 In my reflections and attempts to tie this thin red thread that connects us, I often find myself in close proximity to notions developed by Antonio Gramsci. Gramsci, my companion of solitude during the dictatorship, continues to be an obligatory reference to understand the discontinuity that haunts us. With particular sharpness, he pointed out that the discontinuous and dispersed traditions of the subaltern sectors are always subject to the initiative of the dominant sectors and their alliances, not only of class but also of sex/gender and race (Gramsci 1970: 491).

15 Marx 1957: 160.

16 See Césaire 1939.

each other, thereby becoming sisters... This collective feeling is what has helped us [...] to understand that our problems are not individual... we must examine our reality as "the only oppressed group that is absolutely necessary in history."[17]

Besides, Rosa Luxemburg's vibrant breath was always in the air fuelling the desire, which we felt as inextinguishable and collective, to change *everything*. We were full of a resolute confidence that we would manage to overcome any adversity, and even if moments of defeat awaited us, nothing would stop the revolutionary momentum. Our lives were on fire, volatile and hopeful, the very foundation of a better world. The echo of the voices of Luxemburg and of the greatest inspirer of our generation, Ernesto Che Guevara, stimulated, inspirited and guided us.

Rosa Luxemburg's last writing merits quoting because it provides a sense of the level of hope that drove us:

"Order prevails in Berlin!" You foolish lackeys! Your "order" is built on sand. Tomorrow the revolution will "rise up again, clashing its weapons," and to your horror it will proclaim with trumpets blazing: I was, I am, I shall be![18]

In sum, our experiences and time itself had a particular density. In just a short period of time there were changes in the social sphere, but also concerning new possibilities of understanding the world in novel ways and regarding the connections with others, all of which was illuminated by the light conferred on us by the expectation of the radical transformation of the established order. In those years, the continuum of history seemed to explode day after day. Time had densified, the Kairos of messianic expectations, Benjamin's *Jetztzeit*, opened the door through which the Messiah could enter, establishing a link between past and present, liberating us from centuries of oppressions and defeats, redeeming all the dead generations, at long last making the vindications of the wretched of the earth the order of the day.[19]

Then came the coup, yet shortly afterwards Mario Roberto Santucho (1936-1976), general secretary of the Workers' Revolutionary Party (PRT) and commander of the People's Revolutionary

17 Randall 1970: 20.
18 For the full text, see Luxemburg 1919.
19 See Benjamin 1940.

Army (ERP) issued a summons: *Argentinos ¡a las armas!* Santucho's call accurately illustrates the depth of the revolutionary conviction of many militants: understanding the ferocity of the coup executed in the early morning hours of March 24, Santucho considered the tasks to be carried out in the face of the dictatorial offensive with the certainty that people's revolutionary determination would produce the fall of the regime within a timespan that would entirely depend on the persistence of the revolutionary spirit. Hence the importance of invoking the help, with Benjaminian undertones, of all those who died, our ancestors, in the struggle for a socialist society. The revolutionaries had to get ready to take a "tiger's leap in the open air of history"[20] in order to carry out our second and definitive independence:

> It is a grandiose task that will honour and purify us, that will awaken and activate our best virtues, that will make thousands and thousands of heroes emerge from within our people. The spirit of Che, of Negrito Fernández, of the heroic comrades who fell in the struggle will multiply by thousands in the popular ranks! Responding with honour and vigour to the challenge of the hour, uniting and organizing ourselves for resistance and victory, we will conquer for our children the new socialist world of collective happiness.[21]

$$\bullet \quad \bullet \quad \bullet$$

But the relentless brutality of the enemy would eventually crush all our attempts. Santucho himself fell in combat on July 19, 1976, in the town of Villa Martelli and with him a large part of the Central Committee of the PRT: Benito Urteaga; Santucho's partner, Liliana Delfino, pregnant at the time; Fernando Gertel; Domingo Menna and Ana María Lanzillotto, whose son Maximiliano was abducted by the military at birth and finally recovered his identity 40 years later in October 2016. There was also José Urteaga Augier, Benito's son, who reunited with his family shortly after Maximiliano. The bodies of Santucho, Delfino, Urteaga, Gertel, Menna and Lanzillotto, on the other hand, are still missing. They are part of the bones that we long to recover and for which we have not stopped looking.

20 Ibid.
21 See Santucho 1976.

The abyss underneath

In one aspect Santucho was able to lucidly predict what would happen: the dictatorship was not simply one more in the long series of military juntas that had devastated the country, but one of unlimited ferocity. In fact, the regime carried out a systematic plan to obliterate the pre-existing society operating in all spheres of social life: economic, political, cultural and military. And of course, it also operated in the subjective realm, especially in the subjective realm.

It was not only a matter of the establishment of a permanent state of siege and the control of the country by the armed forces and the repressive apparatus of the state, but of a series of repressive and economic measures that fundamentally impacted on the working class. The scrapping of the productive apparatus went hand in hand with an increase in the level of indebtedness that would have severe consequences for democracy when it was restored after the defeat of the regime in the *Guerra de las Malvinas*/Falklands War in 1982.[22] Carpintero and Vainer affirm:

> During the first months after the coup, hundreds of unions were commandeered by agents of the dictatorship, who prohibited any type of union activity and the right to strike. Public employees were tried by military courts. Almost all the big factories [...] were occupied militarily with the agreement of the employers. At the General Motors plant in the city of General Pacheco [...] army forces surrounded the plant and detained hundreds of workers previously denounced by company managers.[23]

Needless to say, the dictatorship had its own instigators, ideologists, direct beneficiaries and accomplices, such as: large businesses and the US State Department; the CIA and international finance institutions; the leadership of the Argentine Catholic Church; and the members of most of the traditional political forces, for example the Radical Civic Union (UCR), one of the oldest political parties in Argentina, which contributed 53.3% of the mayors, and the Justicialist Party (PJ), which contributed 19.3%.[24]

22 During the period of the dictatorship, national debt increased from USD 8 billion to 45 billion, largely driven by the nationalisation of private company debt during Domingo Cavallo's tenure as President of the Central Bank. After the return of democracy, Cavallo was Minister of Economy under presidents Carlos Menem and Fernando de la Rúa.

23 Carpintero and Vainer 2018: 356.

24 See Marín 1984.

What we could call the most transformative novelty, however, was the course adopted against the regime's political adversaries, who were labelled criminals and anti-national terrorists, demoted to the category of non-humans, against whom unlimited terror and violence was exercised, including the theft of their bodies, prohibiting their families from properly mourning or burying them; a terror destined to produce lasting horror in the general population.

In fact, the exercise of repressive violence had begun prior to the coup, through the implementation of 'Operation Independence,' which began in July 1975 in the province of Tucumán, and the actions of various paramilitary and parapolice organisations.[25] Yet it was March 24, 1976, the day the armed forces assumed direct control, that signalled a qualitative change.

Concretely, political persecution was perpetrated using the state apparatus as an extermination machine, making regular and systematic use of terror, in broad daylight and in night operations whose objective was not only kidnapping, forced disappearance, murder, confinement and censorship, but the methodical inculcation of fear.

The genocidal state dehumanised those it defined as 'political enemies' through the systematic use of torture carried out in a circuit of countrywide Clandestine Detention Centres, and the appropriation of death. The bodies of *lxs nuestrxs* were kidnapped by the genocidaires, who, 46 years after the coup, still maintain a pact of silence about their fate.

What's more, the repression assumed a gendered character, not only due to the organised use of rape and other forms of sexual violence in the prisons of the dictatorship, but also to the stigmatisation of sexual dissidents, on whom the cruelty inflicted was arguably even more vicious.[26]

In total, during the seven years of the dictatorship, 30,000 people were disappeared, around 500,000 went into exile, and

---

25 There is extensive documentation on illegal repression in Argentina. By way of example, the so-called annihilation decrees, namely: 261/75, which authorised the army to eradicate subversion in Tucumán, and decrees 2770, 2771 and 2772/75, through which the Council of Internal Security was formed and the army was tasked with the coordination of all repressive forces. The decrees were preceded by Law 20840, of September 1974, which established penalties for activities considered subversive. Prior to that, in October 1973, the Peronist Superior Council had prepared the *'Documento Reservado,'* which called for the ideological purge of the Marxist wing of the Peronist movement through espionage, and the legal and illegal persecution of its militants.

26 The treatment received by children and pregnant women deserves a separate chapter due to the aforementioned practice of theft/appropriation of those who were transformed into cherished spoils of war, taken from their execrable mothers and fathers, and separated from their 'dangerous' families.

immediately after the coup the number of inmates at the disposal of the Junta rose to 8625 people, approximately 40% higher than the previous year. By 1977 another 1200 people were imprisoned. In the same year, Ibérico Saint Jean, then military governor of the province of Buenos Aires, did not hesitate to say the following about the Junta's plans: "First we will kill all the subversives, then we will kill their collaborators, then their sympathisers, then those who remain indifferent, and finally we will kill all the fearful."[27]

In short, the terrorist state did not just physically eliminate its political enemies: converting themselves into the masters of the life and death of its victims, they tried to erase in them any vestige of humanity. Other elements in this repertoire of infamy included common crimes, robberies, looting, and economic scams against the victims and their families. But the main feature of the Junta's sinister actions as part of their *'Proceso de Reorganización Nacional'* was the systematic erasure of the identities of the living and the dead, the theft of babies, and the refusal to let the dead be buried and mourned by their families.

No doubt, the plan carried out by the dictatorship effectively sought to transform the country from its foundations. To put it succinctly, the aim was to perpetrate a genocide that would change everything from the roots, leaving behind nothing but scorched earth.

Of temporalities, hopes and defeats

The singular experience accounts for the density of time, its condensations and pauses. Having spent my youth in the city of Córdoba – then open to the winds of history that swept through the corridors of my high school, the streets, the student assemblies and takeovers of faculties at the university – I and my *compañerxs* were able to learn quickly the different types of resistance, and how to go on the offensive in the form of street marches and graffities, the erection of barricades and the carrying out of the many tasks and actions of political militancy. What also affected my life were our small reading circles and our first feminist exploits shared with friends, my cousin, and my sister. Forms of activism that were more subtle and light.

While we were going through these intense experiences, what just moments before appeared to be the visceral opportunity to take

27 See Saint Jean 1977.

heaven by storm violently slipped away, leaving us struggling to hold on to and conjure time with our hopes and images of the recent past. *Ñaupax Manpuni*, looking into the past to see the future. In the manner of our indigenous Quechua and Aymara sisters and brothers we looked backwards and forwards, searching for renewed illumination from the times of *'El Ciclo de Azos,'* hoping that the present, against all odds, would redeem the past.[28] However, that time/opportunity soon vanished for good, devoured by the assault of the repressive state apparatus.

Córdoba, which had been one of the cradles of mass movements and mass hopes, an enormous social laboratory, as Marx would have said if he had lived through that time and moved through that beautiful and feverish city, became a besieged place.

In that fleeting and agitated period, I was part of the PRT, a political-military organisation whose top leader was the aforementioned Mario Roberto Santucho. Meanwhile, in February 1975, Isabel Martínez, president of the Nation, had signed the extermination decrees. That it, the coup came as a chronicle of a death foretold, and even so it presented itself to us like a hieroglyph that was difficult to decipher. There was no time to process, no time to think about alternatives, to foresee the unforeseeable, because genocide is ultimately something you cannot prepare for. There are no words, no political imagination that can name the horror that would suddenly overwhelm us. I/we simply couldn't anticipate what would happen even though there were signs...

Not only could we not know in advance of the mortal danger that threatened us. As Marta Vassallo says, having belonged to the 1970s generation and to a sector of that generation that opted for armed struggle, constituted and constitutes an element that hinders the possibility of recovering that experience in its complexity, since for a long time it was (and still is) subject to the harshest of censorship. What I call memory holes, deep breaks in the fabric of one's memories, is something more than a personal matter. It is something we realise

---

28 The *'Ciclo de Azos'* were a series of popular uprisings carried out against the economic and repressive measures of a military dictatorship that called itself the Argentine Revolution (1966-1973). They took place throughout the country between 1969 and 1972 in large cities such as Tucumán (May 1969, November 1970 and June 1972); Córdoba (May 1969; March 1971), Rosario (May and September 1969) and Mendoza (April 1972), but also in smaller cities, such as Jujuy (April 21, 1971) and Trelew (October 1972), and even in small towns like Animaná (July 1972) or Chocón (February-March 1970) (See Fernández and others 2013).

in dialogue with others, the living and the dead. Meanwhile, *lxs nuestrxs* still roam around aimlessly, their bodies stolen... Those of us who survived have barely managed to give expression to what happened, hounded by the need to sustain our lives and convictions in a context of constant danger. Something of their deaths without end endures inside of us.

How to talk about our struggle in the wake of the now hegemonic 'they must have done something to deserve this' and the systematic demonisation of the 'subversive terrorists,' allegedly just as responsible as the genocidal state for the brutality of the repression and its social and human consequences?

The attempt to storm the heavens ended in brutal defeat, in the effective practice of genocide. Yet the experience of terror continued to operate in us long after, as a kind of paralysis, a type of incapacitation to create meaning, unattainable among the absences, the unfinished mourning, the erasure of the political identities of the disappeared, the silence that for a long time hushed their stories with the accusatory mantle of 'it must have been for something.' Or in the words of Vassallo, the defeated are despicable, they reaped what they sowed.[29]

In addition, another part of the bitter fruit of defeat is the conviction, not exclusive to the political right, that one does not question the victors, neither their methods nor their objectives, if the end result is 'positive.' The dictatorship and its spokespeople managed to create an image of themselves as the ones who returned the country to order, civilisation and the precious belonging to the Christian West. In addition, the oh so democratic theory of the 'two evils' has not only become popular common sense but is now supported by a vast academic production with Foucauldian undertones and supposedly neutral aspirations, blessed by the mantra of authoritative citations.

In sum, as a result of the genocide, a large part of Argentine society, even if it has been able to develop critical perspectives regarding the coup, has bought into the condemnation against that generation of alleged 'cultivators of death and sacrifice,' or in Vassallo's terms, "masochists, suicidals, delusionals, a herd of stupid idealists" led by fanatical and irresponsible terrorists capable of imposing onto their own the most atrocious of defeats.

29 See Vassallo 2014.

Dispersed, isolated, subject to mandates of silence even in democracy, the recovery of even a few loose threads of the fabric is still barely ongoing. It is not simply a question of resuming an interrupted conversation: the absences are too many, the time elapsed is too long, the attempts to erase what happened, under the initiative of the ruling class, too recurrent. They insist on summoning us to amnesia, not only concerning the names of *lxs nuestrxs*, but of the past that binds us to them and of the dreams and political projects we had in common.

Internal Exile

> "The secrets that the defeated take with them will always remain unknowable."
> (Marta Vassallo)

On March 24, 1976, a brutal rupture pierced through our lives. The forced disappearance of *lxs nuestrxs*, loved and lost; political prison, exile, the expulsion and displacement of people from their homes and this subtle form of exile that is the deprivation of one's speech regarding what happened, to such an extent that the names of *lxs nuestrxs* became unpronounceable, and even when it was possible to recall them, it was as mere victims, devoid of their stories, their convictions, their struggles and resistances, their desires for another world.

In the days prior to the coup, death was prowling around in the form of police raids, missed encounters between comrades with sometimes fatal consequences, and in attempts to lend a hand to life, to strengthen the ties between us, to welcome fugitives and hide books, to cross checkpoints with your hair untied and with the most casual appearance... "I have nothing to do with anything."

On the day of the coup, the army searched the houses of several of my fellow militants. They were looking for María del Carmen and Adriana, according to their mother's testimony during the recent *Megacausa La Perla* trial. First broken thread.

Later, a very young *compañera* sheltered for a few days at home. I never knew her name. She was very white and petite, she must have been about 16 years old. I don't know if she survived. Perhaps her name was Margarita.

And after that, nothing. Useless to go to the so-called *citas de control,* the control check-ins.[30] And yet I went, and I waited. Five

30 The *Citas de Control* allowed us to know, in a context of political persecution, if the army or the police had taken one of us. If the person did not show up, it was very likely that s/he had been captured. Among the

minutes, the maximum allowed. I knew that I couldn't hold out for much longer. Nothing. No one showed. I had lost contact. What now? I tried to stay engaged following the guidelines of the party. "To Win or Die for Argentina."[31] But it was too late. The fabric was being torn apart. Thousands of loose threads as a result of the kidnappings, the staged assassinations,[32] the murders, the disappearances, the imprisonments, the forced exiles...

On March 31, against all reason, I went to the girls' home. I would ask their mother, I would leave them a little message, something that would allow us to meet again. When I was let in, their mother was extremely upset and sent me away in a very rude manner. She told me that she didn't want to see me there anymore. It was very strange. Truth be told, she had always been somewhere between distant and kind... Then again, she was just another mother, no different from any of ours.

I was alone, as if in a daze... it was no longer just a thread, but rather the entire fabric. A few days later, my father ordered me to pack my suitcase. I was to leave Córdoba. Nothing I said made him change his mind: I had to go.

Expelled by the gale of the dictatorship I arrived in Mendoza, a city where the repression was supposedly less violent. Later we found out that this was not true. At first, I thought I would stay for only a short time, a few months at most. But my stay carried on and on indefinitely. Until today.

I left Córdoba against my will, alone and without ties. Besieged and muted.

Mini (María) and Adriana, along with Elías, whom I had hardly ever met, were kidnapped on April 20 in an operation carried out by the army in Barrio Escobar. They were brought to La Perla, the main Clandestine Detention Centre in Córdoba province, as Cecilia Súzara was able to confirm to me a few years ago, when I described them to her, "one tall and the other small accompanied by a young man..."

Cecilia's description matched exactly. She had seen them in La Perla without knowing who they were. They were tied up, continually

precautions to take was the waiting time: you could not wait for too long because it was risky. Appointments were made to coordinate, to look for and deliver materials, to hear from others, etc. It is important to remember that in clandestine organisations coordination between members of a cell and among cells was not so easy.

31 The rival, equally persecuted, Peronist organisations used a similar slogan: "Free or Dead, Never Slaves."

32 In reality, assassinations in cold blood perpetrated by the security forces but presented to the public as if there had been a confrontation between them and the 'subversives.'

blindfolded... "eyeless," the *milicos* called it. Like most of the people who passed through La Perla, nothing is known about their fate, although we can guess what happened to them. María del Carmen, Adriana and Elías continue to be disappeared even though their families have searched for them, requested habeas corpus, testified...

The year 1976 was one long haze during which I learned to be 'someone else.' A foreigner to myself. Without a past or identity, well-behaved and well-dressed, a 'good girl' in the sarcastic words of my father, who had given me a series of instructions on what I could and could not do in that city unknown to me.

During the same year I met Gustavo, and I fell pregnant with my son Andrés. He was deeply welcomed into my life. He gave it meaning. It took me a long time to understand and learn that it shouldn't be like that, that I should seek meaning for myself, but during the long and sombre night of the dictatorship, this little boy was my only connection to the world of life.

I survived that time in a situation of confinement and internal exile, uprooted from my people, from my political and intellectual worlds, from my home. Alone, unable to discuss with others what was happening, the political and collective tragedy reduced to an almost intimate dimension. Sealed off tightly. Silenced and isolated. Speechless.

My acts of resistance became increasingly minimal: refusing to bear my husband's last name, protecting my young son, born in 1977, from the family pressure to be baptised, singing him quaint lullabies that eventually made him become a convinced Marxist: *'La Guajira del Che,'* songs of Zitarrosa, Víctor Jara, Los Olimareños, themes from the Spanish Civil War. And the beautiful refrain from *"Los dos Gallos"*: "a red rooster only gives up once it is dead..." Oh, how deeply that line resonated with me.

I was also able, once again with my father's help, to hide the few books that were saved from the ruins of my life, covered with magazine papers. And to keep to myself. And to resist. With obstinacy and bite. In the name of *'los míos y las mías,'* my comrades and friends, those whose names I was forbidden to pronounce out loud. I swore that I would not forget, that I would search for them as soon as even the smallest opening presented itself.

The horizon was dark. There was absolutely nothing throughout those eight long years that allowed me to imagine alternatives. But

I insisted on repeating to myself that at least they wouldn't have me. That their ideas and slogans would stay out of my head. And that I would uphold my convictions and the ties to my people, even if only in the form of knowing something that could not be said out loud: they were missing.

It was a time of harsh isolation.

The absences transformed into permanent anguish, the endless searches in the newspapers looking for a name... among the fallen, among those whose names were made available to the International PEN association. The nightmares, recurring and frightening.

Just that, and my little son connecting me to life. Andrés was a strangely wise child who had learned, I don't quite understand how, that there were things that were not to be repeated outside the home. He was very young, but he understood.

I was 'Rara, pero no encendida,' alienated and numb, to paraphrase a sentence from one of my favourite tangos, *Los mareados*. Deep sorrow nested in my soul, and it took me a great deal of effort to remove it. Joy had become elusive, something alien.

Then came the *Guerra de las Malvinas,* the Falklands War, and with it my children Valentin and Martina.

With democracy the street returned, the possibility of pronouncing words that had been erased from the dictionary during the times of "We Argentines are human and right(-wing),"[33] finding oneself among *compañerxs* and shouting for 'Truth' and 'Justice.' Knowing that in the streets, side by side, we were finally more than two again – Benedetti, always Benedetti – recognising ourselves in those personal and political bonds. Still afraid, but also very angry and with the conviction that we would not take a single step back in the search for *lxs nuestrxs.*

My first concrete outlet had been as part of the nascent human rights movement in Mendoza. Towards the end of the dictatorship, Beba Becerra, president of the *Madres de la Plaza de Mayo* in Mendoza, received and welcomed me, and then shortly after the return of democracy, I became a member in the *Frente de Apoyo a Madres de Plaza de Mayo,* the Support Front for the Mothers of Plaza de Mayo.

Little by little, I learned to leave behind my confinement, the solitude, the silence, and my horizon began to be populated with

33 Editor's note: *"Los argentinos somos derechos y humanos"* is a type of perverse fascist humour playing on the Spanish for Human Rights, *Derechos Humanos.*

women who returned from exile. Among them Sofía D'Andrea and Nora Llaver, my friends and colleagues until today. Together we found ourselves amongst the young faces of *lxs nuestrxs* in the streets. We marched together with them, their pictures on our banners, in our hands, in the rituals that we began to develop and perform in a public space that we gradually reconquered in order to demand their lives, their bodies, their children, their fortunes.

Words and books also returned, circulating from hand to hand, from mouth to mouth. The fragmented accounts of what had happened to us. First mutterings tainted by fear, stigma, our own censorship and the censorship of others. In those days, I read desperately to exorcise this period of violent silence and isolation: Gramsci, Luxemburg, Marx, Benjamin...

I returned to the streets and brought along my young children. The banners, the silhouettes of our disappeared loved ones drawn in the streets right next to the symbol of the headscarf, the distinguishing feature of the *Madres*. The marches, the claims for 'Re-appearance with life' and 'Punish the guilty.' Yet it would not be until the beginning of the 1985 'Trial of the Juntas' for crimes against humanity that I would know the stories that connected us all. The testimonies during the trials gave us back the lives of *lxs nuestrxs*, their commitments, their becoming human again: that of Juan Antonio Gutiérrez, Raúl García, Emiliano Pérez, Sara Palacio, El 'Negro' Arroyo, and of so many others.[34]

Connections

So, this is largely what defeat is about. The isolation, the rupture of the threads of the collective fabric, of the connections with others so indispensable for us to think and struggle, of the loss of emancipatory horizons, which can be envisioned in times when the masses become conscious of their powers, when the objective conditions seem precariously to support us, but which painfully fray when time is governed by reaction and defeat, making it seem reasonable to settle for 'the possible.' And yet it has been the repeated occurrence of the impossible that has kept us going throughout all these years, the demand for *lxs nuestrxs* to be brought back to us alive, the efforts to sustain our presence in the streets, even if no one wanted to listen to us, and even

34 See Colectivo Juicios Mendoza 2019.

if we could not hold on to our own past, subjected to censorship and silence, and to the interpretations – consensus, democratic capitalism, etc. – constructed in the field of fashion,[35] as Benjamin would say.

As a member of several collectives that fight for 'Memoria, Verdad y Justicia' (Memory, Truth and Justice), I have often wondered about the threads that unite us, about this delicate warp that connects us across distances and times, and that not only makes present this past that does not pass, but that links experiences and spatialities, and that builds intricate pathways all across the country and across countries and continents. The type of threads capable of crossing even the borders of death in search of the bodies of those that were not returned to us.

Mendoza is by now the place where I have put down roots, although it was once, many years ago, the site of my banishment. Nowadays I can really feel these roots, connected as I am to the Human Rights Movement, to my comrades-in-arms with whom we fight for Memory, Truth and Justice, to the new generation of young feminists with whom we have marched in the streets demanding the right for legal abortion, to the *compañerxs* with whom we struggle in defence of water and life.

Today, we who have been defeated but who have continued to resist, know that in the face of defeats what one needs to do is breathe, to look at and acknowledge ourselves, because one thing is for certain: we are not going to give up. Ours is a collective commitment that we sustain and nourish on the basis of communal listening and affection, and the persistence of the fabric that *connects us,* despite the broken threads, the gaping holes left by the absences and the traces of pain woven into it.

Translated from the Argentine Spanish by hjje.

---

35 Editor's note: For more about Walter Benjamin's ideas on the subject of fashion, see *The Arcades Project* (1999) and the recent *Benjamin on Fashion* (2020).

References

Anderson, Perry (1988), "Democracia y dictadura en América Latina en la década del 70," *Revista de Ciencias Sociales*, 3, 15-23.

Arakaki, Agustín (2011), *La pobreza en Argentina 1974-2006: construcción y análisis de la información*. Buenos Aires: CEPED.

Basualdo, Eduardo (2008), "La distribución del ingreso en la Argentina y sus condicionantes estructurales," *in* CELS *Derechos humanos en Argentina. Informe 2008*. Available at https://www.cels.org.ar/web/wp-content/uploads/2016/10/7-La-distribucion-del-ingreso-en-la-Argentina-y-sus-condicionantes-estructurales.pdf.

Benjamin, Walter (1940/1982), *Tesis de filosofía de la historia*. México: La Nave de los Locos.

Bodoc, Liliana (2019), "Aquella Pregunta." Available at https://elcaminodelasmusas.home.blog/2019/03/24/aquella-pregunta-liliana-bodoc-24-de-marzo/.

Borón, Atilio (2006), "The Truth about Capitalist Democracy", *Socialist Register,* Vol. 42, 28-58.

Calloni, Stella (2016), *Operación cóndor, pacto criminal*. Caracas: El perro y la rana.

Carpintero, Enrique & Vainer, Alejandro (2018), *Las huellas de la memoria* (1957-1983). Tomo II. Buenos Aires: Topía.

Césaire, Aimé (1939/1983), *Cahier d'un retour au pays natal*. Editions Présence Afri-caine. Available at https://susa-literatura.eus/kaierakm/aime-cesaire-cahier_d'un_retour_au_pays_natal.pdf.

Colectivo Juicios Mendoza (2019), *Memorias de los Juicios por Delitos de Lesa Humanidad* (Mendoza, 2010-2018). Mendoza: SIPUC-FCPyS-UNCuyo.

Ekhardt, Philipp (2020), *Benjamin on Fashion*. London: Bloomsbury.

Gramsci, Antonio (1931/1970), Apuntes sobre la historia de las clases subalternas. Criterios metódicos. *In* Manuel Sacristán (selección, traducción y notas) *Antología*. Madrid: Siglo XXI.

Fernández, Juan Manuel and others (2013), "Aportes para el estudio de los levantamientos de masas en Argentina entre 1968 y 1974," VII Jornadas de Jóvenes Investigadores. *Instituto de Investigaciones Gino Germani,* Facultad de Ciencias Sociales, Universidad de Buenos Aires. Available at https://www.aacademica.org/000-076/77.

Larguía, Isabel & Dumoulin, John (1976), *Hacia una ciencia de la liberación de la mujer.* Barcelona: Anagrama.

Luxemburg, Rosa (1919), "Order prevails in Berlin," *Marxists Internet Archive*. Available at https://www.marxists.org/archive/luxemburg/1919/01/14.htm.

Mandel, Ernest (1979), *El capitalismo tardío*. México: Ediciones ERA.

Marín, Juan Carlos (1984), *Los hechos armados, un ejercicio posible*. Buenos Aires: Ed. CICSO.

Marx, Karl (1852/1957), "El 18 Brumario de Luis Bonaparte," *in* Carlos Marx y Federico Engels *Obras escogidas,* Buenos Aires: Cartago, 160-223.

Randall, Margaret (1970), *Las Mujeres*. México: SXXI.

Saint Jean, Ibérico (1977), "Palabras para no olvidar." Available at https://www.nodo50.org/exilioargentino/cambio2013CEAM/2006/Marzo2006/palabras_para_no_olvidar.htm.

Santucho, Mario Roberto (1976), "Argentinos ¡A las armas!," *Marxists Internet Archive*. Available at https://www.marxists.org/espanol/santucho/1976/iii-1976.htm.

Vassallo, Marta (2014), *La terrible esperanza*. Buenos Aires: Colisión.

Walsh, Rodolfo (1969), "Cordobazo," *Semanario de la CGT de los Argentinos*, Nº 46. Available at http://www.memoriaabierta.org.ar/materiales/pdf/cordobazo.pdf.

Walsh, Rodolfo (24 marzo 1977), "Carta abierta de un escritor a la junta militar." Available at https://apm.gov.ar/periplosdememorias/1-1-B-2.html#:~:text=-Carta%20abierta%20de%20un%20escritor,24%20de%20marzo%20de%201977& text=Este%20documento%20testimonia%20y%20denuncia,culturales %20y%20sociales%20del%20Golpe and https://www.inversejournal.com/ 2022/ 01/20/rodolfo-walshs-1977-open-letter-to-the-military-junta-in-argentina-in-troduced-and-translated-by- arturo-desimone/.

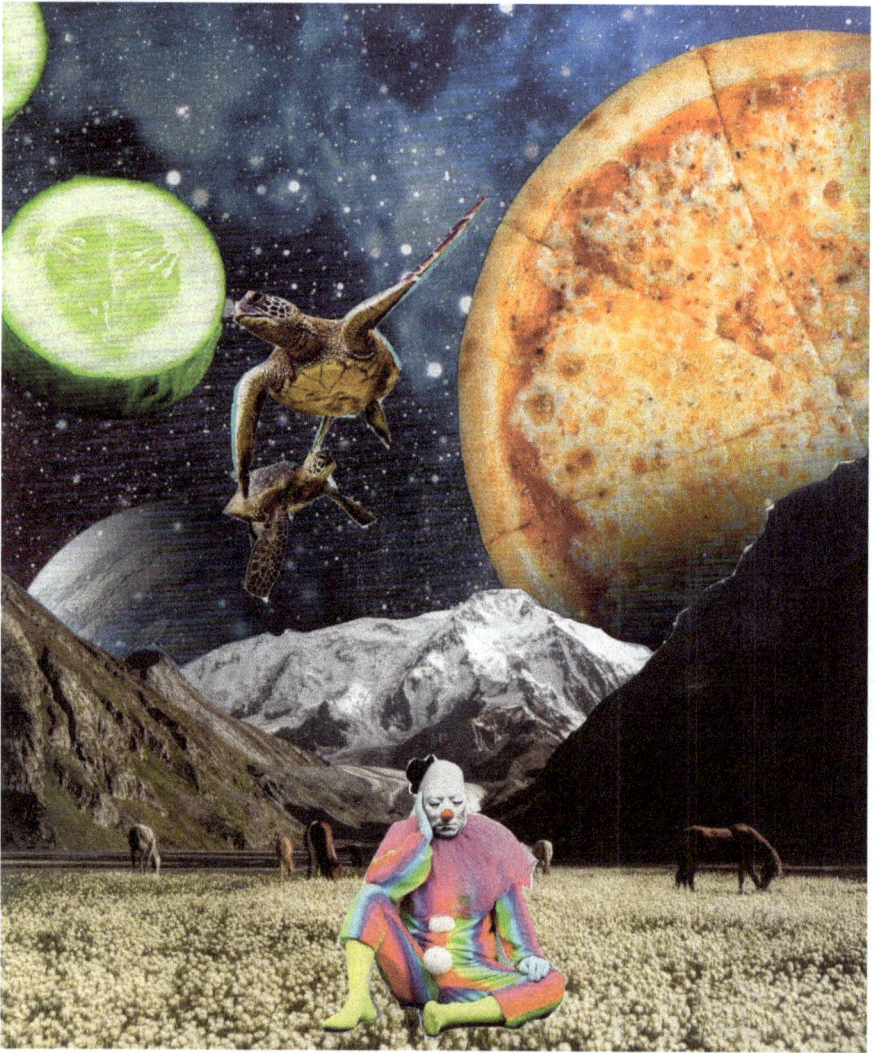

Artist: Mohira Suyarkulova

A Reasonable Doubt – Should I Stay Alone?

Nina Bagdasarova

Left loneliness sounds like an oxymoron. Generally speaking, Leftism implies collectivity, solidarity, understanding the needs and problems of a variety of people. This means that if you are a leftist, there should always be comrades around you and hence you should always have the hope that no matter the situation you will be understood and supported, because you are inevitably part of a larger collective. In my case, I am part of different activist groups, I have my leftist colleagues at the university where I am working (the American University of Central Asia in Bishkek, Kyrgyzstan) and, fortunately, I also have great support from my family. Nevertheless, this topic arose, and many comrades from across the world responded to participate in the project. Is this a mere sign of the moment (which seems to be very difficult and almost hopeless in many places)? Or did such a sense of loneliness arise at other times in history for those who shared leftist views? Considering the biographies of various revolutionaries such as Vladimir Lenin and Rosa Luxemburg, we can assume that this feeling is not unique to our situation, it overtook many at different times and in different historical circumstances. Why is that? What does this feeling of left loneliness reflect and, perhaps more importantly, what can be done about it?

The lone Left among the Left

To begin with, I am sure that there are different types of 'left loneliness' and that we can therefore describe different experiences with these words – in fact, from what I understand, this is precisely one of the intentions of the present book, to explore and investigate different experiences and to try to understand and relate them to each other. The type of left loneliness that I want to describe is based on my personal experience, yet at the same time I am confident one can find analogies not only among many comrades across the world today, but also in history, when people of left beliefs went through the same experience or at least something very similar. I will call this feeling 'the whole world has gone crazy and lost the sense of Reason.' For example, probably something comparable was experienced by many leftists in 1914, speaking out against the outbreak of WWI, when they encountered comrades who suddenly turned out to be fervent patriots and/or those who could not choose between their internationalist convictions and the importance of victory for their own country. Arguably something similar was also felt by many communists when faced with the fact of mass repressions in the USSR in the 1930s, the signing of the Molotov-Ribbentrop pact in 1939 or during the 20th Congress of the CPSU in 1956, when Stalin's awful legacy was revealed.

In post-Soviet Central Asia, the breakdown of the Soviet Union led to millions of people literally feeling homeless after losing their country in the 1991 referendum, in spite of the fact that the overwhelming majority of people voted in favour of keeping the Union (in Central Asian countries it was as high as 95% of the population). In the case of my parents, I remember their sadness and hopelessness at having to deal with the end of a "great country" and its quest to bring a new type of justice and an inclusive social order to humankind. A deep sense of loneliness was part of this complex feeling of abandonment, homelessness and having had their ideals betrayed. And while there were many cases of people across the Union – like the famous theatre director Mark Zakharov – publicly burning their CPSU membership cards, I still hold on to and cherish my father's.

Returning to today's times, concretely, the feeling of loneliness I am experiencing has several aspects. One of them is a strong sense of the irrationality or even insanity of the events taking place around us and the obscurantism looming from all sides. Admittedly, this feeling may not be unique to the Left. Surely, any critically thinking and logically trained conservative or liberal could have felt this way over the past few years. Since the beginning of the pandemic, both political-economic decisions and people's reactions to these decisions have often been strangely violent. And just as the global absurdity of the fight against the pandemic started to finally recede, decisions began to be less improvised and panicky, and more reasonable security measures began to be taken, along came February 24, 2022. The day of Russia's invasion of Ukraine sucked the world into a new funnel of threats and risks that are growing at a tremendous speed and, in fact, seem to have no rational explanation and are therefore without an effective rational solution. Putting it in metaphoric terms, Reason seems to have gone to sleep like in Goya's "The Sleep of Reason Produces Monsters" (or maybe it has just died).

So let me be more precise about what I mean when I say that the Russian war has no clear rational explanations. My personal experience of confronting mass violence directly (during the so-called Osh events in Kyrgyzstan in 2010)[1], as well as many years of experience in studying and teaching the psychology of conflict, have convinced me that not a single conflict can be explained only from rational positions. Rather, something inexplicable always remains – the scale of aggression, the cruelty of clashes, the paranoid belief in one's own righteousness and/or a pathological unwillingness to critically look at one's own, possibly erroneous point of view. This is especially noticeable when there is no significant time gap between the conflict and the proposed explanations. The same applies to the ongoing scenario. There clearly are many explanations for the current war (like Russia's increasing imperialist ambitions, NATO's expansion to the East, the rise of Ukrainian neo-fascists, the latent conflict in the east of Ukraine), but behind each of them there is something that cannot be explained in fully rational terms. It is this 'something' that influences the amount of hate speech in the media and social networks, the broken relationships between friends and relatives, the aggressive street protests. Instead of rational explanations for these reactions, people increasingly resort to defamation and name-calling that do not explain anything. People are called 'zombified' by military propaganda, accused of a lack of critical thinking due to their 'Soviet mentality' or even affected by psychotropic radiation so they do not hear the arguments of reason (admittedly, there is a great temptation sometimes to believe this last hypothesis as the statements of so many seemingly sane people sound so absurd).

Personally, the above-mentioned has contributed to my feeling an acute sense of futility concerning everything that has been done before, the current (quite desperate) situation and the senselessness of continuing to act any further. Years of work devoted to the anti-discrimination struggle and teaching countless students and training participants about reflexivity and analytical skills to be more understanding and sympathetic (because I do believe that the right analysis can make you more compassionate and empathic), seem to have been spent in vain. The sound habit, developed over many years,

1 In June 2010, there was a great massacre with pogroms in which thousands of ethnic Uzbek residents of the city of Osh died along with hundreds of Kyrgyz people. These events were provoked by a huge political crisis that started in April after the overthrow of President Bakiyev.

of answering argument with argument – what used to be called 'dialogue' – has turned out to be ineffective in the current situation. On the contrary, a sharp division into two camps (if you are for Ukraine, then you are against Russia, and if you are against Ukraine, then you are for Russia) deprives one of any choice and the opportunity to discuss matters dispassionately. You see manifestations of imperialism and fascism on both sides, but by saying this, you will receive hatred from everywhere in response. In fact, just being against war and violence is not enough for anyone any longer. The respective positions of the parties are impenetrable to each other's arguments, and if you say that you do not share any of them, that nationalism and the desire for superiority are characteristic of all sides of the conflict, you will receive in response accusations that you cannot distinguish Good from Evil. What is more, even the closest of friends, with whom you shared many views before, are caught up in this dualistic division of views on the conflict.

Another aspect is that the war exacerbated and made more explicit those elements of left-wing loneliness that have always been present in my life, as I now understand, due to the fact that I happened to be born and live in Kyrgyzstan. This type of loneliness can be called 'caught between imperialism and ethno-nationalist anti-colonialism.' To describe this particular form of being left and lonely, let us start with the problem of language. My comrades, in Kyrgyzstan and throughout the post-Soviet space, communicate in Russian. But does this mean that we feel part of the Russian cultural and political space as well? We rather do not. Yes, we all speak Russian, but in different 'languages,' including different 'left' languages. Let me explain. Perhaps because the second language of many of us here in Central Asia is English, we often read different texts and identify ourselves with different leftist authors that are not necessarily being read in Russia. Consequently, many of us focus not only on the Soviet tradition of interpreting Marxism (although it is very important for us[2]), but also on so-called 'Western' Marxism. In addition, for many of us, not only the classical proletariat is important, but so are other oppressed groups – women, migrants, LGBTQ+ people. In fact, most of my comrades share and promote the ideas of Queer Communism (which was

---

2 For instance, we pay a lot of attention to the works of Evald Ilyenkov, Lev Vygotsky, Piotr Galperin and many others.

born in Central Asia)[3]. Hence, for us, the picture of the fight against oppression is much broader than the one painted by most popular Russian left-wing bloggers and publicists with a million-strong audience, like Kagarlitsky, Semin, Rudoy, Zhukov, Puchkov and others, all of whom usually do not accept and at times even ridicule the ideas of feminism, the LGBTQ+ movement and/or intersectionality.[4]

Even if some of them rarely allow themselves openly sexist and homophobic statements, almost everyone trips over the 'stumbling block' of Russian imperial self-consciousness. Seemingly completely without noticing it, they allow themselves to speak arrogantly about the former Soviet republics, and here I refer specifically to the former Soviet republics of Central Asia, the Caucasus and countries like Ukraine and Moldova.[5] Exchanges of opinions with the Left from other countries in the Russian public space are very rare and usually do not include Central Asia, which probably seems too far and too different compared to Belarus or Ukraine. Furthermore, inside Russia, virtually no coverage is given to the life and left movements of those regions that have cultural and political autonomy (the so-called Autonomous Republics or Areas – *Okrugs*). Statements by Russian leftists on the so-called 'national' issue are rare and often sound more like Stalin's (imperialist) than Lenin's (democratic) style, without any reference to contemporary ideas about the formation of nation-states, such as for instance the notion of 'imagined communities' or other constructivist approaches.[6] While these statements may contain the occasional criticism of nationalism (even sometimes Russian nationalism), such criticism generally lacks depth and does not provide an opportunity to see the bigger picture of what is happening in the world (within and around Russia) today. It is this type of 'left imperialism' that creates a distance between us and our Russian comrades, that makes us feel quite alone in the vast expanses of the former USSR. This feeling is important, because historically the people within the Soviet Union shared a common leftist perception of the world, whereas nowadays we feel quite excluded from this sharing. On the contrary, the Russian Left has gradually reprised the role of 'big brother' that Lenin had so

---

3 See Shatalova & Mamedov 2016.
4 I do not mean that we do not have any partners and comrades in Russia – we do, but usually they do not belong to some dominant Leftist discourse in Russia supported by large audiences.
5 People who can read in Russian may have a look at a critique of Russian imperialism by the left youth organization "Kyrgsoc": https://kyrgsoc.org/.
6 See Anderson 1983.

explicitly warned against when he spoke of the "Russian imperialist chauvinism" that may destroy the communist movement.[7] Partly, his prophecy is now coming true. However, it is precisely this feeling of loneliness that also makes it possible to seek and build strong bonds of solidarity with comrades from other former Soviet republics facing a similar scenario. For all of us, Russian remains the language we speak with each other, and it is easier for us to find opportunities to unite with colleagues from places like Kazakhstan, Belarus, Ukraine and/or other countries with which we have a common history and share many political positions. We continue to read and write in Russian and that is also a very important part of our common cause.

At the same time, the struggle against oppression, including the remnants of Russian colonialism and modern practices of neo-colonialism, sometimes leads to the opposite extreme, when this struggle develops into new forms of (ethno-)nationalism, such as the case in Kyrgyzstan and many former Soviet republics today, and which cannot arouse any sympathy in a person of leftist views.

As I said, I was born and live in Kyrgyzstan. Russian is my mother tongue, and I am infinitely ashamed and hurt that I do not know the Kyrgyz language well. This happened historically because of the official state language policy in the Kyrgyz SSR during the 1960s-1970s when Kyrgyz was removed from the majority of schools.[8] Still, I can understand and share the importance of the native language and native culture for many of those with whom I live. Yet, the line separating the fight against cultural oppression from the exaltation of one's own culture over others is often very thin and perilous. Just as imperial lenses are often invisible to those born and raised in Russia, even leftists, so the desire for one's own culture to be dominant is often invisible to people, again even leftists, who nowadays belong to 'new nationalising majorities'[9] and minorities, sharing language and culture with only a few people on a global scale. How aggressive can the defence of one's culture be, when it seems to be disappearing against the backdrop of globalisation? How, while defending one's own culture, not to cross the border between one's own need for autonomy and the desire to dominate others? Moreover, there is the danger, in the heat of the struggle, of perceiving your own minority group as monolithic and

7 See Lenin 1951.
8 A long-term result has been that even today an effective methodology for learning Kyrgyz is still lacking.
9 See Brubaker 1995.

unified without recognising the subtle differences and peculiarities of different groups and individuals *within* one's minority culture.

Quite often, these disputes with comrades come down to different interpretations of the Soviet past, in which the ideas of internationalist equality are bizarrely intertwined with the ideas of the aforementioned 'big brother' represented by the Russian people, and the Europeanised version of modernisation that the Soviet Union brought to our territories.[10] Do these arguments make one feel 'left loneliness'? Yes, definitely. All the more acutely because one experiences it while being among close comrades, who are unable to distinguish certain nationalist convictions 'rationalised' through a rhetoric of 'anti-colonialism.'"

Nonetheless, and in spite of some of the negative emotions produced such as isolation and a certain distancing from friends, I again find this feeling very helpful. In this constant disagreement with the imperial view of Kyrgyzstan from the outside and the limited ethno-national view from within the country, the ability to reflect is honed, ideally allowing one to avoid both of these extremes. Does this mean that I, along with my Queer Communist comrades, take a centrist position – slightly sharing and rejecting the imperial position on the one hand and the ethno-national one on the other? Of course not. Our position is extremely radical; it rejects both of these approaches. Maybe that's why we often feel so alone. As a matter of fact, our position is simple – it is based on the idea of universal equality. As soon as universality and equality are in question, we are ready to enter into discussion, and maybe even fight for these values. Is our position close to abstract humanism? No, it is extremely specific and aimed at protecting every oppressed group, every oppressed individual. Everywhere, all the time.

A third element of my left loneliness is that it seems to me that this and other radical positions we take are not only due to the times in which we live, but are also a consequence of the place we inhabit – i.e. Central Asia – a region not only dependent on the different world centres of power (Russia, the West, the Muslim world, the Far East and South Asia), but at the same time far away from most of them. This remoteness, this 'peripherality' of existence allows us a certain epistemic independence and our own views of what is happening in the 'Big World' out there. However, this remoteness also gives rise to

10 See Shatalova & Mamedov 2016.

another type of leftish loneliness, i.e. not being included in important events and processes generally taking place elsewhere.

By way of example and returning to the current war, having written the statement on behalf of the "Peace Committee of Kyrgyzstan"[11] with our comrades, we received several favourable reviews from various left-wing European media, but none of them dared to publish it as a statement. In response, they merely invited one of the authors of the text to act as a columnist and publish it as his personal opinion. This can be seen as a somewhat perplexing signal from the Left in Europe: "We generally agree with your anti-imperialist position, but we cannot join it publicly." In other words, a voice about the Russian-Ukrainian war from the periphery, even when coming from the territory of the former USSR and from a former colony of the Russian Empire, cannot be considered an argument in the dispute between 'big European and Global' players.[12] Getting a response like this can make you feel very lonely indeed.

Finally, the above thoughts and feelings have arisen in relation to one's very own left comrades-in-arms. But what type of loneliness emerges when I discuss such issues with liberals and conservatives? Truth be told, I have practically no conservative friends, but there are quite a few liberals among them. How do I feel when it comes to discussing politics with them? As a rule, I feel myself to be the object of ironic ridicule, not in a rude way, but behind the statements of the other side there is always a slight tone of condescension, as if the discussion was conducted with a somewhat dull child, and also of surprise: "How can such an educated woman say such nonsense?" Sound familiar? In other words, my arguments are not accepted or even genuinely engaged with in these disputes. Assuming that these reactions are not specific to Kyrgyzstan, I believe that this phenomenon of the impenetrability of liberal and conservative thought to left-wing arguments plays a large role in shaping left-wing loneliness today, when neo-liberal discourse has become predominant in all groups and strata of society. I will thus proceed to analyse this phenomenon as being due to a clash of two types of rationality – 'Right' and 'Left.'

11 The English and Russian versions of the Statement are published on the "Kyrgsoc" website https://kyrgsoc. org/zayavlenie-antivoennogo-komiteta-kyrgyzstana/.

12 The same generally happens with our locally produced publications. They simply do not receive reviews or suggestions for translations, such is the case with books that were published by SHTABpress and also with our most recent book on Left Happiness (See Bagdasarova, Mamedov & Suyarkulova 2020).

Left and Right 'banks' of the flow of events

Analysing these two types of rationality, it is worth recalling how we started the discussion about left loneliness – a reasonable attitude to what is happening today seems to be to create small islands of reason inside the constant flow of information filled with irrational or paranoid explanations and proposals for solving problems. And since it is generally people on the political Left who are among the few to keep a rational attitude towards the current situation, it is this very rationality that can make them feel very lonely in the contemporary world.

Yet, as mentioned above, many of today's conservatives and liberals are faced with the same existential givens as the Left, and hence they may also experience the absurdity of the moment and be in search of rational explanations and solutions for what is happening. While I might not agree with their proposed solutions, it does not seem impossible that they also experience some form of loneliness, for instance the loneliness at having witnessed their liberal values being abused by the 'immoral' and 'irrational' actions of their erstwhile Russian partners.

Therefore, why should the loneliness of the Left be regarded as something special?

In my view, several rationales can be given for this. First, we can follow Roland Barthes and his notion of the Right Myth.[13] The Right Myth (that is, the myth of Right liberals and conservatives) is rooted in the understanding and systematic proclamation of a "human nature," which makes certain social processes appear as natural, i.e. it is "natural" to fight, it is "natural" to want to defeat others, it is "natural" to dominate, it is "natural" to occupy certain social roles that prove the "proper" (proper because it is natural!) social order. Thus, for the Right, their own myth is "natural" – transparent, invisible; they are convinced that they see "reality as it is," that is to say, the "true, undistorted reality" of cruel competition and survival of the fittest. Accordingly, for them, it is always the Left who are the myth-makers, deceiving people with false, utopian hopes and promises of a just society, which will never come true precisely because "human nature" cannot be changed.[14]

For the Left, on the other hand, their vision cannot be mythical, because they are well aware of the particular lenses through which

13 Barthes 1991: 109-164.
14 Ibid.

they look at social processes and events. There is nothing "natural" in a man or a woman, human nature is never predetermined and constant, it depends on the conditions in which a person becomes a person. Or paraphrasing Marx: It is not the nature of a person that determines society, but society that forms and determines the nature of a person.[15]

In our times, after the fall of the Berlin Wall, the neoliberal society that forms and determines our current nature tells us that Left ideas have failed, and that a society built on leftist foundations is not viable. We are told that there is no alternative and that ours, despite all, is the best of all possible worlds. And although works critical of the existing capitalist order began to resurface shortly after the end of the Cold War and have since become more and more popular in academic circles, this has generally not led to the development of leftist ideas and political projects capable of genuinely challenging the status quo. Why is this? What makes the possibility of a left 'renaissance' seem so remote?

Looking at the world from Kyrgyzstan, the reasons are obviously multiple and go beyond the scope of this article, but some of the key shortcomings that I see are: i) the lack of a common 'language,' both conceptually and linguistically, capable of building a common platform for struggle;[16] ii) the corresponding, effective fragmentation and isolation of many left initiatives, thereby preventing the creation of a new 'International' following the example of those that existed in the first half of the 20th century;[17] and iii) on a more fundamental level, the absence of radical alternatives to market-based neoliberal capitalism. By and large, critics are merely debating 'more acceptable and fair' (and so on...) types of capitalism – an 'unconditional basic income,' new, more long-lasting and 'green-friendly' products, new types of economic regulation, i.e. small changes hopefully paving the way for further shifts – but it appears that only very few people are fully ready to give up capitalism as such, despite ever-mounting

15 The exact quote by Marx is: "It is not the consciousness of men that determines their existence, but on the contrary their social existence determines their consciousness." (See Marx 1859).

16 Perhaps one of the most important demands of the Left for modern education is the need for the most multilingual education system possible. At the same time, we need to expand efforts to translate important leftist texts into different languages and hence make them accessible to as many people as possible. In this case, we are talking not only about academic texts, but also popular (re-)presentations of the main ideas of the Left.

17 Currently there are some efforts to organise such a new association like Varoufakis' Progressive International (https://progressive.international/). Still these types of organisations are far from being as large and influential as were the Second or Third International before WWI and WWII, respectively.

evidence that living in really existing neoliberal economic conditions, for the majority of humankind, means always living on the verge of survival at best.

I hear too few people daring to say the R-word, too few daring to touch the core of the system. As Santos notes: "Dominant politics becomes epistemological when it is able to make a credible claim that the only valid knowledge available is the one that ratifies its own dominance."[18] We may paraphrase and say dominant politics has become natural when it is able to make a credible claim that the only valid politics is the one that ratifies its own naturalness. And yet, it is necessary to stop capitalism and to cancel the dominance of right rationality. We cannot just say, "let's change the system and have something new instead." We must begin to imagine this new something and name it in a way that it will attract and fascinate people. For example, the ideas of Queer Communism insist on radical inclusiveness as the main characteristic of the future society. Still, a clear image of this more humane social order and how to get there has not yet emerged. Without question, we have our work cut us for us.

So how lonely does the Left feel in this particular discursive-epistemic space, in a scenario where it is possible to criticise capitalism, but where it appears impossible to offer any genuine alternative, since it will be considered and rejected, both by the academic community and by ordinary people, as a 'utopian deceit,' 'a frivolous perversion' of economic laws and human nature?

Let us go into more detail about what 'human nature' is for the Right. As touched upon already, roughly speaking, it is a 'nature' in which everyone fights for themselves and wants to win, and where everything that builds beyond this desire is already considered 'unnatural.' Only a society where 'natural' impulses are encouraged and developed can be just, because only such a society does not fight against the 'nature' of a person but uses it for the 'common' good.[19] This approach advances Right Rationality step by step – the ascension of the strong, who must ultimately help the weak and keep society whole. There is no Strong without the Weak. The weak are needed. They are the breeding ground for any cannibalistic exploitative order. This logic cannot be disputed, because from the point of view of the Right, this

18 Santos 2018: vii.
19 As it is described in "The Tragedy of the Commons" (Hardin 1968).

type of society is not a myth – it is the 'natural' order of things, the one that is given to us, against which it is not only stupid, but also harmful to fight, since this will 'naturally' lead to the emergence of totalitarian utopias such as 'Communism,' killing millions of innocent people. That is to say, all utopias are simply obliged to be totalitarian, because they will automatically suppress the 'natural essence' of humans.

How can we summarise the main points of the Right Myth in current neoliberal conditions? Clearly, one of the (repeatedly rationalised) grand narratives about human emancipation and liberation has reached its extreme point in neoliberal discourse, leaving far behind all previous conservative and liberal theories:

1. The individual is the measure of all things.
2. The measure of an individual's value is the amount of money and power that (usually) he has.
3. Everyone gets the place they deserve in the hierarchy of success, where they are located in accordance with the set of privileges to which they have access, and access to privileges is always due to the merit of the individual.
4. If this access is limited, then most likely this is the result of irrational self-development, the ill-use of available opportunities, a lack of individual effort, etc.[20]

Is this scheme rational? Undoubtedly yes. It also presupposes a certain social structure – a 'society of equal opportunities.' The whole world has been in this rationality for almost half a century, since at least the 1980s. And in these roughly 50 years in the history of humankind, we have witnessed the most rapid growth in inequality, the impoverishment and marginalisation of millions of people, an unprecedented increase in exploitation, etc. I wonder, how this is possible if, apparently, with the end of Communist 'totalitarianism,' we have all finally become free, we have reached the "end of history" and now all live in a society where everyone gets what they deserve?

For the Left, the answer is obvious. This rationality of inequality and marginalisation is built into the logic of capitalism which, simply

---

20 It is interesting that a lot of people sharing the Right's rationality feel themselves lonely because of the acute individualisation and fragmentation of society. Unsurprisingly, even this is perceived by those on the Right as something 'natural' to be accepted.

put, is the logic of individual success and profit over people. But there is of course nothing 'natural' about this logic. 'Nature' is the name and essence of the Right Myth and this logic is mythological to the core. For the Left, the human being is not a natural being. It is a creature that can think and speak, moreover, it is the only creature on the planet that can think with the help of words. Clearly, many animals can think. Many animals can communicate using a peculiar language of signals among themselves. But no animal communicates with its own kind using words to organise its own thinking. This takes humans out of biological nature once and for all.[21] Humans are from the very beginning such beings as they understand themselves to be. They always organise their lives with other people, otherwise they will not grow up to be human – without people around, a person grows up to be an animal. And they organise this life exactly as they under-stand their own selves. They can understand and consider themselves as people who obey the law of the Strong (Right Myth), or they can understand and consider themselves as beings who live together with other people who help and support each other (what the Right might call the Left Myth).

From a Left perspective, there is hence the need for an alter-native vision, a myth of the Left so to speak, or their story of 'human nature.' In this story, the Left does not resort to biological arguments – after all, among many animal communities, including primates, mutual aid is well developed and helps species survive. Nature cannot be an argument in this dispute. Only the idea of people who together decide *what they should be* (decide, not obey instinct!) informed by a type of (Left!) rationality can underlie a society that is built on univer-sal justice. Naturally, this society cannot only rest on the rationality of individual success and survival, for then we get the society of the Right Myth. Therefore, what kind of alternative rationality becomes accept-able and is this alternative rational at all? For instance, is it rational to care for the sick and weak using common tax money, instead of throwing premature babies into the abyss of privatised healthcare? Should resources be shared equally among everyone and if yes will this be done fairly? Or won't those who put more effort into finding prey receive a smaller share? Wouldn't this seem not only unfair but also totally irrational? Maybe there is a much more rational approach

21 See Vygotsky 1986.

to reality behind the Right Myth after all? Absurd? Perhaps not. By seeking to exclude 'nature' from the equation that underlies society, the Left may appear powerless against the 'rational' arguments of the Right. More about this in the next section.

In summary, the Left feels quite lonely in this discursive space. Of course, a mythological explanation is more 'digestible' – it does not need any further justification, it simply refers everything back to Nature. Barthes puts it as the permanent tendency of the bourgeoisie to reduce History to Nature.[22] Everything is as it is because it is 'natural' – thus you do not need any arguments for your position. It is simply too long and complicated to show people that nobody has some 'eternal human nature' and that in different periods of time different people lived in different territories and their lives were always determined by historical socio-economic circumstances. That is to say, in order to show the connection between economics and people's behaviour, much work must be done. Isn't it much easier to argue that people have always been the same because of their 'natural' characteristics? Wouldn't you feel lonely, too, trying to explain some things that nobody wants to hear (because everybody thinks they already know everything there is to know)? I know I do.

Towards a third rationality: Spinoza's Rationality of Ethics and his understanding of human nature

We can indeed take Nature out of the equation, but if we do, we must then put something else in its place, something that allows Right and Left rationality to be adequately compared using a common basis. For me, in the first instance, this basis is not Nature, but Ethics. That is, the inner Law within us, to which Kant, the greatest researcher of Reason, referred in order to demonstrate Reason's boundaries and limitations. However, this inner law can have another justification referring to Reason, logical enough that it obeys a geometric method[23] that does not allow logical errors to be made. I am talking about the Ethics of Spinoza, in which the Logic of Nature is not separated from the Logic of human existence, and where this existence depends not only on the mind, but also on the body, feelings and desires. Where

22 Barthes 1991: 152.

23 Becoming popular in 16th century Europe, the "geometric method" was a way of demonstrating and proving one's ideas in the form of geometric theorems. The most famous texts were written by Galileo, Descartes and Spinoza, with the latter two disagreeing in many ways.

can Spinoza's ethical reasoning lead us in relation to the question of left loneliness?

There are, of course, many interpretations of Spinozism. Some people see in him the ideologist of late capitalism (Žižek, Fisher), others the predecessor of Nietzsche and Marx (Deleuze, Lenin). Some concepts proposed by Spinoza are even used in subatomic physics. What I want to take from Spinoza, however, is closer to the vision of Deleuze and Marx, although it is obvious that other interpretations can also be important and useful.

For Spinoza, Nature is a comprehensive concept, equal to God and the Universe. It exists around our bodies in space but at the same time it is capable of thinking and, perhaps, it is capable of many other things that we simply do not (yet) know about. In other words, it is infinitely diverse, existing in the form of various modes – bodies and objects that constantly meet each other and influence one another. Where does this ability to influence one another come from? Well, Nature is not just a substance – it is energy. This is what makes us act and influence each other. Every body has a certain potential of action and influence, something that Spinoza called *conatus*, and which today some physicists associate with the momentum of the movement of an elementary particle in a certain direction. Experiments have shown that the trajectory of particles is not random, but that it is built into a complex system of mutual influence, which allows energy not to dissipate, but to grow.[24] For Spinoza, *conatus* is the expression of the eternal and infinite essence of an object, something that helps this object to be fully realised. It is a movement towards the realisation of this essence and this realisation depends on mutual interactions between bodies.

According to Spinoza, the result of the impact of one body on another can be twofold – negative or positive. For bodies that can think, the result of such an impact takes shape in the form of affects or feelings. We experience a positive affect if the impact of another body (including another thinking body, another person) makes us more active and energetic. And we become sad and irritated if the impact takes this energy away from us.[25] That is to say, negative emotions

---

24 "Consequently, everything in Nature permanently evolves, inscribing things in the world by the force of its own activity, a strive from within, innate, like Spinoza's Conatus, starting from itself, no longer in an agonistic and competitive way, but seeking to a concert with the surrounding environment." (Castro, Croca & Moreira 2018: 24)

25 Deleuze interpreting Spinoza puts it this way: "In joy, on the contrary, our power expands, compounds with the power of the other, and unites with the loved object (Spinoza, Ethics, IV, 18). This is why even one

make us passive, which is why, according to Spinoza, authorities generally seek not to make their population happy, but, on the contrary, keep them in a state of sadness and oppression, and thereby passive and harmless. Arguably, today's population finds itself in the even tougher situation of what theorists like Mark Fisher have called "interpassivity," that is, we do not have to protest against oppression by ourselves anymore – we can observe (through the media and mass-culture products, mostly movies and video games) how others deal with, say, the ecological crisis or monopolistic capitalism *for us*.[26] In recent times these 'others' have increasingly taken the form of numerous superheroes on the big screen, with the message being that nobody needs to struggle for justice anymore since there are whole universes of heroes that will help us fight against evil. The most distressing sign in all this is that these movies are addressed particularly to children and young people who grow used to thinking about themselves as helpless unless some extraordinary force will come to support and rescue them.

So, on the one hand, through these products of mass culture, Capital orders all and everyone to "Enjoy!" (Žižek following Lacan), while at the same time, it constantly takes away our time and opportunities to do what is really dear and interesting to us, outsourcing even the most crucial tasks. Is it hence surprising to know that today the level of psychological disorders associated with distress, namely depression and anxiety disorders, is at an all-time high? And is this not one of the reasons for our increasing Left impotence and the Left Loneliness that grows from it? I think it is, and this is why Left Loneliness is something that needs to be overcome as soon as possible.

How? In a situation where the whole surrounding order seeks to make us unhappy and powerless, there is only one way out – to look around for something that will support us in becoming more active and joyful. For many of us today, this can be achieved through the intake of mind- and body-altering substances such as antidepressants, alcohol or cannabis. In fact, Spinoza himself liked to give examples of how the body interacts with different types of food or chemical agents,

---

assumes the capacity for being affected to be constant, some of our power diminishes or is restrained by affection of sadness, increases or enhanced by affections of joy. It can be said that joy augment our power of acting and sadness diminishes it. And the conatus is effort to experience joy, to increase the power of acting, to imagine and find the that which is a cause of joy, which maintains the furthers this cause; and also an effort to avert sadness, to imagine and find that which destroys the cause of sadness (Spinoza, Ethics, III, 12, 13 etc.)." (Deleuze 1988: 101).

26 See Fisher 2009.

and one could hence adopt a Spinozian approach to substance (ab)use on the basis of the interaction of two different bodies. I would argue, however, that it will be more effective if this 'something' is another somebody, and that when two *thinking* human bodies interact, the situation may change dramatically, because *a third, new singularity* can be born as a result of the positive interaction and the reciprocal multiplication of energy, something that is determined by the participation of both bodies and which is not simply the sum of two influences. Ideally, says Spinoza, all people, influencing each other, could become something united, multiplying and supplementing each other's potential. This formula, in fact, anticipates the idea of Marx and Engels that "the free development of each is a condition for the free development of all."[27]

So why can Spinoza perhaps be more effective for our current predicament than Marx and Engels? Simply put, because he cannot be accused by defenders of the status quo of operating on the territory of the Left myth. Rather, he justifies his vision of a healthy and happy humanity using the concept of Nature and absolutely 'natural' explanations, just like liberals do. In my view, a different interpretation of what can be considered 'natural' is urgently needed. It knocks the ground from underneath the Right's feet, and makes it possible to think in a completely different way about what 'natural' happiness is for a person. Moreover, Spinoza's view is extremely *rational*. He proves his correctness with the help of a geometric method, in which each premise necessarily follows from the previous one. As a matter of fact, the rationality of the Right becomes completely irrational through a Spinozan perspective. Neither success nor a (lonely) place at the top of the pyramid of power are sources of happiness. It is simply impossible to be happy alone, being surrounded by unhappy and powerless people who can and must be controlled in order for one's false happiness to exist. It is simply impossible to avoid negative impacts, living in a hostile, competitive environment, in a situation of constant threat and instability. In short, being a 'winner' does not guarantee anything positive. The latter is a myth disguised as a 'natural' explanation and it is this false rationality of the 'Right Happiness' economy that makes the atmosphere of Left Loneliness so suffocating, making those who believe in equality and common happiness for all of humankind feel

27 See Marx & Engels 2018.

marginalised and rather like clowns. In other words, there can be no doubt that true Reason, from the point of view of Spinoza, is on our side.

It should be noted, however, that there is another problem here, much more complicated than the search for a new rationality to overcome Left Loneliness. I am referring to the well-known fact that loneliness, depression and other emotional disorders are very difficult to cure merely by offering rational explanations. Then again, the entire history of psychotherapy, starting with Freud, originates in the process of (self-)awareness and -understanding by individuals of themselves regarding what is happening to them. In the same vein, collectively finding new explanations for our loneliness and understanding these can therefore be an important initial step towards the eventual victory of Left ideas.

To conclude, I am convinced that one can be truly active, realising one's essential potential only when one helps others and accepts their help in return; only when *all* people realising themselves merge into something *singular* capable of changing the world for the better. In the context of Kyrgyzstan, each experience of Left unity and solidarity – such as the much-harassed annual feminist march on March 8 in the capital Bishkek or our regular conferences discussing Queer Communist issues – each book we collectively publish, each protest action in the streets, produces authentic emotions of joy and happiness that allow one to feel not only less lonely but also more alive and meaningful. Of course, the notions of 'all' and 'singular' may once more look like Utopian components in this formula, but then again, we need Utopian horizons in order to understand where to go, both alone and together. In this sense, Вперед![28]

References

Anderson, Benedict (1983), *Imagined Communities: Reflections on the Origin and Spread of Nationalism*. London: Verso Books.

Bagdasarova, Nina; Mamedov, Georgy & Mohira Suyarkulova (2021), *Kniga o schastie dla molodykh (i ne ochen'), dla LGBT (i ne tol'ko) ludei* [Book on Happiness for the Young (and not so) and LGBT (but not only) people]. Bishkek: Knigi dla razvitia.

Barthes, Roland (1991), *Mythologies*. New York: The Noonday Press.

Brubaker, Rogers (1995), "National Minorities, Nationalizing States, and External National Homelands in the New Europe," *Daedalus*, Vol. 124, No. 2, 107-132.

28 "Let's go" in Russian.

Castro, Paulo; Croca, José R. & Rui Moreira (2018), "An Introduction to Eurhythmic Philosophy," *Brolly. Journal of Social Sciences* 1(1), 19-31.

Croca, José R., "Eurhythmic Physics Nonlinear Quantum Physics and Dialectical Thinking. The Search For a Better Understanding of Physics," *World Scientific*. Available at: https://www.worldscientific.com/doi/abs/10.1142/9789813232044_0028.

Deleuze, Gilles (1988), *Spinoza: Practical Philosophy*. San Francisco: City Lights Books

Fisher, Mark (2009), *Capitalist Realism: Is There No Alternative?* London: Zero Books.

Hardin, Garrett (1968), "The Tragedy of the Commons," *Science*, 162 (3859), 1243-1248.

Marx, Karl (1859), A Contribution to the Critique of Political Economy. *Marxists Internet Archive*. Available at https://www.marxists.org/archive/marx/works/1859/critique-pol-economy/.

Marx, Karl & Engels, Friedrich (2018), *The Communist Manifesto*. London: Vintage Classics.

Lenin, Vladimir (1974), "On the National Pride of the Great Russians," *Collected Works Vol. 21*, Moscow: Progress Publisher, 102-106.

Shatalova, Oksana & Mamedov, Georgy (eds.) (2016), *Kontseptsii sovetskogo v Tsentral'noy Asii [Concepts of the Soviet in Central Asia], Shtab Almanac #2*. Bishkek: Shtab Press.

Shatalova, Oksana & Mamedov, Georgy (2016), *Kvir Kommunism eto etika.* [Queer-Communism is an Ethics]. Moscow: Svobodnoe Marksistskoe Izdatelstvo Novye Krasnye.

Santos, Boaventura de Sousa (2018), *The End of the Cognitive Empire*. Durham: Duke University Press.

Vygotsky, Lev (1986), *Thought and Language*. Cambridge: MIT Press.

Artist: Sevgi Doğan

"Solitude is Freedom (Yalnızlık özgürlüktür)" – An Interview with İsmail Beşikçi

Sevgi Doğan

> Darkness flees from light, lies from truth
> Even if the sun is alone, it still shines
> Don't be sad, loneliness is the destiny of the righteous
> Crows fly with the flock, eagles fly alone
> Do not be sad...!
> Loneliness is the destiny of the righteous
> Crows fly with the flock,
> Eagles fly alone.
> (Omar Khayyam)

Prologue

"Solitude is freedom," says İsmail Beşikçi (1939-), one of the most important advocates of the Kurdish people, who has been involved in the leftist political movement in Turkey for many years, who has made/continues to make great contributions to Turkish and Kurdish intellectual life, who has been in prison for a total of 17 years, who has both practically and theoretically defended/continues to defend the rights, culture, history, and existence of the Kurdish people.

In Turkey, as in many other parts of the world, left politics has been divided into different groups. This fragmentation within and between the left-wing groups and parties has at times led leftist movements to be isolated and alienated from each other, and hence to become lonely. In this conversation with İsmail Beşikçi, the aim is to explore the concept of 'loneliness' or 'solitude' – not from a purely emotional or psychological perspective but from within an explicitly political framework. More concretely, what concerns us here is how to combine and associate 'loneliness' and the 'left.' Is that possible, and if so, how does it express itself?

With this purpose in mind, this interview with Beşikçi aims to argue, to demonstrate and to discover (together with the reader) what 'left loneliness' or 'being left alone/being alone on the left' means/ might refer to in our "great and terrible and complicated world," as Antonio Gramsci – himself no stranger to solitude and loneliness – wrote in 1931 in one of his letters to his wife Giulia Schucht. In this respect, Beşikçi's direct and personal experiences of loneliness will shed new light on this matter. Beşikçi, who has been criticised in many different (political-intellectual) circles for his views, studies and writings on the Kurdish issue, tells us what it means to be left alone as a thinker who stands with a people who have been left alone throughout its history. How has he experienced t/his 'loneliness'? What were/are the consequences? How does he relate the left, solidarity and loneliness to each other? Can we describe this situation of left loneliness as a pathology, or does it perhaps have productive elements that can help further the struggle for justice?

SD: *First of all, I would like to thank you for accepting the invitation to talk to me. The aim of this conversation is to discuss, to try to understand and to explain what the notion of left solitude and loneliness may mean in the context of modern Turkey, both in your own experience as well as those of other people involved in left politics. So, what do the notions of the 'left' and of 'loneliness,' and perhaps of 'left loneliness,' mean to you?*

IB: For me, to be on the left means to be on the side of the poor, the oppressed classes, the ill-treated and the disadvantaged. Applying this to the context of modern Turkey, it is debatable whether the Turkish left is really on the side of the oppressed and downtrodden. I say this because I believe that the Turkish left is not truly independent. To be independent, and in a sense to be alone, is to have freedom and free will. Those who are independent/alone cannot accept the supervision of the state's political system. They cannot fall under the influence of the state's official ideology. Those who are independent/alone are not accountable to anyone other than their own reason and conscience. In this sense, independence is a type of solitude in freedom, the condition of being able to fight back against the state's systematic oppression more strongly. Unfortunately, based on what I just said, the Turkish left (at least since the day I was born) is not free in a variety of ways, most concretely in its approach towards the so-called Kurdish question. It is chauvinistic, it is annexationist and it is against an independent Kurdistan. In short, it follows the official (nationalist) ideology, and this ultimately means not being on the side of the oppressed.

You associate solitude with being free. I wonder whether you can elaborate on this? How can an individual be free and perhaps even liberated by being alone?

In every society, there are common, dominant ideas that uphold the oppressive status quo. Hence, behaviours that conform to these common ideas do not set you free. Rather, you only become free when you criticise and do not act in accordance with them. This process of critique will usually encounter a negative reaction and can therefore leave you both independent and alone, in the sense of isolated or ostracised.

One example is that of Socrates. If he had defended not the truth but the common view, he would not have been alone, and his life would not have been ended. Socrates, however, chose the truth. He was hence left alone and thereby freed, even though he lost his life for it. Likewise, Michael Servetus in the 15th century and Giordano Bruno at the beginning of the 17th century were burned at the stake for defending science and truth. In the political arena, however, those engaged in politics must often make painful concessions to their opponents as part of the institutional arrangements. In fact, politicians and political parties generally must develop strategies and tactics to achieve their goals, thereby relinquishing their independence. Scientists and thinkers, on the other hand, conduct scientific studies that are based on observations and experiments, that is, on facts, and one simply cannot make concessions in relation to facts.

When considering the notion of left solitude within the framework of fundamental left-wing principles and aspirations such as togetherness, solidarity, acting together etc., it seems that the left and solitude do not go together. Do you think solitude and solidarity are mutually exclusive?

In the context of modern Turkey, we first need to look at the official ideology, which has historically been Kemalism. Kemalism is not just any ideology, but an ideology that is actively protected and guarded by the Turkish state. Therefore, when you criticise the official ideology, and do not think and act in accordance with it, it is very likely that you will face administrative and criminal sanctions by the state. Nonetheless, those truly independent/alone will not allow themselves to be silenced in the face of such sanctions, even if at first they may end up being isolated as a result. They will continue their resistance without interruption, permanently. And in the process, what sometimes happens, is that we become aware of other people criticising and resisting the official ideology and/or of those who express their solidarity with us, both of which provides much-needed moral strength to those of us who resist and consequently makes us feel less isolated.

Then again, one cannot always count on the solidarity of others. In this sense, perhaps it is safe to say that in certain scenarios one cannot truly be independent and free without solitude and even isolation, and that one's force of resistance comes not from solidarity, but from being able to be and stay alone. In the case of Turkey, when the left becomes isolated, that is, when it becomes free or liberated, it becomes the true defender of the rights of the oppressed and against the official ideology. Yet, the price to pay can be heavy, such as prison, oppression or torture.

You regard loneliness as a type of liberation. Does this mean that for you the individual struggle has priority? Where do you put the collective struggle?

In my view, it is necessary to distinguish between individual and collective struggles. So far, I have been talking mostly about individual struggles, and more specifically the individual struggle of the (political) scientist who works with objective reality and who does so in a disinterested manner. Of course, these types of scientific endeavours can also be collective in nature. They may take the form of the joint work of several thinkers who take on each other's views and suggestions on the same subject. No doubt, when we refer to collective political struggles such as the Kurdish one, these must necessarily be informed by this type of individual and collective scientific work.

In the context of the Khayyam poem cited above, do you think that a sense of solitude and even loneliness is inherent to the intellectual? How are the intellectual's pursuit of truth and solitude related?

Here in Turkey, for those of us who speak the truth, painful experiences of solitude, isolation and even loneliness are almost inevitable. It is something that arises naturally from any process of resistance to the state and the latter's constant oppression in the form of severe administrative and penal sanctions. Yet, our main concern must continue to be the defence of truth under all circumstances, even if it means accepting prolonged periods of solitude. Anything else would be self-denial. Clearly, only those of us who have strong ethical values can do this. In sum, science, the defence of truth, solitude and morality are interrelated concepts.

Where does solitude and loneliness stand in your own life conceptually, physically, spiritually?

Let me give you just one of many possible examples. In September 1996, I was moved from Ankara Ulucanlar Prison to Metris Prison in Istanbul. I was alone and carried only some books and files, including my handwritten notes. When we reached Metris Prison at around 8 pm in the evening, I was 'welcomed' to the prison yard not by the normal prison guards, but by members of the Special Forces. First, I was violently searched, my files and books were thrown into the mud, some of my documents were torn and trampled upon, others were taken by soldiers assisting the Special Forces. After a while, they put me in a ward with some of the things I was able to recover. It was a large cell with double-deck bunk beds. I stayed there alone. Later I was subjected to severe torture.

What I am suddenly remembering is that at the time, the governor of Istanbul was my classmate from the *Mülkiye* (the Faculty of Political Sciences of Ankara University).[1] I knew this from the press, because occasionally his statements would be published there. We had been close friends for four years (1958-1962). We had stayed in the same dormitory, and we had both received a scholarship from the Interior Ministry.

How is it possible that my friend was at the height of the state bureaucracy while I had to face inhumane treatment in prisons, basements and cells? How did that happen? For me, it is about the various types of punishments suffered by those who criticise instead of complying with official ideology. As a result, I have faced repeated investigations, detentions, arrests and prison processes while former classmates and friends worked in various departments of the state bureaucracy. Yet, throughout all these ordeals, I did not feel any need to contact any of these 'friends,' but equally importantly, none of my friends contacted me or my wife, Leman Beşikçi, either. We were on our own.

1 The Mekteb-i Mülkiye-i Fünun-u Şahane (also known as the *"Mülkiye"*) is the former name of the Ankara University Faculty of Political Sciences. It was established in 1859 during the Ottoman period to train the civil ruling class in Istanbul to become compatible with modernisation and Westernisation. It was moved to Ankara during the Republican period. İsmail Beşikçi graduated from the *"Mülkiye"* in 1962.

How do you see the question of left loneliness in the general global context and in the context of modern-day Turkey, in particular with regard to the so-called Kurdish question?

Up until the 1990s, the Kemalist state tried everything in its power to prevent three central issues from being publicly discussed under any circumstances, with very serious, strictly enforced punishment for those who tried to speak and/or write about them: Leftist thought, Sharia thought and the Kurdish question. This changed with the amendment of the Anti-Terror Law No. 3713 in April 1991, after which both left and religious thoughts could freely be expressed while even more severe sanctions were introduced for any expression of views about the Kurdish question. I personally experienced this when my book *Interstate Colonial Kurdistan (Devletlerarası Sömürge Kürdistan)* was banned after the amendment. Yet, paradoxically, this was also the time when the Turkish left could in principle have become independent/alone. But it did not. Instead, by improving its relations with the Turkish state, it was brought somewhat under control and (in)directly began to aid the struggle against the Kurds by accepting the official nationalist ideology. That is why the Turkish left became and remains dependent and not truly free. They simply do not approach the Kurdish question in a healthy way, they continue to argue from within the scope of the Turkish political system and official ideology. Of course, they try to do this by finding many theoretical covers to obstruct the Kurdish national liberation struggle, for example the notion of the 'fraternity of peoples.' Simply put, there is no such thing as a fraternity or brotherhood of peoples between the oppressing and the colonial nation. Even if the Turkish people, and particularly the Turkish left, finally did the right thing and supported the Kurds without any self-interest this could at best be called friendship, not brotherhood.

In the global context, the situation is similar but different. For example, the Communist International sided with the Kemalists during the Kurdish uprisings in the 1920s and 30s. The Kurdish revolts were accused of being reactionary and the Kemalists' genocidal operations were regarded as necessary for the liquidation of feudalism. In the specific case of the USSR, not only did it not support Kurdish National Liberation, it actively backed the Turkish state to suppress it. Another striking example is the key role played by the USSR in the destruction of the short-lived Kurdish Republic of Mahabat.[2] In other words, state interests have always been given priority and hence there was no true independence/aloneness like the one I have been describing.

In sum, the Kurdish people have been left alone/abandoned by both the Turkish left and the international Communist movement for over a hundred years. And while leaving the Kurds alone and leaving a scientist alone may have something in common in their sense of suffering, one must handle this isolation/freedom differently. Scientists may still experience spiritual and intellectual freedom, but it is out of the question for the Kurds as a people and as a nation to experience any type of freedom as a result of their isolation.

You have been extremely outspoken on the Kurdish issue and have paid a high price. You openly criticise both Kurdish and Turkish (left) intellectuals in your "Kurds as Nation Discovering Itself" (Kendini Keşfeden Ulus Kürtler). Nowadays, the Kurdish issue is widely discussed both nationally and internationally, and much research is being done on this subject, in addition to supporting the struggle of the Kurds. What would you say have been the biggest changes so far, starting from the 1960s?

What I would say is that there have been great changes, great achievements, yet the gains were ultimately few compared to the very heavy price paid. A great deal of evidence can be provided for both assessments. For example, about 60 years ago, the Kurds and the Kurdish language were being denied and/or invisibilised. Today, there is TRT Kurdî,[3] which broadcasts 24 hours a day. Before it was also said that the Kurdish language is "a primitive language, [since] it has only around 30 words." Yet today there are 244,000 Kurdish words in the *Kurdish-Turkish Dictionary* published by Zana Farqinî.[4]

The heavy prices paid, on the other hand, are the thousands of Kurdish villages that have been burned down, the millions of Kurds who have been displaced and exiled, the thousands of Kurdish intellectuals whose lives were destroyed in one way or another. Arguably, there may not be any other people/nation in the world that has paid such a high price for what is still an elusive national liberation.

2 The Republic of Mahabat was a non-recognised Kurdish state that was established in January 1946 with the support of the Soviet Union and destroyed in the same year after the Soviet Union's withdrawal.
3 TRT Kurdî is the first national television station in Kurdish languages (Kurmanji and Zazaki). It has been criticised by the Kurds and Kurdish political parties as a propaganda instrument of the Turkish government for the Turkification of the Kurdish population.
4 The dictionary, first published in 2004, was reprinted in 2022 with 44,000 additional words.

I can go on. What about the hundreds of thousands of Kurds who were massacred and assimilated during and after the 1914 Mela Selim rebellion,[5] the Great Kurdish Deportation,[6] Koçgiri,[7] the 1925 Sheikh Said[8] and Ağrı rebellions,[9] the Dersim resistance?[10] Then there were the 1988 Anfal,[11] Halabja[12] and 2014 Shingal[13] genocides, followed by the recent 'Trench'[14] and Afrin operations.[15] Not to forget, the practices in the Diyarbakır prison and the Süleymaniye Central Security Headquarters, which are not much different from those in Auschwitz.

That is to say, yes there have been advances but throughout recent history, the process of genocide, trying to change the demographic structure and assimilating the Kurdish people has never stopped. The so-called "Plan for Reform in the East" *(Şark Islahat Planı)*, initiated in 1925/6, is still ongoing.[16] And yet, despite all this

5 The Mela Selim rebellion was initiated by the Kurds under the leadership of Mela Selim against the governing Committee of Union and Progress (CUP) in the Eastern city of Bitlis in 1914. The CUP regarded the rebellion as reactionary, concerned that it would become a 'Kurdish issue,' and put it down

6 The Great Kurdish Deportation refers to the mass deportations of Kurds from Turkish Kurdistan carried out by the Committee of Union and Progress in 1916. İsmail Beşikçi wrote about this subject as follows: "There are periods in Kurdish history when it was desired to remain hidden, to remain in the dark, and not to be brought to light. The Kurdish Deportation of 1916 is such a period. [...it] did not receive the necessary attention in either Turkey or Western countries. It seems that a special effort was made to keep this period secret and obscure [...]" (see Beşikçi 2019, and Temel 2021).

7 The Koçgiri rebellion, mostly composed of Kurdish Alevis, took place in Sivas in 1921. It was suppressed in the same year.

8 The 1925 Sheikh Said rebellion was an uprising by Sheikh Said (1865-1925), Zaza Kurds and the *Azadî* (Freedom) movement (officially *Civata Azadiya Kurd*, Society for Kurdish Freedom, later *Civata Xweseriya Kurd*, Society for Kurdish Independence). The rebellion was swiftly suppressed and Sheikh Said was executed.

9 The Ağrı or Ararat rebellion refers to a Kurdish revolt against the Republic of Turkey in the Eastern Ağrı province 1926-1930.

10 The Dersim rebellion was an uprising against the Turkish government in the city of Dersim 1937-1938. Tens of thousands of Kurds were either killed or deported.

11 During the so-called Anfal campaign one of the biggest mass slaughters was carried out by Saddam Hussein's Ba'athist regime against Kurds living in Iraqi Kurdistan. Between February and September 1988, systematic air bombings, chemical weapons, the burning of settlements and forced displacement were used against the Kurdish people, causing 50,000-100,000 deaths.

12 A part of the Anfal-Campaign, the Halabja massacre on March 16, 1988, is considered one of the largest chemical weapons attacks ever conducted against a civilian-populated area, killing up to 5000 people.

13 During the recent Iraq War, the Islamic State attacked the Shingal area of Iraqi Northern Kurdistan on August 3, 2014, killing thousands and forcings countless Yazidi women into sexual slavery. Hundreds of thousands of people were forced to flee the region.

14 Upon the collapse of the so-called peace process between the Turkish state and the Kurdistan Workers' Party (PKK) 2015-2016, conflict broke out in the predominantly Kurdish cities of Şırnak, Cizre and Nusaybin between the Turkish security forces and the PKK. In response, in many neighbourhoods local residents dug trenches in order to prevent the Turkish police and army from entering.

15 Also called "Operation Olive Branch," a cross-border military operation launched by the Turkish Armed Forces and the Syrian National Army against the Kurdish-led People's Protection Units (YPG) of the Syrian Democratic Forces in the majority-Kurdish Afrin District of northwest Syria, on January 20, 2018.

16 Prepared by the Reform Council for the East *(Şark Islahat Encümeni)* set up by Mustafa Kemal Atatürk, founder of the Republic, after the above mentioned 1925 Sheik Said Revolt, the main objective of the plan was to prevent future Kurdish revolts and to promote Kurdish assimilation. Many issues addressed

cruelty the Kurdish people have struggled to develop a national consciousness. Why is that? For me, the main reasons are the Turkish official ideology, the actions of the Turkish left, the Turkish Islamist movement and finally, the role of the PKK.

How would you describe the current role of the PKK?

Let me respond in an indirect manner. Today, the Kurds have a total population of over 50 million worldwide, larger than most countries in the European Union, yet the Kurdish people are not represented in international institutions such as the United Nations or the Islamic Conference.[17] Therefore, it cannot be the desire of the Kurds not to demand an independent state and not to be against the Turkish state. If you don't have a state, you can't own anything. You cannot even protect your own cemeteries, you cannot even build and open a museum that commemorates your history and culture. If you do not have your own state, then the state oppressing you can simply send you your children's bones back to you in a body bag and you can do nothing about it. In the meantime, assimilation continues.

What kind of reactions did and do you encounter when you criticise both Kurdish and Turkish intellectuals?

Generally, the reactions were/are in the form of overlooking, pretending not to have heard and not to know, what we might call assassination by silence. Having said that, the criticism and/or insults coming from Turkish circles can be understood to some extent. What is difficult to understand, however, are the insults, discrediting and spread of disinformation coming from Kurdish political groups. The only way I can explain this is by the aforementioned lack of national consciousness, which shows the success of the Turkish official ideology influencing and shaping some of these groups.

Finally, do you think that in recent years there has been any type of awakening or increased awareness by the Turkish people regarding what the Kurds are going through? Has there been a change in their understanding to some extent?

---

by this plan have survived until today, for instance, those articles referring to the prohibition of speaking the Kurdish language in public institutions and the forced use of the Turkish language in the classroom, including in majority Kurdish areas (See Fırat 2008).

17 The Organisation of the Islamic Conference is the former name of today's Organisation of Islamic Cooperation (OIC), an intergovernmental organization founded in 1969 and aimed at political, economic, cultural, scientific and social solidarity and cooperation among member states, with 48 out of 57 being Muslim-majority countries.

Quite the opposite. We can say that the Turkish press, Turkish universities and Turkish society at large have become even more racist and chauvinistic. For instance, we have recently witnessed the violent aggression against Kurdish youth and families who spoke and sang in Kurdish in Izmit and Muğla. We have also witnessed the looting of the market of an assimilated Kurdish artisan who came to Bursa from Mardin 50 years ago. And neither have we forgotten the execution of a Kurdish girl in front of the pro-Kurdish Peoples' Democratic Party (HDP) headquarters in İzmir, right opposite a local police station. The Turkish press ignores these racist actions, and the Turkish judiciary minimises them by imposing very light and symbolic punishments without arrest. In the case of HDP, even though the party now defends the policy of "Turkishisation" *(Türkiyelileşme)*, a sort of voluntary (self-)assimilation, the Turkish media still treats them like a criminal, terrorist organisation. Evidently, this suggests that the Kurds, rather than assimilate, need to further Kurdify, even if this ultimately means a lonely struggle.

Epilogue

Although I originally aimed to conduct this interview with İsmail Beşikçi face-to-face, it was ultimately done in writing due to a series of personal health problems. Luckily, I had the opportunity to meet him in person a few months later. On November 10, 2022, when I met with İsmail Beşikçi and İbrahim Gürbüz, the chairman and founder of the İsmail Beşikçi Foundation in Istanbul, I was able to directly experience the type of loneliness/solitude that Beşikçi described in the interview. It was as if his humble stance and sincere smile were a reflection of his stubborn pursuit of justice and truth, to which he has devoted his whole life. Beşikçi, who recently lost his wife and consequently had to experience a new form of loneliness, continues to work on the Kurdish question with the support of his friends and those who love him. Solitude/loneliness has thus become a moral-political phenomenon rather than an exclusively physical and psychological condition.

According to İbrahim Gürbüz, the greatest example of this is that the Turkish courts, who realised that judicially isolating Beşikçi did not yield the expected results, finally gave up on pestering him because they at long last understood that Beşikçi will never renege on his thoughts and convictions. Speaking of (not) understanding, Gürbüz affirmed that while the people of Southern Kurdistan (located in today's Iraq) have long understood and appreciated the value of Beşikçi's work, exemplified by the prominence of his writings in different university programs, the same does not apply to Northern Kurdistan (located in today's Turkey), where unfortunately his reflections are often ignored and even deliberately devalued and distorted by both Turkish and Kurdish intellectuals. İbrahim Gürbüz and those who do know and appreciate him, on the other hand, define İsmail Beşikçi as a symbol of justice and righteousness, a person who fights for the truth, and who takes conscience and justice as a basis for everything he struggles for, namely true equality between Kurds and Turks, including in the form of an independent Kurdish state. Regarding the question of loneliness, Gürbüz and Beşikçi agree that the left label may be insufficient and that it would be more correct to speak of a *Kurdish loneliness* or the loneliness of those engaged in the Kurdish struggle, independent of their nationality. By way of example, Beşikçi recalled once more the 1988 Halabja massacre, and the lack of condemnation or even reaction by leftists, communists and other self-proclaimed progressive forces. On the contrary, some of them even supported Saddam Hussein, thereby leaving the Kurdish people alone... again.

To finish with an anecdote shared by İbrahim Gürbüz, during one of Beşikçi's countless appearances in court, the presiding judge ordered him to "[finally] give up on this (referring to the Kurdish issue)," to which Beşikçi, who investigated and evaluated the issue from a scientific point of view, answered: "[but] the Kurdish oppression is a fact, so how can I give up on this issue?" Lonely or not, Beşikçi is a treasured example of the defence of science and truth who will undoubtedly continue to illuminate and contribute to our understanding of the Kurdish question through his precious work. In this sense, I would like to conclude with a poem dedicated to İsmail Beşikçi, originally written in Sorani Kurdish by Şerko Bêkes (1940-2013):

To İsmail Beşikci

A tree once said,
We can't do it now.
To a street in Diyarbakır,
We can't give your name.

✳

A flower once said,
We can't do it now.
To a garden in Qamishlo,
We can't give your name.

✳

A stone once said,
We can't do it now.
On the side of Babagurgur mountain,
We can't erect your statue.

✳

A poem once said,
We can't do it now.
To a library in Sablax,
We can't give your name.

✳

Finally, Kurdistan said,
Yes, now we can do it.
Only we can do it.
Like a rose, like poetry, like freedom,
We can keep your name alive in our hearts.

Ji bo Îsmaîl Beşîkçî

Darekê got
Em niha nikarin
Navê te li cadeke Diyarbekir kin

✳

Kulîlkekê got
Em niha nikarin
Navê te li baxçekî nav Qamişlo kin

✳

Kevirekî got
Em niha nikarin
Peykerekî li ser sînga Babagurgur
Ji bo te çêkin

✳

Şiîrek got
Em niha nikarin
Navê te li kutubxabeyeke Sablax kin

✳

Dawî Kurdistan got
Ewê em niha karin bikin
Tenê ev e ku
Wek gul û şiîr û azadî
Te di canê xwe de hilgirin.

References

Beşikçi, İsmail (2019), "1916 Kürd Tehciri," *Zazaki.net*. Available at http://www.zazaki.net/haber/1916-kurd-tehciri-2630.htm.

Fırat, Ümit (2008), "Kürtler ve Şark Islahat Planı Kararnamesi," *bianet*. Available at https://bianet.org/bianet/siyaset/107183-27-mayis-kurtler-ve-sark-islahat-plani- kararnamesi.

Temel, Celal (2021), *Dünya Savaşı Yıllarında 1916 Kürt Tehciri (The 1916 Kurdish Deportation During World War I)*. Istanbul: İsmail Beşikçi Vakfı.

Photo: Rob Bogaerts / Source: Wikimedia Commons

Anarchists should not be lonely (but they are)

James Martel

Anarchists should not be lonely. That really should be (and is) the state of all liberals insofar as liberalism insists on isolating each person, setting them against every other person in a zero-sum competition where relationships are marked by transactionality and mutual suspicion (instead of mutual aid). Anarchism, on the other hand, is about community and, in fact, real individuality; you can only really be an individual in relation to other individuals. Liberalism claims to be about individualism but is distorted by the money economy, so your 'individuality' is given to you, in effect, by your bank account. Nobody knows you as you, but always via mediating forces of capitalism. That is a recipe for deep loneliness. Fascists (I imagine but don't want to think about their perspective too much) are probably even lonelier because their individuality and relationality are all mediated through authoritarian figures, whereby they get their own identity as a ghostly remnant of that being. Both liberalism and fascism are examples of what I like to call 'archism,' a system based on hierarchy and oppression, one that is so ubiquitous that it doesn't even need – and certainly doesn't want – a name. Archism pervades our world, ranking every person from top to bottom, and structures even our sense of reality, of time and space (so the future is better than the present, and over there is better, more important, than over here). How can you not be lonely if you are an archist? You are never at the same level as anyone else, always vying for your place in competition with others. If liberalism is the 'kinder, gentler' face of archism, it remains striated (and upheld) by racism, sexism, classism, homophobia and so many other forms of distinction and ranking.

But in practice, being an anarchist can be a lonely experience, at least politically speaking, precisely because we live in a world dominated by liberalism (and fascism too, increasingly). Anarchists are few and far between and in daily life, most of the people we encounter in the spaces where we live and work are liberals. I often think of a phenomenon that I call getting 'the face' in my interactions with liberals. What I mean by this is the expression that liberals get when they realise that after talking to you for some time, and agreeing with many of your more radical statements, that you actually mean what you are saying. You can be talking about, say, really confronting some kind of unfair advantage. Some liberals will be fine with tinkering around the edges (and I should be clear that by 'liberals' I don't mean the centre left in the US, I mean liberalism in its larger sense as the ideology of capitalism that includes centre left and everything to its right up to fascism). But if you reveal that you wish to take on something lock, stock and root, they suddenly make 'the face.' They've been agreeing with you in principle, so they don't really have the grounds to disagree with you at this point, but it turns out that they never meant to go this far and didn't necessarily even mean or intend to do anything about this situation at all. Try talking to a liberal in the United States about police abolition and you will quickly see what I mean. The minute they realise you are serious, you get the face and it's game over. That feels lonely to me because you thought you were talking to a 'fellow traveller' but then you realise you were on this ride by yourself the whole time. After I get the face, I usually drop the subject, or sometimes, out of desperation, keep going, which only tends to make things worse (then, the face becomes the whole body, a rigidity of rejection, disapproval and embarrassment).

Liberalism is a strange philosophy in that it readily admits many of its faults. This is why you get so many liberals talking to people who are way to their left and thinking that they are in agreement. Yes, there is so much racism in the United States (but let's not truly disturb white privilege!). Yes, it sucks that there are billionaires basking in their grotesque piles of money while other people live on the street (but don't let that homeless person near me! / we *should* tax the billionaires but if we tax them too much they might stop investing and the economy would collapse!).

In other words, liberalism's seeming openness to change is a ruse, a form of gaslighting. Liberalism can act in this tolerant way and readily admit to its own problems because beneath this apparent candour, it is firmly rooted in the assumption that (to quote Margaret Thatcher) "there is no alternative." Insofar as liberalism believes itself to be at "the end of history" (to quote Hegel and then Francis Fukuyama), at the pinnacle of historical progress and unrivalled, especially since its defeat of communism in the early nineteen nineties, it doesn't matter if it has faults because no other system can replace it. This is, of course, not true; fascism, as another form of archism, readily does replace liberalism but this is read as an aberration and, given the fact that fascism is a very unstable and ultra-violent political order, it tends, with some exceptions, to be relatively short lived. The real threat to liberalism comes, not from the right (because, after all, fascists also support capitalism, which is the whole point of liberalism too) but from the left. When liberalism feels more anxious about the possibility of being usurped from the left, it often acts better (that's what the New Deal was all about) or worse (that's what McCarthyism and Trumpism is about) depending on circumstances and which liberals we are talking about. When it feels secure, it can pursue apparently radical goals, but this often amounts to what the Maoists called "waving the red flag to oppose the red flag," that is to use the appearance of addressing a problem to avoid the problem entirely. Diversity, Equity and Inclusion offices in US academia are a great example of this. These actually serve to perpetuate the problem in the guise of solving it. Question: "What are you doing about racism on campus?" Answer: "Well! We have this office, you see..." At that point, we are dealing with an entirely different kind of face, one that brooks no dissension.

Many of the leftists I know (I try not to use the word progressive because progress is a liberal conceit, the idea that we are all advancing through time towards a brighter, better future) share this frustration about dealing with liberals. We do not live in revolutionary times and so those of us who are around and active today must engage with a world view that generally accepts and supports archist practices. We must even acknowledge the way that those views and practices can bleed into our own thinking if we are not careful (liberalism is insidious!).

I'm speaking here more of a political form of loneliness than a personal one, but political loneliness can be just as depressing and frustrating (and it can make you personally lonely as well, of course, if all or most of the people you associate with are liberals). The resolution to political loneliness is to seek out the company of those who are like you; it is always healing, thrilling and restorative to be in the company of fellow anarchists (and communists too!). Part of the fun of that is just to gripe about what it's like to be with liberals (the face!). But far more important than that, there is a sense of common purpose, not just in terms of the politics that we like to practise and would like to see be far more widespread (an understatement!) but in terms of the kinds of relationality that we can experience with one another. There is no question of transactionality when you are dealing with leftists. Quite the contrary, these relationships are anti-transactional precisely because there is no profit to be made, no advantage to pursue; being a leftist in a capitalist/archist world is not a good way to get rich (!!).

One of my good friends and favourite communists, Jodi Dean, wrote a superb book about political comrades.[1] She meant communist comrades, but I am extending that idea to apply to all of us on the far left. A comrade is someone with whom you may not always get along personally, but once again we are not talking about personal but rather political relationality, and this is precisely the form of relationality that is missing for people who are not on the left. Marx himself tells us that people might join a communist organisation for personal reasons (better pay, less oppression, etc.) but when they join up, they discover new needs that they didn't even know they had – the need, above all, for other people, for comradeship.[2]

In my experience, the same thing happens in anarchist circles as well. People join anarchist groups out of curiosity or just from being sick of the kind of mental isolation that liberalism foments. But they discover something quite joyous and unexpected; not just other people but even themselves, themselves as a political and economic agent, someone who has a voice and a power that they didn't know they had because it was hidden under layer upon layer of liberal bullshitting. This doesn't mean that our comrades will always have our back or will never disappoint us (that can lead to loneliness of both the political and personal kind), but the risk of that other kind of bullshit is well worth it (for me, anyway) given the potential for those joyous connections, and the discovery of self and other, which can only come via these comradely forms of association.

Are anarchists going to be stuck in this political loneliness forever? I really don't think so. The best book I've read in years is David Graeber's (now sadly deceased) and David Wengrow's (happily still alive) *The Dawn of Everything*.[3] That book, I would say, is a must read for any anarchist (or any anti-archist too). It has given me a new sense of hope for a non-archist future, even if it doesn't happen in

1 See Dean 2019.
2 Marx 1978: 99-100.
3 See Graeber & Wengrow 2021.

our (i.e., those of us who are alive right now) lifetimes. In it, the two Davids give a sense of how, for most of human history, people organised themselves very differently than they do under current, archist conditions. For instance, they talk about how, when the French Jesuits, who accompanied explorers in the territory that became known as Canada, encountered indigenous communities and learned their languages, they were struck by how everyone, not just the leaders, spoke extremely eloquently. Used to their own class-ridden society where the aristocrats were well spoken and the lower classes were not, they were continually surprised at the ubiquity of beautiful speech. The two Davids conclude that this was because in the indigenous communities in question, political power was not invested only in a few. Every member of society, men and women, the old and the young, were all given a voice and, accordingly, were used to speaking and being listened to.

To me, these were communities that were not afflicted by political loneliness, nor by the allures of archism as a whole. Interestingly, the two Davids note that, when the French Jesuits asked these people what they thought of France itself, they expected them to express feelings of awe and inferiority on their own part, but the opposite was true. To the consternation of the priests, members of these indigenous communities expressed surprise and dismay at how terribly French people treated one another, how they were obsessed with acquisition and had no collective bonds whatsoever. That is what it looks like to have a society marked by political loneliness. That is the society that we still live in today.

This book helps me to understand that we are not, in fact, doomed to this form of political loneliness forever. *The Dawn of Everything*, although it uses neither the word anarchism nor archism, does explain that the (archist) world that we live in today is a horrible accident and nothing was fated or inevitable about us becoming this way. This is critical because it flies in the face of liberalism's own conceit that the world was created to lead to this moment and that the future is just going to be more of the same (only better!). The two Davids show that throughout most of human history, a myriad of different forms of political and economic organisation have been practised and that, assuming humanity survives this current self-destructive archist (again, my word not theirs) frenzy, people most likely will revert to some of those many alternatives, if not creating entirely new ones.

So, to quote Kafka, there is "plenty of hope, an infinite amount of hope – but not for us."[4] That is, we might remain trapped (although I certainly hope not) in the political loneliness of archism but the world will not be this way forever. That might seem bleak, but it actually makes me feel less lonely because the thought of the world being this way forever is really unfathomable.

Perhaps in closing I should say a word about the personal dimensions of relationality instead of merely the political. I know a lot of liberals who have many wonderful personal qualities; they are loyal, caring, kind and generous, and I'm sure if I thought about it hard enough, I could think of some anarchists who don't have these same qualities. This isn't to say that all liberals are jerks and all anarchists are inherently wonderful. It's rather to say that a lot of people have virtues in their personal lives that do not translate into political community precisely because liberalism doesn't allow for that kind of transference. In the times we live in, of liberal triumphalism and fascist threat, one must really go against the grain to access the possibility of political relationality or comradeship. I'm not sure how and why people become anarchists or communists in our time. I'm not sure it's a matter of courage (I don't feel particularly brave) or anything like that but maybe just a form of conviction. If we lived in an anarchist world, maybe we'd be the most doctrinaire and tiresome people. I'm not sure how I ended up being an anarchist but I'm very glad that I did, political loneliness notwithstanding. Besides the lovely way it allows me to encounter some other people politically, it also means that I get to experience myself in flashes as an agent, in charge of my own economic and political life. Even if I can't experience that in its full actuality because there is no widespread political context that supports it, I know that it is possible and that is, to me, something very precious. Personally, I think that is worth a lot of those awkward conversations where I get 'the face.'

....
4 Benjamin 1969: 116.

References

Benjamin, Walter (1969), "Franz Kafka: On the Tenth Anniversary of his Death," *in* Walter Benjamin *Illuminations: Essays and Reflections*. New York: Schocken Books, 111-140.

Dean, Jodi (2019), *Comrades: An Essay on Political Belonging*. London and New York: Verso Books.

Graeber, David & Wengrow, David (2021), *The Dawn of Everything: A New History of Humanity*. New York: Farrar, Straus and Giroux.

Marx, Karl (1978), "Economic and Philosophical Manuscripts of 1844," *in* Robert C. Tucker (ed.) *The Marx Engels Reader*. New York: W.W. Norton, 66-125.

Artist: Sula Gordon

It is going to be alright

Lena Grace Anyuolo

I know how it starts.
When it's hard to wash my face
or change my clothes.
I'm having a banana again for dinner,
my blood sugar is low,
my weight is down.
So my period is late again.
I know exactly what to do to pull myself out of the funk.
Unfortunately, because of capitalist alienation, the journey to being
me will have to be a solo trip.
I switch off my phone and tell the comrades I need a break,
I won't fall victim to the ruse of time scarcity.
Time is on my side.
I'll switch off my phone,
I won't feel guilty to step away.
I have time to fix my house,
I'll clear out the cobwebs gathering at the corners of my soul.
I'll call my sister
and tell my best friend that I'm sorry I've been away for so long.
I won't forget that I'm a human being needing love,
affection, and friendship.
A tired cadre is of no use to the revolution.
I'll give someone else my space because it's time
for fresh ideas on the battlements.
A burnt-out soldier is a liability.

Left Alone

On this break,

however long it takes,

I'll work through the anger,

Write it down then take a walk.

I'll nourish my body and write a poem.

I'll read a novel and take a nap in the afternoon.

I'll check on my comrades from time to time.

The struggle is not a religion

and we are not fanatics.

If you're battered and bruised,

then you have to take a break,

pause for a moment.

Ain't no such animal as an instant guerrilla.[1]

---

1 "[...] Instant coffee is the hallmark of the current rhetoric. But we do have time. We'd better take the time to fashion revolutionary selves, revolutionary lives, revolutionary relationships [...] Ain't no such animal as an instant guerrilla." Toni Cade Bambara 1969 *in* Kalenda C. Eaton (2008), *Womanism, Literature, and the Transformation of the Black Community*, 1965–1980, New York and London: Routledge, p. 59.

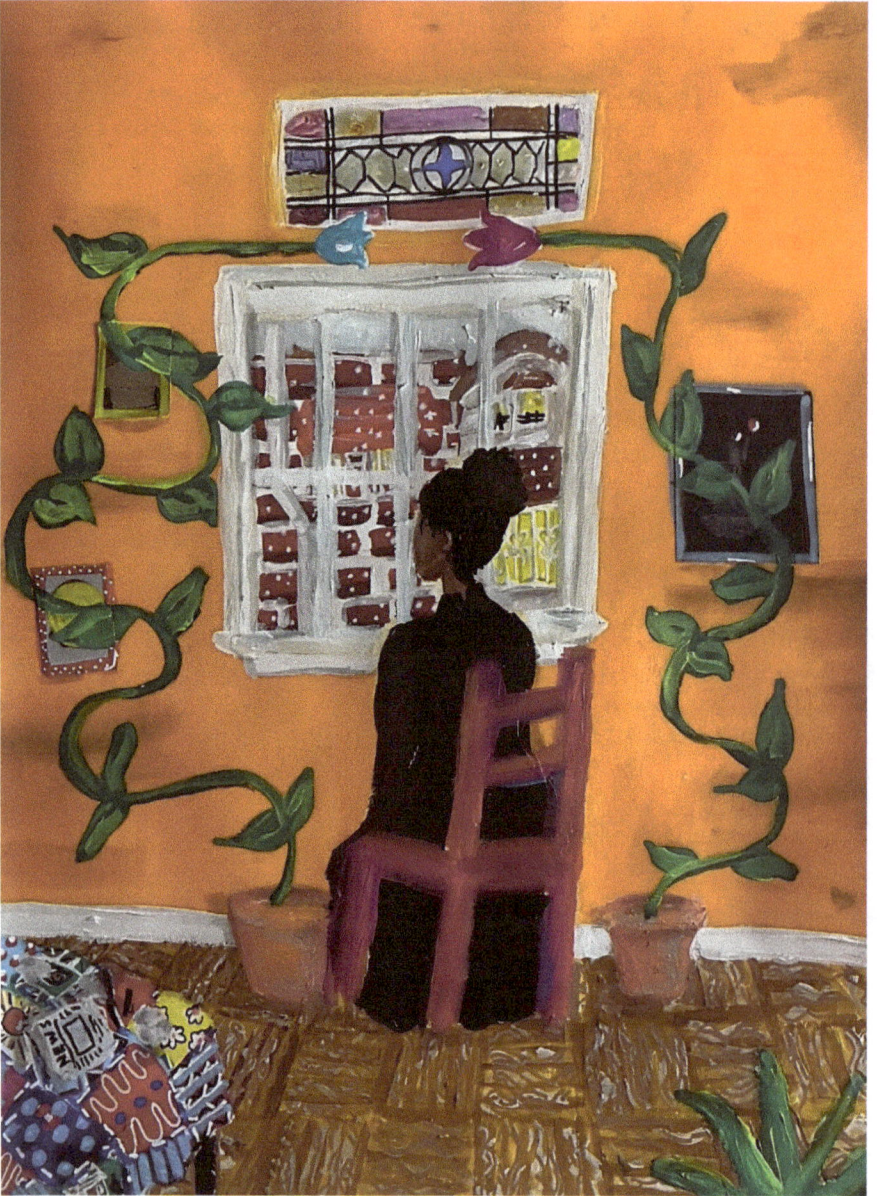

Artist: Sula Gordon

"A Lonely Warrior":
Left-wing Isolation in the Early Adult Life of Ida B. Wells

Jane Anna Gordon

"who's going to help me   make my own glittering nest"
— Julie Choffel (2020)

If there are many faces and facets of loneliness, what unique forms might come of being oriented left?

A defining difference between the political right and the political left is that the former seeks a return to a scripted, if lost past, while the latter knows that meaningful freedoms for the fullest range of peoples are without precedent. They must therefore be created through sustained struggle. Those of the left may therefore, at times, be alone or isolated in their commitment to live in radical uncertainty or to embrace an unchartered becoming. There may be suspicion from those outside the left toward their unflagging attention to how political circumstances overdetermine personal ones. Onlookers, especially if they are kin, may see such a disposition as making excuses or, even if right, imprudent in a finite life where time ticks. They may think the one of the left is arrogant or silly or dangerous for thinking they might do otherwise and may wait impatiently for them to encounter difficulties that buttress this stance. Those of the left will, by definition, have fewer guides in trying to live unscripted.

Similarly, much of the left takes the position that people are transformed through struggle so that, even in moments of real achievement, victory bequeaths new, unprecedented challenges. In other words, the radical quality of left responsibility and its accompanying uncertainty seems never to cease.

Historically and now, there is also a tendency on the political right to more readily close ranks in pursuit of shared ends. By contrast, the left is more unrelenting in its scrutiny. We turn our critical gaze as consistently on our antagonists as on our own. While such rigorous self-questioning may cultivate the most accurate or honest of analyses, it can also cause fragmentation from within and self- as well as externally imposed forms of disappointment and heartbreak. If one finds precious company in kindred spirits, the imperative to unceasing critique might lead to the reinforcement of sustained relationships or to the parting of ways.

Similarly, the singularity of one's resolve in the face of discouragement might fuel one's energy in ways that again make one stand out – as excessive or simply *too much* – to others who have less reason to be driven. Having stood out or apart, one might also be readier to say and to do what might lead to losses in ways that others might admire as courageous and principled or dismiss as a pattern of pathology. One might be less fearful of having to start over, treating it as a risk attendant to one's sense of purpose. In so doing, one may find a meaningful anchor in different temporal terms than many who surround one in chronological time, keeping more nourishing company with the deceased and not yet born, than with living comrades who do not have it in them to begin yet again.

In what follows, I explore this volume's invitation to couple "the left" and "loneliness" through the following questions: *Do people on and of the political left experience distinct forms of loneliness? Do members of the left diagnose their bouts of loneliness in unique terms? Do we offer alternative prescriptions?* I do so through the lens of the early adulthood of Ida B. Wells.[1] In the years during which she was still emerging as the historic agitating journalist, antilynching crusader, and institution-builder she would become, she felt an unrelenting demand to meet exacting standards of gendered, intellectual, personal, political, and racial excellence. Trying to figure out *how to do so* involved careful study and often scathing articulations of the ubiquitous failures all around her. It also required astute calculations as to how to clear and nurture the ground of her own growth as a reader, speaker, and writer through maintaining relations with a small set of primarily Black male political journalists and intellectuals, who, as had her father, urged her on.[2]

Doing so as an orphaned, unwed young woman responsible for her younger siblings meant navigating conventions that thickly surrounded her, beckoning that she trade in the angst occasioned by personal political responsibility for a marriage that would channel

---

1 While many scholars of Wells adoringly refer to her as "Ida" – as I do in the classroom – her daughter, Alfreda Duster's reflections are well-taken. She observed that only Ferdinand Barnett (Wells' husband) called Wells by her first name and stated, "Black women had been trying for two hundred years to be called 'Mrs.,' so it was a breach of etiquette to call her by her first name" (see Sterling 1995: 193).

2 Wells writes movingly of Reverend William J. Simmons, T. Thomas Fortune, and Alfred Froman in this regard. On the role of these and other key figures in Wells' life, see McMurray (1998) and Nelson (2006).

her energies into the supporting roles of wife and mother. Figuring out how instead to prolong and deepen that anxiety-ridden terrain of unchartered becoming led Ida B. Wells into a complex, and often maligned, dance of maintaining multiple suitors through whom she was able to participate in the cultural and social life of her day. But, as someone who had taken on the role of adult in her family while still in her teens, if attracted to not having to protect her own name alone and, more generally, to reducing her own and her siblings' precarity, her life circumstances accustomed her to an unusual degree of personal freedom.[3] While it was extraordinarily taxing – as her reflections on constant indebtedness, poor health, moving and moving again, monotonous work, and ongoing derisive rumouring about her desires and motivations made clear – she did not welcome having to compromise as a basic life condition.

Radical Reconstruction, Interrupted

In the brief span of Wells' early life, her parents, who were fiercely committed to Radical Reconstruction,[4] had gone from enslaved to free to deceased.[5] In the same period, formerly enslaved Black men had begun to vote and be elected to public office, with some quickly earning extraordinary wealth and others building a vast range of Black-run institutions. Almost as quickly, the withdrawal of federal troops from the former Confederacy stimulated rampant retrenchment so that by the 1880s, "Black men still voted in Memphis, but largely due to a stalemate in municipal politics that left the black vote uncontested."[6] Southern Democrats actively barred Blacks from mobilising the political power they had only temporarily gained by introducing prohibitive

3 As such, she shared life conditions with many other historical women intellectuals who either did not marry or, when widowed, opted not to remarry, supporting themselves and thereby occupying the world in a role that, if more precarious and less conventional, was also, for those reasons, less narrowly demarcated. I am thinking here of Christine de Pizan, Rosa Luxemburg, and Anna Julia Cooper, among many others.

4 Bay 2009: 44.

5 *Radical Reconstruction* refers to the period (from the 1866 mid-term elections through 1877) when Radical Republicans seized control in the U.S. Congress and redefined Reconstruction's meaning by passing the Reconstructions Acts of 1867-68. These sent federal troops into the U.S. south to oversee the establishment of more democratic state governments and enacted legislation that amended the U.S. Constitution to guarantee civil rights to freed African Americans, including voting rights for Black men. In this brief period, sixteen Black men served in Congress, including two in the U.S. senate, more than 600 Black men served in state legislatures, and hundreds held local offices. They created the first state-funded public school systems in the U.S. south, made taxation more equitable, and outlawed racial discrimination in public transportations and accommodations. Governments also committed considerable funding to the development of railroads and other infrastructure that would facilitate the growth of economic enterprise.

6 Ibid.

poll taxes, literacy tests, and other legal exclusions. In figuring out how not to compromise in her response to such developments, Wells was deeply informed by the actions of others. At the same time, churches, families, and schools did not speak in unison about how best to forestall intensifying racial terror aimed at re-normalising racial injustice. And even when they did, there remained ambiguities and contradictions that fell to her to navigate with integrity.

As for many others, if particularly acutely in her case, such navigations demanded reconciling often irreconcilable commitments. Even though she would not be able to, she tried to do justice to each. Given that, at the most basic level, these required fulfilling familial obligations while pursuing an unprecedented life as a Black woman political agitator of the written and spoken word, she had to discern how to do so largely alone. There were many who cared about her and her family's well-being and many who perceived, appreciated, and supported the realisation of her talent, but she may well have rightly felt that most others did not care whether she got the impossible balance of her life right or wrong; whether, when breaking from others to act on her conviction, she met with disappointment or defeat. They would surely cheer her on when she did well for herself, and by extension, for them, but would anyone notice – or lose *any* sleep – if she, an orphaned Black woman born into slavery in the U.S. south, abandoned her ambition and collapsed into the isolation of unfulfillment?

Wells' birth in Mississippi to parents who were both profoundly religious and independent, her possessing more uncredentialed cultural capital than economic means, and her formative experiences teaching, while still a teenager, in the rural south, embedded her in distinctive layers of relationship and obligation. Unlike many of the Black elite circles to which her work as a teacher and then major journalist and public intellectual gave her access, she had not completed high school or college. When she thought of her audience, it centred on the Black majorities who more closely resembled her, even if her father had, in his and her words, not known the cruelties of enslavement her mother and so many others had endured.[7] Also, while she

---

7 Ida's father, James Wells, characterised his own "milder" experiences of enslavement as due to his father being his master. Unlike in many other instances, this master did not have any children with his white wife and assured that James Wells was apprenticed as a carpenter and then hired out. James Wells was highly critical of his father's wife who, upon his father's death, had James's mother stripped naked, hung, and beaten. He said to his own mother, who still felt obligated to tend to James's father's wife, "Mother, I never want to see that old woman as long as I live. I'll never forget how she had you stripped and whipped the day after the

was highly attentive to how race and racism were gendered, this, for her, demanded as much concern for the specific ways that racial violence targeted Black men as it did participation in Black women's clubs, especially those focused on the franchise.

Lastly, while she would spend most of her life in the U.S. north, contributing indispensable labour to building up cultural, educational, and political institutions for Black Chicagoans, she insisted that she did so as an *exile* from the U.S. south. She insisted on reminding others that she had been driven from and made to remain outside the place she considered home. At least two consequences followed: While other elite Black Chicagoans would not, she prioritised creating support for Black men fleeing the South, typically with nothing. In so doing, she and her husband, Ferdinand Barnett, regularly drew only on their own funds to offer these refugees of domestic racial terror the range of resources offered recent immigrants from Europe by settlement houses and the YMCA. The Wells-Barnett family forged communities with others who, through political circumstances, had been rendered homeless and made to begin again. Second, while engaging the full range of U.S. political institutions, Wells frequently acted, thought, and wrote from the premise that none treated Black people as citizens. In my own words, if Black people resided in the U.S. and often knew it as their only geographic home, there was a meaningful sense in which they occupied this nation as stateless people. As Wells wrote when the Tennessee State Supreme Court overturned her previously successful case against the Chesapeake and Ohio Railroad:

> The gist of that decision was that Negroes were not wards of the nation but citizens of individual states, and should therefore appeal to the state courts for justice instead of to the federal court. The success of my case would have set a precedent which others would doubtless have followed. In this, as in so many other matters, the South wanted the Civil Rights Bill repealed but did not want or intend to give justice to the Negro after robbing him of all sources from which to secure it. The supreme court of the nation had told us to go to the state courts for redress of grievances; when I did so I was given a brand of justice Charles

---

old man died, and I am never going to see her. I guess it is all right for you to take care of her and forgive her for what she did to you, but she could have starved to death if I'd had my say-so. She certainly would have, if it hadn't been for you" (Wells 1970/2020: 9).

Sumner knew Negroes would get when he fathered the Civil Rights Bill during the Reconstruction period.[8]

In the case of Ms. Wells, her initial loneliness reflected a life situation that seemed to mandate against the pursuit of her passions. The very traits and talents that would be indispensable to her later historic undertakings initially appeared to her and to many in her midst only as personal and romantic liabilities. Once she found and threw herself into her vocation, however, her loneliness took a different form. While she was all too ready to speak *the most unwelcome* of political truths – and would do so unapologetically with life-threatening and -altering costs – the same could be said of only a smallish group of others. Similarly, she treated the project of Black freedom as primary and ultimate and would consider all means for advancing it. She refused resolutely to tip-toe around a ubiquitous white narcissism in her accounts of racial realities basic to U.S. political life. She named the differential consequences whites and Blacks faced when they stole public or private funds.[9] She joined others in asking how to leverage what had been absolutely loyal Black support for a Republican party that was actively backing away from its prior Civil War record.[10] She repeated that white women could and did desire Black men; that not all interracial unions were coerced. She called on other Blacks to arm themselves, as she had already done, so that the price of taking Black life was increased in the terms that spoke most clearly to its would-be attackers.

Although many were staggered by her brutal denunciations of the politically unforgivable, most of them preferred to retain a critical distance, fearing the losses that a less mediated embrace of Ms. Wells' approach might bring. If undeterred by the often relatively solitary nature of her pursuits, she did wonder repeatedly what it meant to fight for a community in which more were not also so willing. Nonetheless, she remained anchored by a political zeal and sacred horizon that reached for the not yet in the here and now. Doing so often meant finding camaraderie in the company of the deceased and the imagined.

8 Wells 1970/2020: 18.

9 As quoted in McMurray "'Negroes are sent to the work house, jail and penitentiary for stealing five cents worth of bread or meat, but whites are made honored citizens, when they steal thousands.' She wryly noted that the Negro 'Is imitating the white man too much with different results. If a white man steals he often times goes to the legislature or congress, and the Negro goes to jail or the penitentiary'" (1998: 128).

10 The Republican Party no longer felt a need to earn the Black vote while she, as Malcolm X would later say, was Black before she had been a Republican (or Democrat).

Unchartered Becoming

> "I am scared   not of what could eat me   but what I could eat
>   going rabid   over what winds up inside of me
>   a tower of lives never lived"
> —Julie Choffel (2020)

In her "Introduction" to Ida B. Wells' autobiography, *Crusade for Justice* (1970/2020), Wells' daughter Alfreda Duster writes:

> The most remarkable thing about Ida B. Wells-Barnett is not that she fought lynching and other forms of barbarism. It is rather that she fought a *lonely and almost single-handed* fight, with the single-mindedness of a crusader, long before men or women of any race entered the arena; and the measure of success she achieved goes far beyond the credit she has been given in the history of the country.[11]

Thomas C. Holt similarly described Wells' steadfast refusal to be deferential or cautious and her blunt forthrightness and outspoken assertiveness as leading her to be "a lonely warrior."[12]

    There are grounds for such assessments. When the yellow fever epidemic hit Tennessee and northern Mississippi, taking the lives of her parents and youngest sibling in 1878, Wells was urged to remain at a physical distance. Instead, "the conviction grew within [her] that [she] ought to be with them."[13] In response to a conductor who questioned her judgment as she boarded a freight train shrouded in black, she stated, "I am the oldest of seven living children. There's nobody but me to look after them now. Don't you think I should do my duty, too?"[14] To the group of Masons who met her at her family's home in Holly Springs, Mississippi with a plan of how to distribute the care of the remaining children, she said that her parents would turn over in their graves if the siblings were separated as would have happened during slavery. Perhaps thereby relieved of the burden, the Masons relented, but Wells was only sixteen.[15] As, in her words, "a young,

---

11 Wells 1970/2020: xxxi-xxxii; italics added.
12 Fradin & Fradin 2000: 81, and Holt 1982.
13 Wells 1970/2020: 11.
14 Ibid.
15 Mia Bay writes, "Although sixteen when her parents died, Wells would always remember herself as only fourteen when she became head of her family. Her slip may reflect simply how very young she felt in the face of the enormous adult responsibilities she assumed after the death of her parents" (2009: 31).

inexperienced girl, who had never had a beau, too young to have been out in company except at children's parties,"[16] she was mortified to learn that members of the community whispered that she wanted to live alone with the children so that she could have sex with a white man for money.

In this same solitary spirit, in the incident that was the focus of the first published story that made Ida B. Wells famous, after purchasing a first-class ticket to the ladies' car of a train, she refused to budge when the conductor said that, as a Black woman, she had to move to the smoking car. As he tried to drag her from her seat, she "fastened [her] teeth to the back of his hand."[17] Two other men joined the ticket collector in physically removing her as the white ladies and gentlemen in the car cheered them on, with some standing on the seats to "get a good view" and "applauding the conductor for his brave stand."[18] Her response was immediately to engage a "colored lawyer" to bring a suit against the railroad. Wells wrote retrospectively:

> I had already secured my appointment as a teacher in Memphis before the railroad case was finally settled; so I had my salary to fall back on to help pay the costs against me. None of my people had ever seemed to feel that it was a race matter and that they should help me with the fight. So I trod the winepress *alone*.[19]

While framed by the State Supreme Court as "harassing" the railroad in a decision that ushered the Jim Crow era into Tennessee, Wells was, as the three-year litigation concluded, "a twenty-five-year-old woman, boarding herself out in various Memphis homes using her own money earned as a poorly paid schoolteacher to hire lawyers to take a major corporation all the way to the State Supreme Court."[20]

None would dispute Duster's assessment of the far greater contributions Wells made than recognition received (especially at the level of national memory). However, while Wells explicitly signals her "aloneness," Mia Bay suggests that Wells' recollection authored decades later "may have been coloured with bitterness over later experiences [...] At the very least, her Memphis diary, written at the time of the

16 Wells 1970/2020: 15.
17 Ibid: 17.
18 Ibid.
19 Ibid: 19; italics added.
20 Washington in Wells 1995: xiv.

trials were unfolding, suggests that she did not in fact battle the railroads alone."[21]

After all, in addition to the foundational bedrock of commitment to her by her deceased parents and their immediate community of Masons and others in Mississippi, there were the dynamic religious communities and fellowship of fellow teachers in which Wells participated through the Memphis Lyceum. There was also a steady stream of suitors she kept in circulation. (Indeed, she documents hankering for the vitality of this Black southern world when she had, at her aunt's insistence, briefly relocated to Visalia, California in 1886.) Similarly, in challenging the introduction of segregation in transportation and other public facilities, Wells joined other Black residents of Memphis, including a fellow older Black woman teacher, whom she admired.[22]

If her writings about her railroad suit furnished the original content that would lead to her finding her "real vocation" as a journalist, this was a largely unchartered terrain. Due in part to her unprecedented position, it was a transition that she experienced with utter elation. While still in her twenties, she reflected proudly on her travels that built the circulation of the *Free Speech and Headlight* newspaper. Crediting the "novelty" of a "woman agent who was also an editor of the journal for which she canvassed,"[23] she described the kindness and helpfulness of many people she encountered. In her words, she was "treated like a queen" as she attended political meetings and church conventions up and down the Delta. At the Masonic grand lodge of her home state, they suspended their labour "to let [her] make an appeal for [her] paper." She reflected, "I was the daughter of Mississippi and my father had been a master Mason, so it was no wonder that I came out of the meeting with paid subscriptions from every delegate."[24] In moments like these, Wells' singularity translated into moments of solidarity that counteracted her sense of relative isolation.

Speaking Unwelcome Truths Without Apology

When she found her vocation and was actively supported by veteran Black journalists, the cause of what might be called her loneliness shifted once more. At stake was less that her energies were drained

21 Bay 2009: 57.
22 See McMurray 1998: 26.
23 Wells 1970/2020: 37.
24 Ibid.

in the tireless work of being an elementary educator as she tried to combine her own continued self-education and intellectual sustenance with supporting kin. Rather, what then singled her out was her distinct readiness to act. For instance, when she was ultimately fired (or not re-elected or renewed) to teach in the Memphis public schools, it was not a function of her ability as a teacher or her character. The "board had a copy of the *Free Speech* on file in the office showing criticism of them. They didn't care to employ a teacher who had done this."[25] She reflected later that the "worst part of the experience was the lack of appreciation shown by the parents. They simply couldn't understand why one would risk a good job, even for their children."[26]

Her reply was that she "thought it was right to strike a blow against a glaring evil and [she] did not regret it."[27] She added, "Up to that time I had felt that any fight made in the interest of the race would have its support. I learned then that I could not count on that."[28] In acting as she had, it was not that she acted alone, even if, at times, she acted in the company of the deceased. When realising that she could not rely on or assume automatic and broad support, she took her cues from different segments of the Black community, and especially from how she understood the commitments her father had modelled for her. After all, when his employer (who was also his wife's former master), locked him and his family out of their home upon learning that James Wells had not voted Democratic as he'd been instructed, Wells, without pause or word, moved across town, rented a new home, and began his own business.

Similarly, when Wells printed the name of a Black preacher who had been sleeping with a congregant's wife, he rallied fellow ministers to boycott the *Free Speech* for its revelations. In response, she published the names of every minister who had agreed to participate, telling "the community that these men upheld the immoral conduct of one of their number and asked if they were willing to support preachers who would sneak into their homes when their backs were turned and debauch their wives."[29] While her early Puritanism would mellow with time, in part through realising some of the dangerous fall-out

25 Ibid: 33.
26 Ibid: 34.
27 Ibid.
28 Ibid.
29 Ibid: 37.

that it could produce for the most vulnerable, her readiness to speak the truth as she saw it never wavered. As John Hope Franklin reflected in 1970, "[s]he did not hesitate to criticize southern whites, even before she left the South, or northern white liberals, or members of her own race when she was convinced that their positions were not in the best interests of all mankind."[30,31] This unusual confidence in her own judgment is what T. Thomas Fortune was describing when he observed that, "If Iola [Ida's pen name] were a man she would be a humming independent in politics."[32] As a matter of fact, Wells had no sense that she was beholden – not to those who employed her, not to those who preached to or educated her, not even to her most committed supporters. For her, appreciation, which she most certainly felt when warranted, did not mandate silenced disagreement or criticism. Still, her fierce independence meant that, even when in the company of others, she could face isolation. It was evident in moments when she asked herself whether she was foolish to fight in the ways that she did, knowing that she would continue to do so regardless of how others answered.

While an unusual degree of verbal sparring among Black journalists was the norm and the often-gendered jabs at her were seen as a sign of her achieving genuine belonging, Wells' commitment to brandishing truth with no accommodations generated a rather different response when it came to white southerners. As is now marked with a statue in her honour, they burned her newspaper's office, destroyed her printing press, and put a bounty on her head. She, of course, was only just getting started.

When "the leading White male citizens of Memphis threatened to kill her, Wells bought and carried a pistol."[33] The growth of "Jim Crow despotism and Black conservatism"[34] only made her militancy more resolute. Wells resented the "lack of activism among other middle-class black contemporaries, who sometimes used money to bypass the indignities of discrimination rather than defending their

---

30 Ibid: xiv.
31 There are many instances of criticisms she made internal to the Black community. These vary from calling out Black leaders for failing to use their wealth to create opportunities for Black employment, to criticising Black families, such as those in Visalia, California, for opting for a segregated school which led to vastly inferior learning conditions and a seeming admission of inferior Black talent, to calling out Booker T. Washington for criticising fellow Black leaders in the wrong venues.
32 Fortune, quoted in Wells 1970/2020: 30.
33 Wells 1995: xvii.
34 Ibid.

race"[35] and worried that few Black leaders, especially clergy, felt compelled to centre or speak directly to the people she had observed in country schools and churches – *or most Black people*. She reflected how, even when she had known nothing beyond what she had read, as a teenage teacher, people would "come to [her] with their problems because [she], as their teacher, should have been their leader."[36] They "needed guidance in everyday life"[37] that those typically expected to leaders were not offering. In her weekly letters to the *Living Way*, she acted from "an instinctive feeling" of what "people who had little or no school training" would want "coming into their homes weekly," something "which dealt with their problems in a simple, helpful way."[38] She continued, "I wrote in a plain, common-sense way on the things which concerned our people. Knowing that their education was limited, I never used a word of two syllables where one would serve the purpose."[39] This was a criticism of the many Black leaders, especially Black male leaders, who would soon eclipse her prominence following the death of Frederick Douglass. It was the systematic passing over of Wells that fuelled the "later resentments" to which I referred earlier, which in part propelled her to write an autobiography. Wells hoped it would counteract her sudden decline in national prominence which came, in large part, from her refusal to be diplomatic and accommodating when doing so fundamentally compromised her truth-telling. Put differently, if her insistence on speaking unwelcome truths put her in prophetic company, living and dead, it was also a source of intensifying isolation as political tides turned rightward.

Constant Self-Questioning, Relentless Self-Doubt

But before she had found a purpose through which to pursue her passions, when still a woman coming of age, it was not at all clear that it was her unqualified commitment to truth-telling action that separated her from many. Instead, this "nonconforming, fiercely independent, often angry, powerful female self"[40] frequently wondered *what was wrong with her*. It was not easy for her to see the configuration of the world – and her situation in it – as what made her strengths a

35 Ibid: 57.
36 Ibid: 21.
37 Ibid: 20.
38 Ibid: 22.
39 Ibid.
40 Washington in Wells 1995: x.

temporary liability, as what contributed to her sense of loneliness. In her *Memphis Diary* she reflected:

> I don't know what's the matter with me –, I feel so dissatisfied with my life, so isolated from all my kind. I cannot or do not make friends and these fits of *loneliness* will come and I tire of everything. My life seems awry, the machinery out of gear and I feel there is something wrong.[41]

Wells was frustrated by the norms and rituals she was supposed to engage in to forge meaningful, even intimate, connections with others. She wrote, "I will not begin at this late day by doing that which my soul abhors; sugaring men, weak, deceitful creatures, with flattery to retain them as escorts or to gratify a revenge."[42] Still, it was through such courtship that she was able not only to have male company but, through it, access to much of the social life of Memphis. It was not that there was no room for Wells to express herself openly and to exercise leadership through Black cultural institutions and organisations. It was instead that women were not to participate in cultural and social activities alone.

Rules of romance also intensified the challenges of Wells' desire to live in ways unscripted for a late nineteenth-century Black woman. Even as she worked to refute the racist and sexist (misogy-noir) myth of Black women as 'harlots,' Wells in fact accepted Victorian conceptions of the lady. For instance, if she was in no rush to take up the mantle, she affirmed the indispensable role of Black mothering in uplifting the Black race. She supported conditions for the emergence of Black men and the flourishing of Black manhood and wanted a life defined by similar degrees of self-expression and self-realisation. She did not see her own professional and political accomplishments as endangering or reducing what was available to her Black male counterparts.

Also frustrating her was the sheer expense of participating in Black elite life on a teacher's salary. Even if the sixty-dollar a week Memphis city school salary was seen as relatively generous, she could not rely on being paid on time. And while teaching gave her stature and access to opportunities for continued education and self-improvement,

41 Wells 1995: 59; italics added.
42 Ibid: 37.

she understood very clearly that she only preferred it to the other available options. Central among them was menial work at which she thought she would be worse. Intensifying her sense of teaching's dead-endedness was that despite her conscientiousness, she was never promoted beyond a fourth-grade classroom. Detesting any labour that had to be repeated from scratch over and over, she found the elementary focus tedious.[43] But before there was a clear exit, which she steadily built for herself, it appeared that this might be all there was.

As she moved into her vocation, the readiness of hostile others to create denigrating rumours about her did not subside. This would remain true even later when she married Barnett, a man who enabled her to continue the work that mattered most to her.[44] At the same time, she found the writing itself, the work of building the paper's regional readership, and the world of professional journalism invigorating. Enlarging her pedagogical reach and autonomy, she was exposed to considerably more news content and varied prose styles through regularly reading coverage in other papers. She also participated actively in a range of journalistic associations. Her paid work, in its many dimensions, contended with all the unfolding political matters of the day.

Her self-questioning thereby began to shift into a more political frame. Through it, she could see that what had appeared as personal inadequacies or limitations were not only or even primarily that. Nonetheless, even then, she would periodically, until the end, chastise herself for her quick temper. This is poignant given, as Linda O. McMurry observed, one of her special strengths was how uniquely she articulated anger, disillusionment and frustration of Black people in a world indifferent or hostile to their flourishing.[45]

43 Wells' daughter, Alfreda Duster, is quoted as saying, "Mother was very displeased by the fact that if you swept the house today, there'd be more dust there tomorrow. That bothered her – the fact that you had to clean up the place today and tomorrow you had to do the same thing. She didn't feel that she was accomplishing anything."

44 Alfreda Duster reflected, "[Father] was just as outspoken and just as militant as Mother, but by nature he was more easygoing. [...] He was always very supportive of whatever she got into. [...] Mother didn't worry about the house. Dad had somebody there to clean it up. [...] She said we should always know how to keep house, how to wash, how to iron, so even if we had someone else to do it, we would know how it should be done. [...] my dad did most of the cooking. He liked to cook – she didn't – so he'd go into the kitchen, put on an apron. [...] Mother was always busy, always reading, always writing" (1970/2020: 193-194).

45 See McMurry 1998: 98.

An Isolated Sense of What is Merited

Differences of political orientation were no less saddening. The disappointment they occasioned just had a different tenor. It is evident in Wells' reflections like these: "I am wondering what a fool am I to sacrifice so much and suffer so much and work so hard for a race which will not defend itself or protect me in defending it. Not for myself alone do I weep." She continued, "lastly and most of all, I weep because the manhood of the race knows itself slandered... its mothers, wives, sisters and daughters insulted and despoiled [...] and still fails to assert its strength [...] Is mine a race of cowards?"[46]

Wells wonders not about whether such sacrifices were correct to make but about her isolation in recognising their merit. Especially given their aim was collective, shared, and social. She laments that others won't also act as they so obviously should (and would, were they not so fearful) and at the harm of their own inaction to their souls and psyches. The resulting loneliness, if we can call it that, is no less real. In some ways it is yet more profound. Why were others willing to accept the compromising of their freedom for the sake of retaining a job or other form of position when one could, as Wells did, simply begin over? Why were they so ready to muddy their commitment to the unfinished promise of Reconstruction? If it fell to them to make and remake the world, why were so many so easily distracted? Why did they not feel – in a way that was impossible to ignore – the interwoven natures of personal and political self-realisation?

We may attempt an answer through consideration of a related but different question: what was it about Wells that enabled her to be so resolute and *so brave*?[47]

Some of the answer lies in the relationship between her parents and her brief taste of the actual project of reconstructing the U.S. nation on democratic terms. The fact that her parents and this project died simultaneously enabled her to romanticise both in ways that

46 Wells 1894, cited in Giddings 2008, 312.
47 In Eve L. Ewing's "Foreword" to the 2020 edition of *Crusade for Justice* she retells this story: Wells' "ten-year-old son awakened her in the middle of the night, saying her husband wanted her to get on the train. 'Mother,' he said, 'if you don't go nobody else will.' Wells travelled to Cairo, unearthed the details of the incident, and appeared before the governor as 'the official representative of all the black people of Illinois,' to argue that the sheriff who permitted the gruesome event to happen should not be reinstated. She spoke against the sheriff's attorney, who was a state senator, and stood toe-to-toe with the state's attorney. With no formal legal training, she won the case" (Wells 2020: xi).

were galvanising.[48] What was not exaggerated was a liberating faith anchored in the pursuit of Black independence through active literacy and political participation or the clarity with which Wells had been instructed that *her work* was going to school and helping to maintain a home in which her pride of place was tied to an ability to read through which she shared the news of the world with adult others.

She was also someone who, while losing much early on, experienced support in navigating that bereavement on adult rather than a child's terms. That meant taking on strenuous and uncertain work that she would not have chosen and, while doing it, trying to expand her options through joining intellectual and political circles that widened her horizons. In them, she embraced opportunities for leadership, whether through organising and participating in readings and theatrical productions or editing and writing weekly journals. All contributed to cultivating a widened Black civic life and each time she spoke or wrote it seemed to enlarge interested audiences.[49] The attributes that she was thereby able to transform from personal liabilities to political resources were a quickness to anger, a readiness to be disputatious, a keen eye for contradictions, and an organic sense of the relatedness of what were treated as disparate, individuated challenges.

In the preface to Wells' autobiography, she mentions a young woman who compared her to Joan of Arc. In Wells' daughter's assessment, the analogy was "at best, strained."[50] It was true that Joan was a peasant girl "in a time when peasants and girls had nothing to say to the ruling class of France," however, Joan had enjoyed the "rallying [of] a generally sympathetic French people to a common patriotic cause."[51] Wells, by contrast, was born into racialised enslavement in a "South bent upon" degrading Black people. She therefore did not only face opposition by whites, but from many of her own people who, fearing what her strategy might unleash on them, "impugn[ed] her

48 See McMurry 1998: 55.
49 McMurry (1998: 88-90) shares fascinating sociological observations from Garland I. Penn's (1891) *The Afro-American Press and Its Editors*: of the nineteen Black women journalists profiled in the book, most entered journalism at a young age, were unmarried or deferred marriage, had been born in the South, first wrote for church-related papers, and had received some formal school. Nine of them had lost one or more parents while young. Ida began writing at twenty-one for a newspaper run by a minister, was born and orphaned in Holly Springs, Mississippi, took some formal classes after leaving high school at sixteen, and wed at 30. McMurry also notes the number of Black male editors who were actively supportive of Black women journalists, giving them jobs, forums and praise.
50 Wells 1970/2020: xxxi.
51 Ibid.

motives."[52] Still, from the moment she entered public life to campaign against lynching and for civil rights, human rights, and women's rights, her relentless commitment to a vocation of public agitation brought her into relationships with kindred spirits. Unlike many others, they supported and applauded her transcending of existing confines of race and gender, seeing in her highly visible acts of subversion openings for so many others to meaningfully expand what they could do and be.[53] As Wells reflected, their courage and vision enabled her to act with and for her own.

Some Concluding Reflections

> "we don't know its real name   so we say sadness"
> —Julie Choffel (2020)

To return to the questions that framed this chapter – of whether the political left experiences distinct forms of loneliness, diagnoses such bouts in unique terms, and offers alternative prescriptions – the readiness of those on the political left to centre the systemic relationship between the personal and the political is a double-edged sword. While such a diagnosis shifts what otherwise might be experienced as individual or private failings as the function of a shared predicament that could – *and should* – be otherwise, doing so also involves breaking with the many who invest in forcibly adjusting us all to standards that don't fit rather than mobilising such energy in struggles for collective transformation. If a promise of the left is to try to address sources of potential personal isolation as shared problems, it is a wager that relies on ongoing collective mobilisation that will inevitably face wins and losses and always uncertainty. There will be many onlookers who see such a gamble as risky and foolish and will therefore instead seek advancement in a system with rules that, if unfair, are at least familiar. Their opting for what is known is likely to be expressed in forms of hostility toward those on the left that can be difficult to bear, especially if one is already in relative isolation.

Still, if one throws oneself into shared struggles, they can offer rich antidotes to such isolation or loneliness. After all, as we saw in the case of Wells, progressive collective movement can crystallise or

---

52 Ibid.
53 See Nelson 2006.

become one's vocation, helping one to realise one's distinct talents and passions in and with others in pursuit of freedoms that are historically unprecedented. After all, it is increasingly rare to be able to devote most of one's energies to enacting what really matters to one; in constructing spaces and relations through which one can express oneself fully. Instead, too much time is usually spent in activities that are tiresome, or even compromising, often encouraging us to turn on and individualise our predicaments rather than building solidarity with others. At best, much paid work, which fills most of our time (if we are lucky to be fully employed), is only adjacent to what compels us. And we share little more with the many people we are paid to work alongside than training.

Yet, even at their most successful, such struggles will be incomplete and imperfect, begetting new and often unforeseen projects and challenges. At every stage, those who participate will do so with different investments, resources, and degrees of commitment. Some will delight us with their contributions; others will surely disappoint us. Disagreements will brew; personal differences will stew. Some will be negotiable in ways that expand our understanding. Others will generate impasses and profound hurt.

There may be a small few who enact an unqualified left praxis. In the face of their clarity and resolve, some will see them as pushing too far, too fast; as over- or under-estimating friends and foes; as dangerous and making others look afraid, or otherwise limited.

The fragility of the world the left seeks to build, one that is ever responsive to the fullest range of existent and emergent ways of being human, is frightening in a small globe marked by bigger fascisms. Our necessary, relentless questioning and analysis can so easily lead to our destroying ourselves through fissures that render us a weak foe, making legitimate differences a liability rather than a strength. The outside challenges we face – those that would render the Earth inhospitable in every way – are so dire.

As we look with unflinching intensity at our obligations, we must remember that they are not only to others, but also to ourselves. For us, the wasting of each of our potential is a crime. Each of us and we together should not tolerate it. We must instead, even if sometimes as lonely warriors, furnish conditions for its cultivation, nourish domains for its deployment.

As we continue to try, sometimes in moments of relative or prolonged isolation, we would be wise to celebrate prototypical embodiments of what it means to be left, not only when they have become martyred ancestors. Their singularity is not that of messiahs or of gods but of what it can mean for us all to be human. Their exemplary qualities are not an indictment of our limitations. They should not be met with maligning that leads to their isolation and alienation. Instead in life and in death, they clarify our work, calling on us to nurture a terrain in which they – and ideally no one – is alone or lonely. We will fare better in such indispensable work if we keep company with the likes of Ida B. Wells. We are strengthened by engaging her as one of *our* heroines and by admiring – rather than fearing or resenting – her extraordinary clarity and bravery that were rooted in much, including irredeemable loss and an unwavering commitment to building a freer and more just society.[54]

References

Bay, Mia (2009), *To Tell the Truth Freely: The Life of Ida B. Wells*. New York: Hill and Wang.

Berry, Daina Ramey & Gross, Kali Nicole (2020), *A Black Women's History of the United States*. Boston: Beacon.

Choffel, Julie (2022), *The Inevitable Return of What We Do Not Love*. Georgetown, KY: Finishing Line Press.

DeCosta-Willis, Miriam (1995), "Introduction," *in* Ida B. Wells *The Memphis Diary of Ida B. Wells* (Edited by Miriam DeCosta-Willis), Boston: Beacon Press, 1–16.

Ewing, Eve L. (2020), "Foreword," *in* Ida B. Wells *Crusade for Justice: The Autobiography of Ida B. Wells*, Second Edition, edited by Alfreda M. Duster, with a new foreword by Eve L. Ewing and a new afterword by Michelle Duster. Chicago: University of Chicago Press, vii–xi.

Fradin, Dennis Brindell & Fradin, Judith Bloom (2000), *Ida B. Wells: Mother of the Civil Rights Movement*. New York: Clarion Books.

Franklin, John Hope (1970/2020), "Foreword to the 1970 Edition," *in* Ida B. Wells *Crusade for Justice: The Autobiography of Ida B. Wells*, Second Edition, edited by Alfreda M. Duster, with a new foreword by Eve L. Ewing and a new afterword by Michelle Duster. Chicago: University of Chicago Press, xiii–xiv.

Giddings, Paula J. (2008), *Ida: A Sword Among Lions*. New York: Amistad.

Holt, Thomas C. (1982), "The Lonely Warrior: Ida B. Wells-Barnett and the Struggle for Black Leadership," *in* John Hope Franklin & August Meier (eds.) *Black Leaders of the Twentieth Century*, Urbana: University of Illinois Press, 39–62.

....
54 For further reflection on the relationship between political imagination and loss, drawing insight from the life and work of Wells, see Hooker 2017.

Hooker, Juliet (2017), "Black Protest/White Grievance: On the Problem of White Political Imaginations Not Shaped by Loss," *South Atlantic Quarterly*, 116 (3), 483-504.

McMurry, Linda O. (1998), *To Keep the Waters Troubled: The Life of Ida B. Wells*. Oxford, UK: Oxford University Press.

Nelson, Claudia D. (2006), "The Men that Influenced Ida B. Wells-Barnett," *Making Connections: A Journal for Teachers of Cultural Diversity*, 10 (1-2), 25-44.

Penn, I. Garland (1891), *The Afro-American Press and Its Editors*. Springfield, MA: Wiley & Co.

Sterling, Dorothy (1995), "Afterword," *in* Ida B. Wells *The Memphis Diary of Ida B. Wells* (Edited by Miriam DeCosta-Willis), Boston: Beacon Press, 191-199.

Washington, Mary Helen (1995), "Foreword," *in* Ida B. Wells *The Memphis Diary of Ida B. Wells* (Edited by Miriam DeCosta-Willis), Boston: Beacon Press, ix–xvii.

Wells, Ida B. (1894), *Indianapolis Freedman*. 21 July.

_____. 1970/2020. *Crusade for Justice: The Autobiography of Ida B. Wells,* Second Edition, edited by Alfreda M. Duster, with a new foreword by Eve L. Ewing and a new afterword by Michelle Duster. Chicago: University of Chicago Press.

_____. 1995. *The Memphis Diary of Ida B. Wells* (Edited by Miriam DeCosta-Willis). Boston: Beacon Press.

Artist: Meghan Markin

The Problem of Pathology:
Meditation on Race, Disability & Loneliness

Derefe Kimarley Chevannes

Introduction

The affective implicates the political in formative ways. Frederick Douglass observed his Aunt Hester's scream as she was raped by her white slave master, "I have often been awakened at the dawn of day by the most heart-rending shrieks of an own aunt of mine, whom he [the Master] used to tie up to a joist, and whip upon her naked back till she was literally covered with blood."[1] Aunt Hester's scream stands as an affective protest against the anti-human machinery and machinations of black chattel slavery. The scream was a cry against anti-black racism and the anti-democratic practices that upheld it. Yet, the scream, or as Douglass notes, the visceral "shrieks" of Aunt Hester, also stand to indicate the pathology of blackness within European modernity, so much so, that the black voice – its cry, its scream – would register no democratic response or reprieve.

For example, the Black Lives Movement (BLM) centres precisely the historical silencing of black lives – indeed, of black cries. It was the cry of Eric Garner, whose famous last words – *I can't breathe* – would become a death cry and a rallying one as well. "On July 17, 2014, Garner was confronted by Staten Island police for selling cigarettes on the street. When the police moved to confront Garner, the matter became physical, and officer Daniel Pantaleo placed Garner in a chokehold, an illegal manoeuvre. The incident was caught on video, and viewers can hear Garner telling Pantaleo he can't breathe."[2] Those same fatal three words would yet bellow from the existence of another black man, George Floyd, whose neck was arrested by the jackboots of American policing. Floyd's cry, *I can't breathe*, echoed over twenty times[3] against an institutional refusal to hear. That cry would still reverberate both in life as in death. These cries, black screams, would move beyond the Aunt Hesters of the 19th century and haunt the George Floyds and Eric Garners of the 21st century. Death by somatic,

1 Douglass 2003: 20.
2 Lebron 2017: 5.
3 See Singh 2020.

and socio-political, asphyxiation is a lonely affair. It is a fatal suspension of black political life, one summarily cut off from the vast world of social intercourse. In a word, it is an assassination of futures, that is, the death of existential revelry with, and in a world of, human others.

To be sure, narratives of blackness are not monolithic. The inclusion of deaf people, and even, the black deaf, raises additional lines of inquiries about the relationship between race and disability in the formation of the supposed problem of pathology. For example, "[b]eing both Black and deaf is in many ways a 'double whammy' because of society's abrogation of each of these two minorities. When the conditions of Blackness and deafness are combined in one person, the individual effects of prejudice, discrimination, and negative self-image are compounded exponentially."[4] In what follows, I argue that both black and deaf people summon an existential scream in order to telegraph the violence of being treated as pathology, and therefore, being located as an anthropological problem. I begin by centring the question of blackness and modes of anti-black racism within the Euromodern world. In doing so, I meditate on questions of loneliness as affect and its liberatory possibilities. From there, I turn to the question of deafness by exploring the intersection of race and disability and the black deaf relationship with loneliness. In the final analysis this chapter offers a mediation on the epistemic-affective dimensions of loneliness as constituted in raced and disabled terms.

Black Loneliness and the Possibility of Liberation

In order to deal with the question of the human being as pathology, by which I mean a sense of being diseased, or a diseased sense of being, one is left a singular remedy: to be cured. As such, violence against the black body was imagined as a form of Euromodern corrective. The affect and the political are thus inseparable facets of the lived experience of the (black) human being. As such, it is only fitting to ask a central question: How does it *feel* to be a pathology? Deeper still, how does it feel to be not only wronged, as a question of (in)justice, but also to *be* wrong – an ontological error – the wrong form of a human being? This is precisely the question W.E.B Du Bois posed concerning what was dubbed 'the Negro Question.' And so, Du Bois asks: "To the real question, How does it feel to be a problem? I answer seldom a word.

4 Smith & Hairston 1998: ix.

And yet, being a problem is a strange experience, peculiar even for one who has never been anything else."[5] Blackness was pathology and therefore, became an embodied problem. Or, as it is so often expressed in contemporary vernacular: the crime of being born black. This is to say the theory of the raced problematicity of the human being – the 'Negro Problem,' as some termed it – is deeply intertwined with a presumed pathology.[6] Much like problems, pathologies too have remedies. In a word, problems demand solutions and pathologies demand cures. In the end, we are confronted with something akin to existential dread: the tiredness – the sheer exhaustion – of being someone's else 'problem.'

As an Afro-Caribbean – Jamaican – immigrant to the United States, I recall very well my early days. I was in a predominantly non-diverse, racially homogenous setting – more than 9 of 10 people who lived there were white. This was the first time I found myself completely immersed in a non-black, entirely white environ. I left Jamaica with an incandescent youthful exuberance. I had so much shine, so much hope shored up like a message-in-a-bottle tossed in the sea of possibility, waiting for someone to find it – to find me. I was a black teen then, on the cusp of my 20th year, wanting to explore the world, to see what was beyond my relatively small orbit. What was to come, unbeknownst to me, were important years – they were my college days. Prior to leaving my tropical homeland, one filled with the vibrant, yet complex, colours of life, I recall vividly, the overflowing excitement to explore and engage cultures beyond my own. I was what many philosophers and thinkers called a social being. Yet, as it turned out, I found myself encountering a reality completely divergent from my own dreams and aspirations. For instance, I recount meeting a few black students (by which I mean, I could count them all on one hand) – one from Trinidad and Tobago, another from the Democratic Republic of the Congo. There was a shared mutuality – a shared humanity – that we recognised in each other. Of course, the circumstances of American life, and its grim raced realities, came to bear heavily on us; we all found ourselves sitting at the proverbial lunch table together. All of us, all black faces in an ocean of white gazes – admittedly, we were castaways. We encountered a distinctly American phenomenon, what scholar and educator

5 Du Bois 1994: 1.
6 See Du Bois 1994.

Beverly Daniel Tatum interrogates as, *Why Are All the Black Kids Sitting Together in the Cafeteria?: And Other Conversations About Race*. There was a palpable, piercing human loneliness that we felt, paradoxically, in the midst of an embodied black collectivism. The white gaze cordoned off our sense of self and normalcy – it was as though, by sitting together, we were self-incriminating. What was our avowed crime? Racial separatism and its rather specific charge of black segregation. Perhaps this is partly what it means to be an American *problem*?

The Negro problem is to be expected in a world that is decidedly Negrophobic. Though we were diasporic black and not African Americans, as a technical manner, through the white American gaze, our shared blackness condemned us equally. bell hooks spoke to this "separatist" phenomenon, "[t]hroughout my tenure as a Yale professor, I was often confronted with white students who would raise the issue of why it is black students sit together in the cafeteria, usually at one table. They saw this as some expression of racial separatism, exclusion, etc."[7] This racialist white grievance clamours in an unrelenting register, "'blacks are just as racist as whites – we are all racists',"[8] and so represents a chilling reminder that black humanisation, situated in the midst of a hegemonic Eurocentrism, is reduced to white dehumanisation. It makes sense, then, when Martin Luther King Jr. wrote, "[t]here is not even a common language when the term 'equality' is used. Negro and white have a fundamentally different definition."[9] A Negrophobic normativity turns reality on its head – it is a cataclysmic distortion of truth, occasioning the sedimentation and regimentation of an economy of racial lies, falsehoods and untruths. It is a neo-colonial situation and with it, all its raced social and political phenomena emerge. For this reason, Fanon implores us to abandon the old political vocabulary of Euro-American humanism: "Two centuries ago, a former European colony took it into its head to catch up with Europe. It has been so successful that the United States of America has become a monster where the flaws, sickness, and inhumanity of Europe have reached frightening proportions."[10] And so, in the cafeteria, the blacks sit together, all of us, in our unashamed, yet publicly shamed, blackness. Our affective response, of seeking mutuality, or

---

7 bell hooks 2015: 16.
8 Ibid: 15.
9 King Jr. 2010: 8.
10 Fanon 2004: 237.

escaping the quicksand of a raced loneliness, stood as an epistemic architecture – of building new lines of thinking, and of relations. It is a grounding of black reason through black affect. In a word, it constructs a new political reality. It is as bell hooks contends: "all social manifestations of black separatism are often seen by whites as a sign of anti-white racism, when they usually represent an attempt by black people to construct places of political sanctuary where we can escape, if only for a time, white domination."[11] In this sense, black resistance, at micro or macro levels, amounts to the collapse of an internal and external pathology of difference. Acts of black resistance that are born out of affect, whether black loneliness or outright black rage, become a praxis of emancipatory struggle, whose impact produces a depathologizing outcome. It is a coming to terms with blackness as socio-political prescription to the ailments of Euromodern society.

Black loneliness, that is, race and affect in dialectical relations, produces not only subjugation but at the same time, engenders the possibility for *something more* – that is to say, it reformulates black reason as a phenomenological moment where black loneliness becomes a formative moment of, and for, liberatory praxis. After all, it was within the four walls of American incarceration, that is, in the bowels of solitary confinement, the space of black loneliness and a violent separation from black (and human) sociality, where MLK penned "Letter from Birmingham Jail," whose discourse on segregation as racial exile produces new avenues of epistemic resistance: "All segregation statutes are unjust because segregation distorts the soul and damages the personality."[12] The effect of a segregation is both socio-political and affective. In my own moments of black loneliness, where anti-black racism within academia treats the black subject – me – as an exceptionality, through the fetishization of black existence, that is, I am exceptional for being black, or conversely, I am an exception to blackness and therefore, not quite black. Or, as a final turn, because I am black, I am excepted from being human. In the end, all anti-black treatments, in the scientific sense, reduce my blackness to a mere object. The Negro problem is always a problem of being imprisoned in a state of exceptionality – a lonely existence, to be sure, in what is a predominantly white milieu.

11 bell hooks 2015: 15.
12 King Jr. 1963: 3.

In other moments, I vividly recall the struggles of pedagogy as a black academic within the classroom. I once taught "Introduction to Contemporary Political Thought," a general education requirement for incoming freshmen (and other students). At the end of the semester, one student anonymously wrote that I had turned a political theory course into "an African American Studies" class, for which, the student complained, they did not register. The syllabus listed fifteen assigned thinkers or texts. Of that number, three of the assigned readings were written by black theorists, twelve by white. Though the canon taught was eighty per cent white, still, it was not white enough. This, of course, is compounded by the fact that I, a black, was read within the classroom as a raced text, my existence reduced to an (em)bodied textuality. Therefore, there were four black texts read in the classroom – four too many. My blackness and the blackness of the canon became diagnosed as pathology within Euro-American normativity. Put simply, I was an existential fetter, a black problem, to proper knowledge-production. This lived experience of anti-black racism within a Euromodern world can engender a deep sense of loneliness by inducing psychosocial and epistemic isolation.

Frantz Fanon's *Black Skin, White Masks* diagnoses the question of black pathology as a psycho-existential condition. He argued:

> To come back to psychopathology, let us say that the Negro lives an ambiguity that is extraordinarily neurotic. At the age of twenty – at the time, that is, when the collective unconscious has been more or less lost, or is resistant at least to being raised to the conscious level – the Antillean recognizes that he is living an error. Why is that? Quite simply because – and this is very important – the Antillean has recognized himself as a Negro, but, by virtue of an ethical transit, he also feels (collective unconscious) that one is a Negro to the degree to which one is wicked, sloppy, malicious, instinctual. Everything that is the opposite of these Negro modes of behaviour is white. This must be recognized as the source of Negrophobia in the Antillean. In the collective unconscious, black = ugliness, sin, darkness, immorality. In other words, he who is Negro is immoral.[13]

13 Fanon 2008: 169.

For Fanon, the question of pathology is immediately a question about the wrongness of being,[14] or as he puts it, "he [the black] is living an error." The consequence is a form of self-negation or self-denial. Are we surprised, then, some whites often say, "you're pretty for a black girl" or, as was often said of me, "you're articulate for a black man"? In this sense, a prized blackness was always existing in a delimited zone of exceptionality. This is to say, beautiful or rational blackness was a punctuation of blackness – it was a pause or a suspension of Afrocentricity,[15] not its predisposition. Of course, the result of this condition, that is, an attempted assassination of the condition of being black, is a lonely affair because, ironically, it represents a lonely existence while living in a world of others. But such is the often terminal effect and impact of anti-black racism within European modernity. The question of "Left Loneliness" is hence, sometimes, about finding one's self in the social world; it is navigating and finding a sense of homeliness, a restoration of homeland and a retrieval of self. It is enacting self-integration in the midst of racial segregation. Put differently, a project of homeliness requires building black communities and economies of political exchanges and thus, sustaining black precincts of radical thought toward a freedom enterprise. The Euromodern world makes of blackness a problem, to be sure, a pathological problem – an embodied criminality. For this reason, we witness many black families without black mothers, fathers, sons and daughters because they have been locked up and jailed.[16] Being a problem is a lonely affair because, apparently, its diametrical opposite is the solution itself. In European modernity, whiteness is remedy, blackness is toxicity. The consequence, as Fanon identified, is Negrophobia. The Negrophobic world is invariably a Europhilic world, where the dislike, hatred and fear of the black is a consequence of the valorisation and veneration of whiteness. From every facet of the social and political world, blackness is disavowed: in education (Jim Crow separatism); in law (prison industrial complex); in politics (disenfranchisement); in medicine (scientific racism and the Tuskegee Experiment[17]); in policing (George

---

14 See Wynter 2006.
15 Given that "Afrocentricity seeks to enshrine the idea that blackness itself is a trope of ethics" because it "is a transforming power that helps us to capture the true sense of our souls" it follows, then, that the Afrocentric order is one of "human regeneration [because] [i]t challenges and takes to task the perpetuation of white racial supremacist ideas" (Asante 2003: 2, 62 & 2).
16 See Haley 2016 and Alexander 2012.
17 From 1932 to 1972, the United States Public Health Service conducted a racist scientific study on the

Floyd); in housing (redlining[18]); in Caribbean and African regionalism (European colonialism). Negrophobia is the rational articulation of the social and political logics of a Eurocentric world order. But like most, if not all, phobias, its root is indeed a pathological condition. It is a flight from reason, particularly black reason – human reason. And so, in a lonely world, up appears down – it is an inversion of reality, so much so that what manifests is life as surreal, as absurdity. Accordingly, black reason problematises pathology and therefore, depathologizes blackness as a problem. The result leaves intact only a condition, not blackness as remedy per se, but blackness as a human condition.

Therefore, in the midst of an imposed and instituted black loneliness, paradoxically, the possibility of humanistic social transformation becomes a lived reality through dialectical change. The afflicted sense of loneliness at the thought of Steve Biko's assassination, the South African anti-Apartheid activist and thinker, did not kill 'black consciousness,' instead it breathed into it the certainty of posterity – it was an intergenerational and transgenerational restoration of South Africans, and other diasporic blacks, formulating, in the process, a renewed sense of selfhood against moments of Euromodern alienation.[19]

Race & Disability: The Black Deaf Problem

Yet, in the grand scope of human history, race represents but one of many conditions of pathologizing the human being. Within the domain of disability, take, for instance, the pathologizing of deafness. Disability, understood through ableist logics of difference, have been known to rupture belonging and reproduce loneliness as a site of social isolation, "[a]bleist narratives present disability as an unwanted difference [...] Bodily difference was narrated as the source of social isolation and emotional loneliness."[20] The deaf subject has, historically,[21] been viewed as an apolitical subject, that is, (s)he is thought to be outside

evolution of syphilis in the black people. Black men were injected with syphilis and were not informed of its effects for the purposes of scientific medical advancement. Black participants were not medically treated. Many died from the disease, their spouses infected, and their children born with congenital syphilis.

18 See Richard Rothstein's *The Color of Law* (2017) for further reading on the history of the United States' discriminatory, anti-black racist housing policies and laws instituted against African Americans.

19 See Biko 2002.

20 Tarvainen 2020: 878.

21 For a more nuanced take, one may want to explore Soviet construction(s) of deaf identity outside the hegemonic register of Western conceptions of deafness as disability. Claire L. Shaw's (2017) profiles of Soviet deafness proffer meaningful contrasts to the dominant Western, capitalistic construct.

the realm of the political.[22] That is to say, the deaf subject lacks human reason due entirely to their 'auditory deficiency.' For this reason, deaf culture rejects the nomenclature of being diagnosed with 'hearing loss.' And so, deaf scholars have reformulated an alternative narrative, not 'audiological impairment' or even 'hearing loss' but rather 'Deaf Gain.' This position is defined by Bauman and Murray: "Whereas popular constructions of deafness are defined exclusively by the negative effects [...] a Deaf Gain perspective brings forth a number of social, psychological, and cognitive benefits. In calling attention to Deaf Gain benefits, we are not claiming that it is necessarily better to be deaf than hearing, but we are saying that it is not necessarily better to be hearing than deaf."[23] The transition to Deaf Gain away from hearing loss is but one of many attempts at an epistemic turn, a movement away from an 'auricularised' (hearing) ontology of deafness towards a more deaf-centric epistemology. Carol Padden and Tom Humphries further argue that "[d]eaf people for the most part have always lived within the world of others,"[24] the immediate result is, then, to create a deaf world, one that stands not so much in opposition to the hearing world, but rather in contrast to it. The use of sign language, for example, immediately suspends notions of political speech, as a disclosive state of being, as being exclusively phonocentric, that is to say, reduced only to the *phonos* (Greek for sound). Yet, the signed languages of the deaf have sometimes been disavowed as either *gestures* or *sentiments*: "Others believe that Deaf people are protective and romantic about signed languages because they are 'dependent' on them. Lacking the ability to use speech, it is said, they become overly sentimental about their 'adaptive means.' In contrast, hearing people surely do not think of themselves as 'dependent,' in any pejorative way, on speech."[25] Other scholars, such as Owen Wrigley, similarly contend, "[s]ign languages are most often considered by hearing officials either to be only a manual form of the dominant spoken language or to be a set of gestures, pantomime, or semaphore signals without distinct linguistic status."[26] It is precisely this denial of linguistic viability that seeks to deny deaf communicative existence.

22 See Owen Wrigley's *Politics Of Deafness* (1996) for further reading.
23 Bauman & Murray 2014: xxiv.
24 Padden & Humphries 1988: 56.
25 Ibid: 69.
26 Wrigley 1996: 67.

Historically, this has been true of deaf lives and the result sometimes led to an apolitical, lonely state of affairs: "The situation of the prelingually deaf, prior to 1750, was indeed a calamity: unable to acquire speech, hence 'dumb' or 'mute'; unable to enjoy free communication with even their parents and families; confined to a few rudimentary signs and gestures; cut of, except in large cities, even from the community of their own kind; deprived of literacy and education, all knowledge of the world; forced to do the most menial work; living alone, often close to destitution; treated by the law and society as little better than imbeciles – the lot of the deaf was manifestly dreadful."[27] Once more, to be made a pathology – a human problem – in law, politics and sociality invariably result in the elimination of human relations with others. To be disavowed from the enterprise of communication itself is always a lonely experience, the consequence of which is existential dread. Yet, despite these rituals of disavowal of deaf subjectivity, those who are a part of the deaf community have utilised sign language in order to assert their own political subjectivity. The communicative labour of the deaf is to assign value to intercorporeality, that is, an embodied collectivisation of selves, in such a way that political speech itself transcends its phonocentric episteme.

Audism functions as an overdetermination of the human being as an auricular being, that is, the person who *hears*. It is a fatal reduction wherein being human means being able to hear. The result, then, is a dehumanisation of the deaf subject because s/he is without hearing and therefore, without *sound* reasoning. Audism becomes articulated, much like anti-black racism, through a co-opted historical project. Its justificatory practices emanate from the audist impulse of the European sciences and the concomitant philosophies born from them, not the least of which includes the science of politics. For instance, as a figurehead of evolutionary science, Charles Darwin, in his *The Expression of the Emotions In Man And Animals*, equated the sign language of Deaf people to the gestural motions of so-called savages, "With conventional signs which are not innate" he says, "such as those used by the deaf and dumb and by savages."[28] The savage, as a matter of definition, is located outside society, namely, in the woods or the wild, for he is outside the social contract and ergo, ungovernable.

27 Sacks 2000: 12.
28 Darwin 1872: 61.

He remains untouched by the civilising sentiments and sensibilities of society. Of course, the deaf becomes fossilised in primitivism due to being incapable of rational speech. The upshot is a presumed turning away from reality, from a sober accounting of political life to an indulgent discounting of it – a hedonistic madness. The British founder of modern cultural anthropology, observed in the work of Edward Burnett Tylor, would note, in his *Researches Into the Early History of Mankind*, "Savage and half-civilised races accompany their talk with expressive pantomime much more than nations of higher culture."[29] The development of European scientism, in its quest for modernity, hypothesised and sought to make empirical justifications for the exclusion of the deaf from civilisation and as a result, the domain of the political. It is of little wonder, then, the deaf would be classified as "half a man."[30] Alexander Graham Bell, famed American scientist, in his *Memoir upon the Formation of a Deaf Variety of the Human Race*, remarked: "I have shown that sexual selection is at work among the deaf and dumb, tending to produce a deaf variety of the human race. Those who believe as I do, that the production of a defective race of human beings would be a great calamity to the world"[31] must curate remedies for the elimination of deafness. To do so, he prescribes "the segregation of deaf-mutes, the use of sign language, and the employ of deaf teachers to produce an environment that is unfavourable to the cultivation of articulation and speech-reading." For further experimentation into the elimination of "the deaf variety," Bell concludes: "I commend the whole subject to the attention of scientific men."[32]

The cauterisation of the deaf from the genealogy of the human being emerges from the abnormality of the 'deaf variety' – a splitting away from the faculty of the senses such that a particular 'deaf idiocy' occurs. The deaf variety is considered to be a sub-human malformation of the aural human being. The agency of the deaf becomes captive to phonocentric logics – the demand of sound in order to be human – as the deaf subject labours fatally to produce another's world: a hearing world. For example, what is known as 'oralism' is a common audist approach to remake deaf people to be hearing, "[o]ralism, the belief that spoken language is inherently superior to sign language, played an

29 Tyler 1878: 15.
30 See Lang 2017: 212-213.
31 Bell 1883: 41.
32 Ibid: 48.

important role in deaf education."[33] Oralism was viewed and used to remedy the problem of deafness as pathology: "oralism is as much an ideology as it is a method, and one with a distinct teleology. As speech was considered God-given, that which separated man from beast, it was a sin to permit the deaf to remain silent."[34] Therefore, phonocentric speech became a substitute for sign language. Denial of language acts as a disavowal of being human in a world of human beings. Such denials engender isolation and thus generate a sense of non-belonging or social loneliness due to a violent removal from human history.

Paul C. Higgins speaks to the relationship between exclusion and loneliness: "Since childhood, members of deaf communities have experienced repeated frustration in making themselves understood, embarrassing misunderstandings, and the loneliness of being left out by family, neighbourhood, acquaintances, and others."[35] Yet, these same moments of deaf loneliness, such as they are, "help to strengthen a deaf person's identification with the deaf world."[36] Externally imposed loneliness becomes a portal for internal transformation. Moreover, our meditation on deaf positionality must also reflect on the intersection of disability and race, that is to say, the space intersected between deafness and blackness. Linwood Smith and Ernest Hairston critically examine the subjectivity of black deafness:

> To dismiss the racial aspect of deafness would be naïve and presumptuous because the Black deaf person is already at a disadvantage from the time he is born. It can't be explained away and it won't go away easily. Attitudes die hard. Black deaf individuals have seldom been provided with a good educational foundation and with upward mobility opportunities to do meaningful work and to grow on the job. We live in a 'hearing' and 'color-conscious' society.[37]

The logics of both audism and anti-black racism locate the black deaf subject at the threshold of multiple sites of social and political exclusion. But that exclusion is not merely binary or dual, meaning, it is not only a racist and audist exclusion, but sometimes, for the black deaf, it is white deaf anti-black racism: "At many segregated schools for the

33 McCaskill, Lucas, Bayley & Hill 2011: 26.
34 Wrigley 1996: 16.
35 Higgins 1980: 42.
36 Ibid.
37 Smith & Hairston 1998: 3.

Negro deaf, emphasis was on vocational rather than academic training."[38] Like black hearing people, deaf black people felt and bore the heavy weight of racial segregation. Yet, unlike the former, the question of deafness meant that black disability was a dual problem, a double pathology. In light of the history of the pathologizing of deafness, or a decidedly pathological history of deafness, it is of no surprise, then, that deaf communicative agency becomes estranged. The negation of sign language in order to overvalorise phonocentric discourse immediately calcifies reason as partly being a sonic phenomenon. In such a scenario, the deaf cannot reason and thus, are reduced to a sub-human being. The deaf world, however, proffers a radical alternative that produces an embodied labouring of communication – that is, communicative praxis becomes incorporated within the corporeal. It is a labouring towards explicating the terms of the deaf world. This labouring produces a different language, a new linguistic phenomenon with all its political implications. This linguistic phenomenon occasions a new discursive reality, one that asserts, "signed languages are human languages."[39] It is exactly this humanistic *telos* that becomes the *sine qua non* of communicative agency, for in the production of collective value, a world beyond sound materialises – a deaf, signed world emerges. However, the severing of intersubjective relations through projects of audism is not due to any internal deficiencies within deaf people but instead represent instances where communicative agency has become alienated. Put otherwise, the alienation of communicative agency disavows its teleological imperative for creating collective value; it is an estranging of the human being from other human beings. The consequence is that listening and interrogation, as a recognition of the other, is negated – communication replaced by the demand to command and control.

It is for this reason Paddy Ladd turns to linguistic colonialism, denoted in part as a seizure and denial of modes of deaf valuation for the expressed purposes of institutionalising hearing normativity and comfort, noting, "it speaks volumes about the conceptualisation of the liberal hearing–Deaf relationship – all that matters is to ensure the Deaf person understands what you desire to tell them"[40] and therefore, deaf valorisation is displaced for hearing domination. Yet, to decolonise not merely linguistics as such, but broadly, communicative existence, there must be attempts of epistemic and

38 Ibid: 31.
39 Padden & Humphries 1988: 73.
40 Ladd 2003: 179.

political resistance[41] in order to generate new ways of deaf being or being deaf, outside the old audist paradigm. Drawing from Du Bois' colour line, this necessarily means a demolition of what Christopher Krentz names "the hearing line," wherein hearing people "associate [deafness] with what is outside human language and understanding."[42] Therefore, a decolonial approach includes forms of resistance that are both anti-audist and anti-racist within the political domain. The result leads to a transformation of the category of the human being. In such a space, loneliness becomes not a source of subjugation, or an affective signifier for political isolation and social exclusion, but a normal process of quotidian human living.

Coda: Problematising "Problems"

Whether on the Negro Problem or the Deaf Problem, or when both intersect, the question of race and disability (deafness) returns us to the mediation with which we began: How does it *feel* to be a problem? The resolution lies in a constant act of defiance – of resistance. It is a refusal to be a problem, to be pathology. Yet, paradoxically, some problems can only be resolved by problematising them. Only at this level of the meta-discursive, where there is a problematising of the problem itself, can there be the possibility of dialectical transformation – the opportunity to create a new phenomenon, a new reality: freedom through disability and black revolutions. To be sure, there is an anchoring of politics that comes from the space of the personal. We write what we write not simply because it is important; indeed, its own importance almost always emanates from a space of personal trial or conviction. That personalised space of struggle is the source of an embodied voice. Political speech, as redefined above, has the capacity of world-making, of charting a new trajectory of what it truly means to be a human being. Thus, the question of our times is most certainly a question of resistance, of revolt, of liberation from forces, be they racist or audist – or both, racist-audism – that seeks to deny our voice and in so doing, make an attempt to dehistoricise the oppressed, where we cannot usher in a new civilisation, whose purpose is to make us known to ourselves

41 As a stratagem for political resistance, deaf people sought sovereignty over their own affairs through a rejection of hearing paternalism and domination: "An example of effective Deaf intragroup linkages surfaced during the 1988 Deaf President Now protest, when students, faculty, and community members banded together to successfully push for the enactment of Gallaudet University's first Deaf president" (Lockwood 2014: 333).

42 Krentz 2014: 432.

and those around us. This process of systemic denial, self-negation or human erasure is to forcefully render the oppressed speechless – to be without a voice. The consequence, as I have limned it, leaves one experiencing an agonal sensation: What does it mean to *be* a problem? In my own space of Left Black Loneliness, there begins an ongoing battle to be heard – a violent cry or even a gentle whisper – and with it, the emergence of not only individuality, but a grounded, fully-formed humanity. As bell hooks writes, "[t]heorizing black experience in the United States is a difficult task. Socialized within white supremacist educational systems and by a racist mass media, many black people are convinced that our lives are not complex, and are therefore unworthy of sophisticated critical analysis and reflection."[1] Reflection can and must be a critical enterprise of self-interrogation, a process that generates political consciousness, without which there can be no social transformation. That is, reflectivity is a sustained mediation on relations to self and others; as a phenomenological process, it is a suspension of normativity – of everyday practices, assumptions and ways of life. As such, a reflexive approach to affect, particularly as a feeling of loneliness, becomes a multi-dimensional phenomenon with social, political, and even epistemic implications. The fact is deaf people "saw themselves as being 'alone' after having the opportunity to interact with like-minded peers who had had similar experiences of what it means to be deaf in a hearing society."[2] Loneliness may thus constitute a generative site of possibility for a freedom project.

For these reasons, I mediate, through critical reflection, on the revolutionary potential of speech, politics and communication, through an application of black and deaf lived experience in order to concretise our theoretical prescriptions for the ultimate end of material and socio-political transformation. To do this meaningfully, there must be an engagement with the affective-epistemic dimensions of political life; this explains Fanon's seminal observation: "Total liberation involves every facet of the personality."[3] Therefore, for both black and deaf subjects, the movement from being a problem, as existential pathology, to being a human being with historical contingency and political futures, begins with a rather simple interrogative meditation: how does it feel to *be*? Not as others would will it, but as we would and must have it.

1 bell hooks 2015: 2.
2 Leigh, Morere & Pezzarossi 2014: 366.
3 Fanon 2004: 233.

References

Alexander, Michelle (2012), *The New Jim Crow: Mass Incarceration in the Age of Color-blindness.* New York: New Press.

Asante, Molefi Kete (2003), *Afrocentricity: The Theory of Social Change.* Chicago: African American Images.

Bauman, H-Dirksen L. & Murray, Joseph J. (eds.) (2014), *Deaf Gain: Raising the Stakes for Human Diversity.* Minneapolis: University of Minnesota Press.

Bell, Alexander Graham (1883), *Memoir upon the Formation of a Deaf Variety of the Human Race.* Washington, DC: U.S. Government Printing Office.

bell hooks (2015), *Black Looks: Race and Representation.* New York: Routledge.

Biko, Steve (2002), *I Write What I Like: Selected Writings.* Chicago: University of Chicago Press.

Darwin, Charles (1872), *The Expression of the Emotions In Man And Animals.* London: John Murray, Albemarle Street.

Douglass, Frederick (2003), *Narrative of the life of Frederick Douglass.* United Kingdom: Bedford/St. Martin's.

Du Bois, W. E. B (1994), *The Souls of Black Folk.* New York: Dover Publications.

Fanon, Frantz (2004), *The Wretched of the Earth.* New York: Grove Press.

Fanon, Frantz (2008), *Black Skin, White Masks.* London: Pluto Press.

Gordon Lewis R. & Gordon, Jane Anna (eds.), *A Companion to African-American Studies.* Hoboken, NJ: Blackwell Publishing.

Haley, Sarah (2016), *No Mercy Here: Gender, Punishment, and the Making of Jim Crow Modernity.* Chapel Hill: The University of North Carolina Press.

Higgins, Paul C. (1980), *Outsiders in a Hearing World: A Sociology of Deafness.* United Kingdom: SAGE Publications.

King Jr., Martin Luther (1963), "Letter from Birmingham Jail." United States: American Friends Service Committee.

King Jr., Martin Luther (2010), *Where Do We Go from Here: Chaos or Community?* (Edited by Coretta Scott King and Vincent Harding). Boston: Beacon Press.

Krentz, Christopher (2014), "The Hearing Line: How Literature Gains from Deaf People," *in* H-Dirksen L. Bauman & Joseph J. Murray (eds.) *Deaf Gain: Raising the Stakes for Human Diversity,* Minneapolis: University of Minnesota Press, 421-435.

Ladd, Paddy (2003), *Understanding Deaf Culture: In Search of Deafhood.* Clevedon, UK: Multilingual Matters.

Lang, Harry. G. (2017), *Fighting in the Shadows: Untold Stories of Deaf People in the Civil War.* Washington, DC: Gallaudet University Press.

Lebron, Christopher J. (2017), *The Making of Black Lives Matter: A Brief History of an Idea.* United States: Oxford University Press.

Leigh, Irene W.; Morere, Donna A. & Caroline Kobek Pezzarossi (2014), "Deaf Gain: Beyond Deaf Culture," *in* H-Dirksen L. Bauman & Joseph J. Murray (eds.) *Deaf Gain: Raising the Stakes for Human Diversity,* Minneapolis: University of Minnesota Press, 356-371.

Lockwood, Elizabeth M. (2014), "Effective Deaf Action In The Deaf Community In Uruguay," *in* H-Dirksen L. Bauman & Joseph J. Murray (eds.) *Deaf Gain: Raising the Stakes for Human Diversity,* Minneapolis: University of Minnesota Press, 321-340.

McCaskill, Carolyn; Hill, Joseph Christopher; Lucas, Ceil & Robert Bayley (2011), *The Hidden Treasure of Black ASL: Its History and Structure.* Washington, DC: Gallaudet University Press.

Padden, Carol & Humphries, Tom L. (1988), *Deaf in America: Voices from a Culture.* Cambridge: Harvard University Press.

Rothstein, Richard (2017), *The Color of Law.* New York: Liveright Publishing Corporation.

Sacks, Oliver (2000), *Seeing Voices: A Journey Into the World of the Deaf.* New York: Vintage Books.

Singh, Maanvi (2020), "George Floyd Told Officers 'I Can't Breathe' More than 20 Times, Transcripts Show," *The Guardian.* Available at: https://www.theguardian.com/us-news/2020/jul/08/george-floyd-police-killing-transcript-i-cant-breathe.

Smith, Linwood & Hairston, Ernest (1998), *Black and Deaf in America: Are We that Different.* United States: T.J. Publishers.

Shaw, Claire L. (2017), *Deaf In The USSR: Marginality, Community, And Soviet Identity, 1917-1991.* Ithaca: Cornell University Press.

Tarvainen, Merja (2020), "Loneliness in Life Stories by People with Disabilities," *Disability & Society,* 36(6), 864-882. Available at: https://doi.org/10.1080/0968 7599.2020.1779034.

Tatum, Beverly Daniel (1997), *Why Are All The Black Kids Sitting Together in the Cafeteria? And Other Conversations About Race.* New York, NY: Basic Books.

Tylor, Edward Burnett (1878), *Researches Into the Early History of Mankind and The Development of Civilization.* New York: Henry Holt and Company.

Wrigley, Owen (1996), *The Politics of Deafness.* Washington, D.C.: Gallaudet University Press.

Wynter, Sylvia (2006), "On How We Mistook the Map for the Territory, and Reimprisoned Ourselves in Our Unbearable Wrongness of Being, of Desêtre: Black Studies Toward the Human Project," *in* Lewis R. Gordon & Jane Anna Gordon (eds.) *A Companion to African-American Studies,* Hoboken, NJ: Blackwell Publishing, 107-118.

Artist: Sula Gordon

Bridging the Gaps[4]

Lena Stoehrfaktor

These days, it's hard for me to find some peace of mind.

I can balance out the escapades and marks left by my day
A thousand little shocks and traumas, I can keep at bay
Come what may, I can still make hay
The exceptions to the rule don't make me lose my cool

I find my way through all the things I'm asked to do
The days when I need to protect myself are now among the few
My mind and my capacity – I trust in their veracity
Until they steal this very trust from me

Out there they draw a line
Between what is there/theirs and what's mine
But when the divide opens wide
Between you and your physical capability
Then you'll see it, your own destructibility

My body is a loyal friend, it's right here by my side
But all my little missteps it will someday not abide
I can push it, but in the end I reach my limit
At some point it's over no matter how I try to spin it

Before our outer shells can no longer hold us
We must reach out to each other, so isolation won't enfold us
If we can bridge the gaps between us, it won't be so crushing
When the songs of exploitation tell us we're good for nothing

For years my body sustained me, but I paid it no respect
I ignored it until it became a constant source of stress
The pain that manages to thwart your everyday life
The crunch and pop of joints that are no longer lithe

---

4 A translated excerpt of the track, *Wenn wir die Lücken füllen*. For the full track, in the German original, see: https://www.youtube.com/watch?v=D5gKaJ0lTLk.

Left Alone

The aches and scleroses, revealed in scans and diagnoses
Now... I *know* what health means.
Crying from a young age at bagatelles,
which healed so quickly it makes me envious now
Depressing when the effort is no longer what I'd like it to be
And I find myself dependent on pills or other people
Out of politeness you have to say, it's fine
Try to keep your composure when all you feel is pain
Helping hands, like constricting bands
The resulting fears become states of anxiety
And they change your personality
Until you see only the negative in any possible reality

Before our outer shells can no longer hold us
We must reach out to each other, so isolation won't enfold us
If we can bridge the gaps between us, it won't be so crushing
When the songs of exploitation tell us we're good for nothing

These days, it's hard for me to find some peace of mind.

Translated from the German by Patrick Anderson

Artist: Mohira Suyarkulova

A diabolo, qui est simia dei[1]

Georgy Mamedov

My eyes are glued to a greyish hardcover in a second-hand bookshop. The title, in brown letters, reads *Latinsky Yazyk* – it's a Latin textbook for foreign language students. I feel almost a magic urge to have this book. To own it. I do not resist and buy it; it costs pennies anyways. I skim through the yellowed pages filled with the familiar font – typical of Soviet-era books – and get a strange satisfaction from understanding random words in a language I never learned. *Accusatīvus. Actīvum. Infinitīvus. Gerundium.*

I studied English and German in college, but we did not have a Latin class for some reason. I always felt bad about that, as if my knowledge was incomplete and defective. I felt that without the basic knowledge of Latin I missed some foundation, continuity, tradition.

Tradition ties. Tradition bounds. Tradition bonds.

• • •

I ask an Estonian comrade what it means to be a leftist in Estonia. She answers: it means being lonely. Lonely.

Why are we lonely?

• • •

Lonely like a child that nobody wants to play with in a playground.

What does the child do? They imagine friends for themselves. Imagined friends. Superhero-friends who will always stand by. Who will play. Who will love.

I know this bitter feeling of loneliness, of being left out; and a strong desire to compensate for that in one's imagination.

All traumas originate in childhood.

• • •

I was smoking on the outdoor terrace of my favourite pizza place in Bishkek. It was a short lunch break on a regular weekday. A couple passing by drew my attention. They looked odd, mismatched. A Kyrgyz man, my age or younger. Average height and weight. He wore a backpack. Something in his look betrayed him as a provincial guy, not from Bishkek.

1 Where God has a church, the devil will have his chapel.

She was a white woman, a foreigner. American or European? She gave me a strong queer vibe. Let me be honest, she was a towering fat dyke. What brings them together – I was almost ashamed of my presumptuous curiosity. Are they colleagues in some international NGO? They looked too casual for that. Is she a tourist and he her guide/translator? Might be... They entered the café and I forgot about them.

On my way out I lit another cigarette on the terrace. My couple left the place few moments later. Now there were four of them. A young Kyrgyz woman had joined them, and the dyke was carrying a boy 5 or 6 years old. His eyes were all grey, there were no pupils; his legs were dangling, most likely cerebral palsy. The white lady was holding him gently. The man and the woman – who were an actual couple – helped her with the door. The woman carried a big bag.

The mystery of the misallied couple is solved. Like in a fast reel I saw how in the morning the parents had chosen the best clothes for their son. It's an important day and they must give the best impression possible. What if she says no? They had also put on their Sunday best. After all, going to the city is not a casual thing.

I saw the dyke and her beloved fem wife going through numerous adoption catalogues during the calm, cosy evenings in their ranch in Milwaukee. They saw his photo and looked in each other's eyes and simultaneously said – "yes, that's the one." The dyke rushed to her phone to google the country she had never heard of before – Kyrkyrstan, Kyrgyzistan, ahh – Kyrgyzstan!

They all act out of love. The Kyrgyz parents want nothing but the best for their son. Who was unlucky to be born in a country and culture which not only provides no support to people like him but despises them. Over there he will get all the care he needs and be free of the awful stigma. This sacrifice is worthy. The white lesbian couple will love him. They will call him Nick Nourbek. It is very important that he stays connected to his culture of origin, that he knows his roots. Maybe they will allow him to phone his birthparents sometime. And they for sure will return on holiday to this beautiful and hospitable country where the people are so nice and kind. The parents love Nourbek.[2] The lesbians will love Nick Nourbek.

Fuck this love. Fuck them all.

• • •

2 Editor's note: Nourbek is a common Kyrgyz first name.

It's not silly at all to say I love you to someone you haven't spent much time with. In love, it is intensity and not duration which defines time. You can spend months and years with people and still really know nothing about them, because the time you share is loose or even empty. It's very true about many of our relationships, especially with those closest to us, like family. And with the one you love, time becomes thick and intense. Hours can matter more than months. The time I've known you has been very thick. Also, in love, time apart matters no less than time together. I had enough time to learn something about you and examine my feelings towards you. I love everything about you. And I know that you will never be an easy person to love. There is a lot going on inside you, but I wanna embrace you just the way you are.

Letter to A., May 2019, Bishkek

• • •

On a sunlit terrace of a coffee shop in Bishkek, Ahmad enthusiastically tells me about a small cultural centre in Kabul where he and his friends host film screenings and poetry readings. On his mobile he shows me the trailer of a film by a female Afghan director and shares his plans to start a film production studio after he completes his studies in Bishkek, where I happen to teach him an art history class in a film and media arts program.

Ahmad persuades me to visit Kabul and is probably somewhat offended by my reluctance. He insists that it is safe, that Afghanistan is much more than the misery, violence and suffering that news media only bother to show in their coverage of the country. This conversation took place exactly a year ago, in September 2020.

A few days ago, Ahmad and I met for coffee again. He was lucky to catch one of the last commercial flights out of Kabul in August. We clinked our cups to him being safe and able to continue his studies, but neither my clumsy attempts to cheer him up, nor the warmth of the afternoon sun amid the chill of an early fall breeze, could disrupt the heaviness that hung around him. The cultural centre he invited me to last year was closed by him and his friends as soon as the Taliban started advancing and capturing cities around the country. "We did not want to wait for them to come and destroy everything we built; we destroyed it ourselves." Ahmad recalls his last Skype conversation with his parents, who decided to stay in Kabul and adapt to the new circumstances.

"We lived through the Taliban's rule in the 1990s, we'll live through it again, but we do not want you to ever come back here. We love you, but from now on you are on your own." I asked if he recorded the call. He did not. We joked grimly about the lost opportunity for a dramatic art project that could have been made out of that recording.

September 2021, Bishkek

• • •

Procedat ex amore in odium. "There is just a step from love to hatred." Perhaps, it is the solution. Hate what you (have been told to) love. I hope Nick Nourbek hates his sweet mombians. I hope he hates his degenerate birthparents. I hope he grows full of hatred to his promised American dream (I'm convinced the dyke was a Yank). I hope he hates Kyrgyzstan. May out of this hatred the new world be born!

Hate thy Mother, hate thy Motherland. Hate thy Father, hate thy Fatherland.

But does this work in reverse? Must we love what we (have been told to) hate? This would be a dialectical choice much harder to make than the one above. It is easier to start hating what you used to love, than to start loving what you used to hate.

• • •

I once felt love towards Putin. It was short, momentous, but deep and intense, as true love usually is. I loved Putin with all my heart. And the tears started pouring from my eyes, so deep was my love for that little, miserable motherfucker. I wanted to embrace him, to kiss him gently and whisper in his ear that I love him, that we all love him.

It was Psylocibin, of course. Who on earth would feel that when sober? But was it just delusional? Didn't it reveal some truest truth about the world, one that we are not ready to accept?

> Imagine all the people
> Lovin' Putin with their hearts
>
> You may say I'm a dreamer
> But I'm not the only one
> I hope someday you'll join us
> And the world will be as one

• • •

I can easily hate what is (seemingly) lovable. I hated Amsterdam, I remember. All those relaxed, gentle people, bestowing upon you their unasked-for, wide toothy smiles. All those little tiny tidy houses along the canals. All that unshiny yet solid wealth. Stolen wealth, accumulated for centuries. The foundation, the solid base for a casual smile. A smile is a luxury. In Bishkek strangers rarely exchange smiles, probably never.

I feel like an angry barbarian, an uninvited guest, at this feast of life. Perhaps it is just envy. You are jealous of the solidness and solidity of their socially secured life. No wonder you envy that – you never learned Latin, did you?

• • •

We want to weave our lives, and not just lives – the entire world – into a solid, seamless canvas. My Grandma loves to say – *gde tonko, tam i rvetsa* – it breaks where it is thin. In these breaks, ruptures, ragged holes, the logic of the world order falls apart and we get a chance to see what that solid compound is made of. Benjamin called it a dialectical image.

• • •

Right after Benjamin turned 40, he went to Nice with the aim of ending his life. In the dark, stuffy room of a cheap boarding house he wrote a will and a few letters to friends and exes. He did not die that night.

Writing helps, I assume. This is what a shrink would say – write out your pains. You'll feel relief.

I write.

• • •

Wherever I go there is a shadow of you

I climbed the Sulaiman's Mountain[3]
And looking through the mist at the city with never healing wounds
I was thinking of you

I watered the tips of my beaten boots
In the waves of the hot lake[4]
And the sand and the breeze and the blue
Filled me with the sweetest thoughts of you

3 Editor's note: Sulaiman-Too is a sacred mountain in the city of Osh, Kyrgyzstan.
4 Editor's note: The "hot lake" refers to Lake Issyk-Kul, one of the largest lakes in the world, located in the Northern Tian Shan mountains in Eastern Kyrgyzstan.

I entered the wooden church[5] which was full of beautiful plants
And while lighting the candles to my namesake saint
I was thinking of you

In the meditative silence of the medieval Nestorian monastery[6]
Following the shadow of a solemnly flying falcon
I was thinking of you

In the empty mosque after Juma I saw a boy
Protruding his fit butt in a prayer
What a beautiful boy – I could not take my eyes off him
But his beauty made me think of you even more

November 2019, Bishkek

• • •

I have been thinking of George Grosz a lot lately. He continuously spiralled between love and hatred all his life. He hated Germany and everything German in the 1920s so much that he even Anglified his name – originally Georg Groß. Germany paid him back in full. Three blasphemy charges, regular death threats. He hoped that after the years of hatred in Germany he could finally turn to love in the United States. That did not happen. Instead, he realised that he was too German, even Gothic in his blood, and the American glossy life did not fit his Nordic origins. He started loving what he used to hate. His Germanness. From a fierce communist in the early 1920s, he grew into a sinister unmasker of the hypocrisy of the Bolshevik leaders from Lenin to Trotsky and Lunacharsky, all of whom he happened to meet during his short trip to Soviet Russia. He started hating what he used to love. What a dialectical life!

He returned to Berlin in 1959 denouncing his American dream as "a soap bubble." A few weeks later, after a night of drinking, he slipped on the staircase of his apartment and died unconscious the same day. *In vino veritas!*

• • •

Do we all have an American dream?

• • •

5 Editor's note: The "wooden church" refers to the Orthodox Cathedral of the Holy Trinity in Karakol, Kyrgyzstan.
6 Editor's note: The "Nestorian Monastery" refers to Task Rabat in Naryn Province, Kyrgyzstan.

... Defending his carrying out of the withdrawal [of US troops from Afghanistan] in a casual interaction with reporters after a 9/11 memorial event at the Shanksville Volunteer Fire Department in Pennsylvania, Joe Biden made a revelatory remark that went almost unnoticed by the major media outlets in the US. "For example, if we were in Tajikistan and we pulled up with a C-130 and said, 'We're going to let, you know, anybody who was involved with being sympathetic to us to get on the plane, you'd have people hanging on the wheel as well. Come on."

Well, I bet Biden nailed it. I was born in Tajikistan and lived there through the bloody civil war triggered by the dissolution of the USSR in the 1990s. I am one of those "sympathetic" to the US from Biden's mumblings. Throughout my student years I was a beneficiary of multiple educational programs, grants and exchange trips funded by the US government and philanthropists. Even my career as a leftist intellectual and my radical queer activism have been wholly dependent on foreign grants that supposedly 'promote democracy and human rights.'

Watching in the news people storming Kabul airport, desperately clinging to the wheel of an airplane as it was taking off, and eventually falling from the sky, I was thinking how long it would take until I and many of my friends and comrades would find ourselves in similar circumstances. And it is not an emotionally manipulative stretch. The biggest crimes of American imperialism are not those committed through 'boots on the ground.' Those are just the most obvious ones.

The biggest imperialist felony is the monopolisation of the very concepts of liberation, democracy and human rights. Nobody asks one to be "sympathetic" to America for the sake of America or its dusty 'American dream.' What is being traded for that "sympathy" is the very desire to live a decent life, to be able to, let's say, create and watch films, to study and understand the world and to take control of your own bodies and lives. And Afghanistan was not the only place in the world where many of these things were contingent on foreign aid.

With all the heart-breaking imagery of desperation and suffering we saw in the news, and even more that will remain unseen by the world, Afghanistan is not unique and what is happening there right now is not an excess. What we see in Afghanistan is just a condensed example of the state of things around the world. Illusionary islands of 'democracy' and 'freedom' sustained by imperialist monetary and military interventions in the sea of disillusioned, impoverished and deprived masses finding their only hope and refuge in the most reactionary ideologies.

September 2021, Bishkek. From an unpublished op-ed commissioned by an American leftist magazine

. . .

I hate y'all and there is no one to love.

. . .

"If I wanted to be nice to everyone I don't sleep with, I'd have a lot to do. So I'm nice to the ones I sleep with. That's politics." (Ronald M. Schernikau)

If I wanted to be nice to everyone I sleep with, I'd have a lot to do. I'm not even close to Schernikau, my politics and my desires never match. I'm more like Kollontai. She is a hero. She is an icon.

. . .

Champion of free love
Great revolutionary
Sasha Kollontai
Shot at her man
Revolutionary sailor Dybenko
No matter how hard she tried
[to] love [like a] communist
It didn't turn out very well

I want to love [like a] communist too
When a person is not a means
But the goal
When there is no anxiety drug addiction
At which each meeting is replaced [by]
hangover
brittle
Desire for a new dose
Human-dose

We are consumers of people
and replacement therapy
Doesn't help us anymore

You are my heaviest drug
Even though you weigh only 50 kilos
I lift you up with ease
You wrap your legs around me
And we spin in a ridiculous dance
By the crumpled bed

I don't want to consume you
I don't want to consume anyone
I don't want to shoot you
I don't want to shoot myself

I just hope
Communism
Coming soon
And everything will be different
Well, except
Crumpled bed

August 2019, Bishkek. Google translation from Russian

• • •

"If you're not a socialist at 20 you've got no heart, if you're still one at 40 you've got no head."

I'm 38 and I'm looking forward to my 40s with fear. What if I fall into this stereotypical trope? What if I betray my principles, what if I suddenly fall in love with the tiny streets and cosy houses of Amsterdam? What if I fall in love with Putin without any damn psychedelics?

• • •

One must remain solid in one's hatred.

Artist: Marcello Sessa

Left Loneliness and Feminist Love

Giulia Longoni

Loneliness. When Hjalmar invited me to write this essay for the first time, we immediately wondered if there was an Italian equivalent of this word. Perhaps, we agreed, the term could be translated with *solitudine,* for which the Treccani Encyclopaedia proposes the following definition: the condition, the state of someone who is alone, as a temporary or lasting situation, as a familiar expression of relief; but also, the condition of those who live alone, from a material, emotional and other points of view. In this respect, the Italian meaning seems to suggest a state of malaise or well-being related to the condition of people who find themselves alone for an unspecified period. What this definition lacks, however, are all the profound nuances which accompany the true feeling of *solitudine*, as it fails to express the strong existential pain that those who have been living in a state of loneliness for a long time easily recognise as familiar (where loneliness is thus understood in its most negative connotation). As far as I'm concerned, although my first language is Italian, the complexity of this feeling is best conveyed to me by the English term loneliness, which I associate more easily with the deeply rooted pessimism and discouragement that seizes me whenever I find myself thinking that, for a series of contingent circumstances, it sometimes appears impossible for me to be able to build authentic and lasting bonds within the social reality I live in.

In my psycho-affective reality, loneliness is accompanied by two other key notions: that of the political left *(la Sinistra)* and that of feminist love *(amore femminista)*. I will try to explain this, starting with what the Left means to me and why it is often linked to a feeling of abandonment. As a Marxist feminist philosopher, politics has always been a substantial area of everyday life for me, not only in the more traditional and partisan dimension of understanding this practice but also regarding the importance of feminist militancy, which I practice inside and outside the academic environment, as well as in collectives and movements in which I have been actively involved from my university years and to which I try to devote most of my available time outside of work. The feminist networks I've been a part of over the years, and feminism as such, which I've studied for most of my adult life, have taught me a great deal about myself, the world of collective reality, politics, and interpersonal relationships. Yet, they have also taught me that feminism, in our current situation, if it is not accompanied by a strict structural critique of the capitalist system in its neoliberal form, can become a very dangerous tool in the hands of the nationalist right. As seen in the last Italian general elections, under the false pretence of defending the rights of emancipated white women in the 'free and civilized West' from the 'retrograde cultures' of which non-Western migrants are supposedly the bearers, the nationalist right will adopt only some of the main points that characterise feminist claims, while uniting them to openly racist and conservative agendas that result in the creation of a phenomenon that Sara Farris describes as femonationalism, in her book *In the Name of Women's Rights: The Rise of Femonationalism.*

Unfortunately, the awareness of this critical positioning is not yet widely shared in the world of mainstream feminism. And whereas the political right has found a way to take on some of the most popular positions of the feminist movement today with the sole aim of garnering a percentage of voters with whom they would otherwise have nothing in common, the left in Italy (and not only in Italy) is becoming increasingly moderate. The final historical goal of Marxian scientific socialism is completely forgotten by the contemporary left, which not only does not express any desire to overthrow the capitalist system but no longer even proposes a critical analysis of it. The rights of workers and/or other subjectivities, oppressed by capital in a broader sense, are nowhere near the centre of any party program. Instead, the attention has shifted entirely towards a functional support of the current economic model. Also, the discussion of issues such as 'women's rights,' queer subjectivities and environmentalism, are part of the party management only as issues addressed from a mainstream point of view. This, in turn, undermines the radical effectiveness of their structural criticism and ultimately makes them subservient to the current neoliberal system.

In other words, the left seems incapable of adopting the positions of an intersectional Marxist feminism, which advances a more complex examination of the issues relating to gender-based discrimination vis-à-vis the exploitation of capital towards subordinate subjects, be they women, workers, queers, migrants and/or precarious workers. However, this is exactly where I position myself politically: in a transfeminist stance that is located at the intersection between the critique of the capitalist system and the subordination of gender, class, 'race' and sexual orientation. This is what it means for me to be on the political left in Italy today: to work for and with the masses of what Judith Butler defined as "precarious lives,"[1] because I myself live this precariousness on a daily basis and because I think that a Marxist feminist position can represent a valid alternative solution, not moderate but convincingly realistic, to the nationalist, xenophobic and racist tendencies of the far-right, which in recent times seems to be acquiring ever more ground in the world.

For me, feminism has never been something to be understood as an issue that affects only women – the very concept of woman, in itself, is extremely reductive and problematic, as Paola Rudan so accurately explains in her *Donna. Storia e critica di un concetto polemico*. On the contrary, feminism concerns anyone who recognises themselves as exploited, marginalised or oppressed. In short, all those human beings that left political parties should in fact be representing within a parliamentary system. Unfortunately, however, this idea is not shared by most of the contemporary Italian left and perhaps not even by mainstream feminism, which focuses instead on the promotion of self-help programs with the aim of allowing a small number of the women in the world – the 'privileged 1%' to quote the authors of *Feminism for the 99%: A Manifesto*[2] – to climb the heights of power and reach more relevant positions within the capitalist labour market. In a sense, therefore, my aforementioned loneliness expresses a double political dimension: a feminist one and that of a left-wing political orientation.

On the one hand, identifying yourself today as a feminist means being associated by most with the mainstream positions of the neoliberal current, which allows women in positions of power, non-feminists, such as the new Italian prime minister Giorgia Meloni, to appropriate the concept and exploit it for political ends that have nothing to do with an authentic feminist positioning.[3] In her first speech as Italy's new PM on 26 October 2022, Meloni expressed herself as follows:

1 See, e.g., Butler 2006 & 2015.
2 See Arruzza, Bhattacharya & Fraser 2019.
3 See Farris 2022.

Among the many burdens that I feel resting on my shoulders today, there is naturally that of being the first woman head of government in this nation. Reflecting on the importance of this fact, I inevitably find myself thinking of the responsibility I have towards the many women who currently face great and unjust difficulties in affirming their talents or the right to have their daily sacrifices appreciated. But I also think, with reverence, of those who built through their example the rungs of the ladder which today allows me to climb up and break through the heavy glass ceiling placed over our heads. Women who dared and defied the odds, out of passion, reason, or love. Women like Cristina (Trivulzio di Belgioioso), the elegant organiser of salons and barricades. Or like Rosalia (Montmasson), stubborn to the point of participating in the 'Expedition of the Thousand,' who created [modern] Italy. Like Alfonsina (Strada) who pedalled hard against the wind of prejudice. Or like Maria (Montessori) or Grazia (Deledda) who with their example opened the gates of education to girls all over the country. And then there are Tina (Anselmi), Nilde (Iotti), Rita (Levi Montalcini), Oriana (Fallaci), Ilaria (Alpi), Mariagrazia (Cutuli), Fabiola (Giannotti), Marta (Cartabia), Elisabetta (Casellati), Samantha (Cristoforetti) or Clare (Corbella Petrillo). Thank you all! Thank you for demonstrating the value and valour of Italian women, as I hope to be able to do as well.

This fragment of the long speech by the representative of the *Fratelli d'Italia,* the 'Brothers of Italy,' clearly aims to identify her as a feminist icon, the first female Italian premier. However, the only feminism in which Meloni can actually insert herself (and in any case forcibly) is the neoliberal one, of which some fundamental key slogans appear in her speech such as the "great and unjust difficulties in affirming their talent or the right to have their daily sacrifices appreciated," "those who built through their example the rungs of the ladder which today allows me to climb up and break through the heavy glass ceiling," or the reference, only by their first names (the surnames were added by me but are completely absent from Meloni's speech), to some women who, in her view, built the ladder that made it possible for her to climb the hierarchies of power.

Among these appears Marta Cartabia, who from 13 September 2011 to 13 September 2020 was a judge at the Constitutional Court, of which she was also the President from 11 December 2019, thereby becoming the first woman to hold this position. At the same time, it is necessary to mention that Cartabia exercises her political offices informed by a staunch Catholic orientation and that she is close to the Catholic *Comunione e Liberazione* (CL) movement. Her contribution in the field of religious freedom, also expressed through her academic publications, can be characterised by the defence of the positive secularism of the state, i.e. the right to display religious symbols in public spaces. Cartabia also took a stand against the equivalence between same-sex unions and heterosexual marriages, recalling, among other things, judgement no. 138 of 2010, which states that the Italian Constitution protects the family, as distinguished from other forms of cohabitation and therefore not including non-heteronormative marriages. These positions have evoked repeated criticism of Cartabia from various LGBTQI+ associations, reiterated on the occasion of each new assignment conferred or suggested for her.

Another female politician mentioned by Meloni is Nilde Iotti, the first woman in the history of republican Italy to hold the third highest position of the state, that is, the presidency of the Chamber of Deputies, a position she held from 20 June 1979 to 22 April 1992, eventually becoming the longest-serving Speaker of the Chamber in the history of modern Italy. Iotti is also remembered for having been part of the resistance to fascism from 1943 when she became a partisan dispatch rider. In addition, she actively participated in the struggle for liberation through women's defence groups, and in 1945 the UDI (Italian Women's Union) entrusted her with the task of investigating the conditions of the most financially vulnerable families. On 31 March 1946, Iotti was elected to the municipal council of Reggio Emilia and in June 1946, at the age of twenty-six, she entered the Palazzo Montecitorio together with twenty-one other female deputies, the first women elected to the new Italian Parliament. Iotti also actively partook in the work of the Constituent Assembly and was chosen, alongside Angela Gotelli, Maria Federici, Teresa Noce and Lina Merlin, by the Commission of the 75 to draft the Constitutional Charter. Her report on the family remains current today, and she ended up co-writing articles 29-31 of our Constitution.[4]

4 Article 29 establishes the recognition by the Italian Republic of the rights of the family as a natural society

On the one hand, therefore, in Meloni's speech we note the use of the name of a woman who 'made it,' Cartabia, and holds a position of power that allows her to carry on with her reactionary positions, in particular concerning LGBTQI+ rights and women's bodily autonomy in relation to the guarantee of the right to abortion; and on the other hand, the instrumentalization of a partisan woman, Iotti, who participated in the resistance and actually contributed to making women's rights one of the key topics of the Constituent Assembly. Meloni's speech is doubly painful for those who, like me, try to actually live feminism, resistance and revolution, because it contributes to the spread of a wrong but functional idea to the reactionary right of what it means to be a feminist – in this case understood only as the possibility for some women to hold institutional positions of power – and also because it rewrites the personal and political history of key symbols of the struggle of Italian women with genuinely left-wing origins, such as Nilde Iotti, who would never have wanted to be associated with the neo-fascist forces represented by Meloni's party and the right-wing governmental alliance headed by Meloni.

This situation painfully affects me on several levels: the attack on the history of the Italian resistance, the elitist resignification of important feminist issues for media purposes, the further isolation of transfeminist networks created by this propaganda, the idea that everything can be manipulated, even the meaning of entire lives dedicated to a communist struggle for which there seems to be no space any longer, all of which gives rise to what could be defined as a feminist loneliness,[5] experienced by me on a personal level as the physical and emotional invasion of a deep sense of impotence, isolation and anger. Giorgia Meloni's swearing-in meant all of this to me. It was a day marked by a strong feeling of emotional exhaustion, a feeling

founded on marriage. Marriage is ordered on the moral and juridical equality of the spouses, with the limits established by law to guarantee family unity. Article 30 stipulates that it is the duty and right of parents to maintain, school and educate their children, even if born out of wedlock. In cases of parental incapacity, the law ensures that their duties are fulfilled. The law ensures that children born out of wedlock have every legal and social protection compatible with the rights of members of the legitimate family. The law dictates the rules and limits for the search for paternity. Lastly, in article 31, the Italian Republic undertakes to facilitate the formation of the family and the fulfilment of related tasks with economic measures and other provisions, with particular regard to large families. It protects motherhood, infancy and youth, promoting the institutions necessary for this purpose. Although these articles may seem antiquated to us today since they are based on an idea of femininity closely linked to motherhood and the family understood in a heteronormative sense, at the time they represented a significant turning point in sanctioning the protection of the rights of women and children born outside of marriage and therefore considered 'illegitimate.'

5 See Magnet & Orr 2022.

typical of someone who has lost an important battle for the future. It will forever remain in the history books that the first female Italian prime minister is a mother and a Christian, politically right-wing and reactionary, and yes, a woman, but a woman, who despite trying to make us believe otherwise, is definitely not a feminist.

Given that the personal is political, as the feminist claims of the 1970s taught us so very well, this *solitudine politica* is reflected in the constant feeling of loneliness that accompanies the frustration of identifying oneself instead with a political and personal position that could really speak to the large masses, in the sense in which Rosa Luxemburg understood them. That is, a set of subjectivities which, by experiencing tools that prepare the working class for the revolution, acquire ever greater consciousness of their subordinated condition and the dialectical form of the class struggle. The instrument that Luxemburg considered most useful to acquire this consciousness is *lo sciopero di massa*, the (mass) strike.

> But strike action itself does not cease for a single moment. It merely alters its forms, its dimensions, its effect. It is the living pulse of the revolution and at the same time its most powerful driving wheel. In a word, the mass strike, as shown to us in the Russian Revolution [of 1905/6], is not a crafty method discovered by subtle reasoning for the purpose of making the proletarian struggle more effective, but *the method of motion of the proletarian mass, the phenomenal form of the proletarian struggle in the revolution.*[6]

For Luxemburg the mass strike is thus the tool of the proletariat in the revolutionary struggle but precisely for this reason it cannot be decided *a priori*, it must instead arise spontaneously from the working masses, and must be understood as a phase, a preparatory exercise which allows the proletariat to conceive of itself as a *unicum*, a network or collective of subjectivities that becomes a heterogeneous totality in the struggle against the bourgeoisie, owners of the means of production. The mass strike therefore precedes the revolution, prepares the ground for it and at the same time accompanies it, but it does not coincide entirely with the revolution, since it is only one component among the many different mechanisms of history that

6 Luxemburg 2008: 141, emphasis added.

constitute it. It is, however, the place of the collective and the community, the moment in which, inside the historical dialectic, the mass of the workers become the proletariat through, on the one hand, opposition to the bourgeoisie, and on the other, thanks to the construction of relationships and support networks, starting from the recognition of a mutual condition of exploitation.

This way of conceiving the left as a political position stems from the assumption that by sharing the experience of solitude, originating from precariousness, it is still possible to build a collective and even a revolutionary subject through the re-elaboration of the very idea of what it means to be human. The neoliberal *zeitgeist* in which we live constantly forces us to think of ourselves only as singularised individuals, in constant mutual competition with each other. Its guiding principles are not (and perhaps never have been) collaboration, association, mutualism or solidarity, all that matters is to 'get there,' to 'make it,' no matter how, no matter whether in climbing to the top we must crush colleagues and friends we meet during the course of our lives. What's more, not only does how you get there not matter, creating authentic and deep human connections could even be an obstacle to success. Instead, what is required is 'networking' in the most commercial sense of the term: knowing as many people as possible in order to be able to exploit them to achieve one's personal goals. Our shared bodies, lives, and solitudes don't count, all that matters is personal success in line with the notion of an egocentric victory, that is, in line with the neoliberal idea that one always wins *over* someone else, because at the peak of the hierarchy of privilege there is only room for one seat.

Against this background, the notion/proposition of the Marxist feminist revolution takes on a Copernican connotation, no longer Man with a capital M, in an Arendtian sense responsible for genocide, violence, discrimination and totalitarianism – the epitome of individualised and non-shareable loneliness – but human (and non-human) beings who populate the earth in their constitutive and necessary vulnerability. A Marxist feminist movement, in the current context, is hence doubly revolutionary to the extent that, on the one hand, it assumes the need for radical critique in order to eradicate the foundational structure of the capitalist system of production starting from a perspective of the intersecting discriminations of gender, class, 'race' and sexual orientation; while on the other, it proposes the explicit construction of a completely new society, not metaphysical but rooted in the most fundamental reality of the human being: its constitutive relationality in vulnerability. As highlighted by Adriana Cavarero in her *Inclinazioni. Critica della rettitudine*, subjectivities are not born as self-placed and vertical, as proven by the figure of the newborn, who at the time of their birth needs constant care in order to survive. Similarly, old age is equally characterised by a strong dimension of care. That is, the human being is born and dies, always and inevitably, in care. Cavarero, therefore, emphasises how the idea of subordination and dependence, which we are used to thinking of in profoundly negative terms, conceals within it a positive potential: if conceived of as constitutive of all subjectivities, it can act as counterfactual to the neoliberal capitalist construction of the 'authentic' subject as absolutely independent and dominant. Just as Luxemburg rethinks the revolution starting from the proletarian masses who, through the instrument of the mass strike, experience their own subordination and consequently the condition of vulnerability in the exploitation they share, in a similar vein it is precisely from the realisation and sharing of human precariousness that a feminist vision sets out to re-signify the world in a necessarily non-hierarchical sense. In the subordination of exploitation, subjectivities experience their own constitutive shared vulnerability, and in the process reveal the false foundationalism of the Man/ Human built by the Western tradition, self-placed, completely independent and inherently patriarchal. Subordination is the foundation of a different feminist politics, to the extent that it makes necessary the rediscovery and collectivisation of all-human relations, thus becoming the revolutionary locus of the reaction against exploitation itself. Because it is in the horizontality of care, in the associative spontaneity of the masses, and from the pain of exploitation transformed into networks of vulnerability, that we can find the fertile ground for revolution and social re-signification, in a direction that makes the inherent human necessity for relationality its all-important starting point.

There is, therefore, room for love in this feminist perspective, indeed I would say that love is precisely the key starting point. A love understood not in terms dictated by the law of bourgeois property, but rather considered according to the theorisation proposed by another communist woman: Aleksandra Kollontai. The Russian revolutionary presents the relationality of a precisely feminist love, one not based on possession and jealousy but instead living in the collectivity of political activity and which can thereby be(come) the antidote to the negative loneliness experienced by isolated subjectivities.

> The 'individualists,' who are only loosely organised into a collective with other individuals, now have the chance to change their sexual relationships so that they are based on the creative principle of friendship and togetherness rather than on something blindly physiological. The individualistic property morality of the present day is beginning to seem very obviously paralysing and oppressive. In criticising the quality of sexual relationships modern man is doing far more than rejecting the outdated forms of behaviour of the current moral code. His lonely soul is seeking the regeneration of the very essence of these relationships. He moans and pines for 'great love,' for a situation of warmth and creativity which alone has the power to disperse the cold spirit of loneliness from which present day 'individualists' suffer.[7]

Kollontai is arguably the only Russian revolutionary to seriously consider the problem of rethinking not only economy and politics, but also morality and with it, certain societal customs, highlighting how, in a communist society, it is/will be necessary to abandon the notion of property even in the field of love, contrasting it to the individualism of bourgeois society which gave preference to competition over the founding value of friend- and comradeship. One concrete example could be the love shared by Rosa Luxemburg and Leo Jogiches,[8] about whom Clara Zetkin expressed herself as follows: "He was one of those very masculine personalities – an extremely rare phenomenon these days – who can tolerate a great personality of a woman in loyal and happy comradeship, without feeling her growth and development to be fetters on his own ego."[9] Another example of this feminist and revolutionary love might be found in the relationship between Lenin and his wife Nadezhda Krupskaya, which Jodi Dean describes in her text "Lenin's Desire: Reminiscences of Lenin and the Desire of the Comrade" as...

7 Holt 1978: 240.
8 See Luxemburg 2019.
9 Frölich 1994: 33.

a strange duck. Krupskaya was Lenin's wife, yet she doesn't describe how they fell in love. Instead, the two have discussions and take walks. She shares with him the details of her work teaching in an adult education school and producing and distributing agitational leaflets. There is no endearing marriage proposal. [...] From a communist perspective, the desire that suffuses, shapes, and informs the text is familiar. The collective intimacy of comrades replaces the romantic intimacy of the couple; the two are two of many. Absorption in the political struggle for the Party, for the emancipation of the working class, for the revolution, and for socialism remakes familial relations.[10]

This type of love, a love which as far as I'm concerned constitutes itself as profoundly feminist, is shared between people who live their lives in full awareness of what it means to fight politically and constitute themselves as people who inhabit their own vulnerability.[11] Today, this type of sharing often seems no longer possible. In a world in which we are frequently told that there is no room for revolution anymore, and in which we are increasingly alienated in our polarised subjectivities, which come into contact only to be in competition and outperform one another, having a different outlook at the world comes with the terrible premonition that one will forever be condemned to experience the deepest and most radical loneliness. It is therefore time to (once again) quote a famous text by comrade Lenin: *Che fare?/What is to be done?*

Personally, although the feeling of loneliness often becomes so suffocating as to submerge my whole body and mind, what helps me every time to emerge from the deep darkness of my soul is the passion and the politics that continues to exude from women who have inhabited and struggled before me. Rosa Luxemburg, Aleksandra Kollontai, Clara Zetkin, Angela Davis, bell hooks, Simone de Beauvoir, Luce Irigaray and Carla Lonzi are just some of the women of the revolution whose life stories – or *"chi narrative,"* narrative voices as Andriana Cavarero would say – guide me towards the search for my authenticity whenever I happen to lose it as a result of the distortions of the world. Their extraordinary example emboldens my imagination

10 Dean 2020: 125.
11 For additional readings on "revolutionary romance" and "red love," see Proctor 2019 and Hardt 2017.

in a heroic way. It is important to stress, however, that these women are not Marvel heroines who defeat 'absolute villains' with only their strength and/or intelligence. Rather, the women of the feminist revolution form part of collective identities who have lived and acted within flows of bodies and thoughts, and which inhabited the masses, changing the world of politics together with comrades who, like them, were willing to make the revolution (of thought, of actions, of culture, of the Party).

It is in the relationship that I can establish with their leadership without paternalism, with their inherent relationality, their love for the cause that led them to risk everything, without compromise, that my loneliness transforms into agency. These women are alive in every feminist movement that aims to challenge the current system, they are present in the squares occupied worldwide by *Ni Una Menos/Non Una di Meno*, they are present in every conversation that talks about them/ with them/through them, they are present in the books that recount their militancy and the political communities they belonged to and those in which they are still alive today, created thanks to and through them. An example of this is the recent book *Post Rosa: Letters against Barbarism*, a set of letter exchanges between political activists, academics, etc., who, beginning with the figure of Rosa Luxemburg and their personal encounters with the Polish revolutionary, weave relationships and share with each other their own political experience from within the territories they inhabit. From the words of the editor clearly emerges the will to place the Polish revolutionary at the centre of a collective aimed at establishing itself as a possible antidote to the individual lonelinesses of the authors that compose it, Luxemburg as the source of the revolution of today's world, Luxemburg as a collective and as the construction of an alternative that fights the political and existential loneliness of a global Left adrift:

> The starting point of this book was an intense and still outgoing bout of Left Depression, Left Loneliness and re(-encounter) with Rosa Luxemburg, "[the] lone voice in the wilderness," just a few weeks before the 150th anniversary of March 5 this year (2021). More precisely, the meeting was one between my increasingly disintegrating self and Luxemburg's Letters – from inside prison and the prison inside her – with the surprising outcome being a sense of (temporarily?) resurrected vitality

and desire to move, once more, against my inner and our outer chains. The next thing I know, I am frantically reaching out to Luxemburgians from across the globe, truing to cajole them away from their busy schedules and enthuse them about contributing to a slightly unorthodox, deeply personal Luxemburg publication in the midst of a barbarious(ly handled) pandemic. The responses were overwhelmingly positive [...].[12]

Let me cite two examples that had, in my personal life, the ability to transform my loneliness into feminist love and political agency. First, I recently participated in the National Assembly of the *Non Una di Meno* movement, held in Reggio Emilia on 29 and 30 October this year [2022]. Despite having been a member of the movement for some time, due to the Covid pandemic I had not yet had the opportunity to participate in a national gathering in person. The experience was a genuine shock to the system, about 300 people converged in the city, whose different venues all became transfeminist for the two days of our stay.

In general, due to my political and personal loneliness, I often find myself struggling with managing my body and behaviour in shared environments. I wonder, how should I move? How should I speak? Am I be dressed appropriately? Am I smart and prepared enough to express my views in a space where I know these will almost certainly not be agreed with? Consequently, my body stiffens and my mind takes over in order to hyper-control and censor my entire personality, bending it to the will of a hostile environment. Loneliness reappears even in the modality of a factual sharing of spaces with other people. In this sense, it takes the form of an existential solitude in which, although sometimes I am even asked to speak, in doing so I do not feel safe and therefore I try, every second, to think about what others would like me to say, but which I then refuse to say because my internal resistance is too strong and doesn't want to yield, so I find myself motionless, in body, mind and emotions, captured by a strong sensation of constant anxiety. I feel, one might say, under attack.

The experience of the *Non Una di Meno* national gathering, on the other hand, showed me how it is in fact possible to share a space with so many others – informed by practices that are attributable to a feminist love as defined above and therefore not traditionally romantic

12 Joffre-Eichhorn 2022: 1.

but militant, relational and combative – and inside of which my sub-jectivity can find a place. My body moved in space without censorship, my thoughts found themselves inserted in a flow that freed them, my emotions were no longer captured only by anxiety but unfolded in all their strength and heterogeneity. To the chant *"siamo il grido, altissimo e feroce, di tutte quelle donne che più non hanno voce"* ("we are the loud and ferocious cry of all those women who no longer have a voice") my subjectivity responded, raising its fist, with a spontaneous participa-tion in actions that I know well, share and feel belong to me, in the revolutionary force, in the spirit of sisterhood, I too have found my voice and my bodily agency.

As for the *Post Rosa* book: I was lucky enough to be able to review it and therefore to read and study it carefully. For those who, like me, work in the academy on subjects not included in the classi-cal tradition of Western thought, writing in a 'scientific' way is always difficult because it implies a constant negotiation with the self. How much of my themes and my authors am I willing to sacrifice to bring them back into a 'scientific' canon which, inevitably, is based precisely on the exclusion and/or disregard of the issues that are closest to my heart? The *Post Rosa* book too poses this problem and then proceeds to respond: nothing. What matters to the authors is not academic rec-ognition but the genuine engagement with Rosa Luxemburg's thought and practice, as resulting from the different experiences that each subjectivity, militant or not, has made of and with her. What emerges from the book is not an infinite list of pompous references and critical literature; nor is the goal to legitimise Luxemburg's activity through its inclusion in the traditional canon, but to highlight that there is no need for this, because the relevance of the thought and political prac-tice of the Polish revolutionary still guides, after decades of history, the lives of many subjectivities for whom the encounter with Luxem-burg became the engine that ignited actions and connected revolu-tionary political practices across the globe.

It is thus the legacy of Luxemburg and of the other women of the feminist revolution that we must protect and nourish, taking it up and letting it flow at the intersections of collective bodies and non-tra-ditional narratives. It is in their revolutionary force that we must house our lonelinesses, in order to weave them together in a web that sup-ports all precarious subjects, because vulnerabilities in subordination, if combined, create the passion of hearts that beat together for the love of freedom.

Translated from the Italian by hjje and Daria Davitti,
with the support of Anastasiya Kotova

References

Arruzza, Cinzia, Bhattacharya, Tithi & Nancy Fraser (2019), *Feminism for the 99%: A Manifesto.* New York: Verso Books.

Butler, Judith (2006), *Precarious Life: The Powers of Mourning and Violence.* New York: Verso Books.

Butler, Judith (2015), *Notes Toward a Performative Theory of Assembly.* Cambridge: Harvard University Press.

Cavarero, Adriana (2013), *Inclinazioni. Critica della rettitudine.* Milan: Raffaello Cortina.

Dean, Jodi (2020), "Lenin's Desire: Reminiscences of Lenin and the Desire of the Comrade," *in* Hjalmar Jorge Joffre-Eichhorn (ed.) *Lenin150 (Samizdat),* Canada: Daraja Press, 125-133.

Farris, Sara R. (2017), *In the Name of Women's Rights. The Rise of Femonationalism.* Durham: Duke University Press.

Farris, Sara R. (2022), "Giorgia Meloni is a Female Face for an Anti-Feminist Agenda," *Jacobin.* Available at: https://jacobin.com/2022/12/giorgia-meloni-far-right-feminism-nationalism-family.

Frölich, Paul (1994), *Rosa Luxemburg: Ideas in Action.* London: Pluto Press.

Hardt, Michael (2017), "Red Love," *South Atlantic Quarterly,* 116(4), 781-796. Available at: https://read.dukeupress.edu/south-atlantic-quarterly/article-abstract/116/4/781/132975/Red-Love.

Holt, Alix (ed.) (1978), *Selected Writings of Alexandra Kollontai.* Westport: Lawrence Hill Co.

Joffre-Eichhorn, Hjalmar Jorge (ed.) (2022), *Post Rosa: Letters against Barbarism.* New York: Rosa Luxemburg Stiftung.

Luxemburg, Rosa (2019), *Lettere di lotta e disperato amore. La corrispondenza con Leo Jogiches* (Felix Tych & Lelio Basso (eds.)). Milan: Feltrinelli.

Magnet, Shoshana & Orr, Celeste E. (2022), "Feminist Loneliness Studies: an introduction," *Feminist Theory,* 23(1), 3–22. Available at: https://doi.org/10.1177/14647001211062734.

Proctor, Hannah (2019), "Revolutionary Romance," *Jacobin.* Available at: https://jacobin.com/2019/02/russian-revolution-love-kollontai-luxemburg.

Rudan, Paola (2020), *Donna. Storia e critica di un concetto polemico.* Bologna: Il Mulino.

Artist: Kimberly Chiimba

2084

Leo Zeilig

Truly, I live in dark times!

The innocent word is foolish. A brow unfurrowed
Bespeaks indifference. S/he who laughs
Has not yet heard
The terrible news.

What times are these, when
A talk about trees is almost a crime
As it silently shrouds so many evils!
S/he who walks calmly crossing the road
Can surely no longer be reached by friends
Who are in need?

[...]

But you, when the time comes at last
That wo/man is helper to wo/man
Think of us
With forbearance.
(B.Brecht)[1]

This story occurs at a few places in time, some near to us and others far. Ricky lives in 2084 and is an old man, he is a lifelong activist and socialist, reminiscing about a planet that has been transformed. He recalls this planet sixty years ago – in 2024 – when he was a child, that was undergoing radical change and the people he knew involved in that change. But we must allow ourselves to laugh on reading this phrase 'radical change': once we would have called it by its true name – 'Revolution' – the real-life struggles of the working people. In 2024, a new generation of activists, dreamers and doers rediscovered the language and vocabulary of working-class people – imperialism, revolution, liberation, etc. –, words which had become 'profane' with the seemingly never-ending onslaught of neo-liberal ideology on the right, and the idiocy of post-modernism on the left, especially in the Global North. Suddenly, however, in the years after 2024, that vocabulary was seized on again by those whose task was to make the revolution – though I pause here, for how much mole-like, patient labour had been put in by countless people for years before this 'suddenly' became possible?

---

1 For the full poem (translated by Patrick Anderson) see Joffre-Eichhorn, Anderson & Salazar (2020/2021), *Lenin150 (Samizdat)*, Hamburg: KickAss Books (1st edition) and Canada: Daraja Press (2nd edition), pp. 269-271 & 313-315.

Revolutions, as we know, had been raging almost uninterrupted during the period after the collapse of the state socialist regimes in 1989. As a matter of fact, Revolution had been the choice of the people in the Global South for decades. So, to be precise, the events after 2024 were nothing but the beautiful contamination of a long-overdue revolutionary wave that had begun much earlier, in those places that we used to call 'underdeveloped'.

In 2024, these revolutions began at long last to echo in strikes and rebellions in the hardened cores of global capitalism in Europe and North America, in Japan and Australia. Working people in the self-proclaimed 'developed countries', in Germany, France, the UK and Canada, finally stopped playing their game of sleeping beauty – from South to North, from periphery to centre, the global revolution had begun.

Ricky was Sarah's son, and Sarah was a revolutionary. She had recently separated from her partner – Ricky's father – Godfrey, and now she was throwing herself into the frenzy of a world in radical mutation. Yet, right in the middle of this explosive summer, she met Joe, and they fell in love. Joe became close to Ricky.

The story of this world – in two places, 2024 and 2084 – is narrated by Ricky and Joe.

Enjoy the story, it is [y]our history, [y]our past, [y]our present, and possibly [y]our future.

Leo Zeilig

1 – Summer, 2084

Joe Stein was my mother's lover 60 years ago, in 2024. They were lovers and comrades for four months. My father had recently returned home; he had been away for three years. When he returned, I didn't recognise him, but I remember that he cried and lifted me above his head as though I had just been won.

2024 was the year that today we regard as our beginning, when the old ways faded or whatever they say about the revolution now. In the years before these events, Joe was a practising revolutionary, and Sarah was raising me. And then Joe unravelled. In the summer days of the revolt that gave birth to the new world, Joe unravelled.

My name is Ricky Ujobolo. I have always used my father's name although I never really knew him. I know that today there is a certain fashion with names, taking them, and changing and refiguring them. But this story is not really about me, it is about my memories. I should have written it down when it happened, but I lacked the inclination and words, I was only eight.

Anyway, it is still one of the shibboleths of our time that children don't understand or remember. After everything we've done, the changes we have made to the world, we still make this mistake occasionally, but I am confident we will get there sooner or later. Optimism of the will.

These were the days when I was a schoolboy, but when I learnt the truly essential lessons on the street. I was a revolutionary by the time I was eight and as Joe promised I felt sometimes as though I was in charge.

The memories of these events have not faded. Particularly of Joe, or Joey as I called him – I wanted him to have a 'y' like me, and for his name to curl in the same way mine does. Joe always said to me, "Ricky I'm not going to stop fighting until the children are in charge."

So, this is what I am trying to do here, to resuscitate from the dreadful mists of time the story of Joe Stein, my mother Sarah Simons, and some of their comrades to whom we shall look back with forbearance.

For a few short months Joey held Sarah's hand, but they are all dead now. Let me explain.

To start with I should say a few words about my mother. Sarah had become, long before she died, the truest exponent of our revolution. These were, as they used to say, her days. In a manner of speaking, they were her events. If you want to date the events, you might as well give the days of her birth and death. Historical moments always start before their official beginnings and so ours can be said to begin with Sarah's birth in 1990 – a moment in time that was labelled by reactionary historians and journalists as the 'end of history'. Of course, Sarah begged to differ.

Sarah and Joe's brief love marked the dramatic changes that spread across our islands for the next fifty years. These changes were not much reflected in the old parliaments; I was only nine when I threw my first, clammy fistful of stones at the old government buildings.

Rather, the revolution took place in the palaces – there were still palaces that had been abandoned (and occupied) – and even more in the streets that had become ours.

We did things like old-fashioned revolutionaries: burnt down police stations, fraternised with the army, and never stopped arguing amongst each other; but we didn't feel old-fashioned and most of us never stopped to see if we were doing it correctly. We just did it. We exported our revolution in tweets, blogposts, DMs, and hashtags in five minutes. And we won.

I don't like the way these events are written about today, as if everyone knew exactly what they were doing, and that we were like ancient heroes who were destined to succeed. Even our failures are nowadays made to look spectacular, as though we were always going to make them (take your pick, comrades: Russia in 1917, Spain in 1936, and on and on, the Arab Spring in 2011). No, we did not proceed in the clear light of day, and we didn't do these things so they could be made clear for us in the future. We were like any revolutionary – clumsy, hopeful, and impatient.

It didn't have to happen; we didn't have to win.

Yet amid those heady days of revolt, when for once it seemed like we were beginning to win, Joe unravelled.

What follows is a peculiar account of what happened to a few good people in 2024, pieced together from Joe's notes, Sarah's stories, and my own memories. Of course, recounting history always involves an element of fiction to join the pieces, and tell the story, but don't fool yourselves – this really happened.

Also, remember to look at them with indulgence, and if this story seems far-fetched, or even ridiculous to you, then you must realise that our world has irrevocably changed for the better.

2 – April 2, 2024

Meetings had been held at the community centre for several years. Before this, The Rising Star, the forlorn high-street pub, had allowed the group to use its back room. Yet when local children had attended a meeting organised to help prevent the closure of their school, it became clear that a more neutral place to meet was needed.

The community centre, like a thousand across the country, was a neglected building that had been saved by a church from total ruin after the council had withdrawn its grant.

The church was called The New Temple for the Glory of Our Father and the reason why the New Temple tolerated meetings of Solidarity Action for so long was entirely down to the ingenuity of Arnold Jones. Arnold had managed to convince the church that they were, in their own peculiar way, also pursuing the Kingdom of God. He had trained as a priest, knew the Lord's words and with his arms flying, he would describe the Sermon on the Mount as if he had been a witness to it. Amen!

Arnold was addressing the weekly meeting on, "What do we mean by revolution?" Richard Crosson had been the first to arrive, to prepare the room and set up a well-thumbed book stall, which he kept in his car boot – "for quick release," he would say. Richard was the real inspiration of the group, the dynamo that powered everything. He was a 34-year-old history teacher and held the energy and hope of the entire branch in his hands.

Richard was chairing and he started the meeting to a slightly forlorn audience of eight, "Welcome to this week's meeting of Solidarity Action."

Joe Stein sat at the back of the room scrolling through the group's paper, *The Fire this Time*, on his phone. Richard made the introductions and nodded to Arnold who sat beside him.

Arnold, a tall thin man, stood slowly, then leaned on the table in front of him and spoke. "They call us extremists, friends, but I will tell you where the real extremists are to be found..." – he always started like this, half way through a thought or an idea – "... among the 1300 individuals who own over half of the world's wealth, who own the companies that dump grain into the sea to keep prices artificially high, and the politicians who order bombs to be strewn across our towns and cities, or the forests to be burnt to clear land, not for the landless, mind you, but for the few bastards who have stolen it. Perhaps you want something closer to hand, so take the money wasted on military equipment which could be spent on schools and hospitals..."

No matter the size and composition of the audience, Arnold always spoke as if he were addressing a crammed hall of students and workers – a period in the 1970s that he remembered as having unfathomable possibilities. His words rushed out, scattering over the group, pausing only to gulp in mouthfuls of air. He spoke for almost thirty minutes.

Finishing, Arnold concluded, "We are faced with a challenge, and one we have confronted since at least the start of the last century. We can accept to live in this everyday, torturous hell that contemporary capitalist society imposes on us, or we can try with the force of our combined hands to uproot the world. To build an alternative that will take us out of these dark ages, of climate catastrophe and war, out of these times of darkness."

This was vintage Arnold. Even a brief conversation with him left you with the impression of an imminent end, or a momentous new dawn. Recently he had warned Joe in a phone call of the threat of fascism. "Fascism with nuclear weapons," he'd said. Joe took the news very seriously and did not sleep for a week.

As a matter of fact, in recent times and despite the familiarity and routines of left activism, the worn diagnoses etc., something really was beginning to change. Even Joe had felt it during the latest wave of strikes and picket-lines, had detected a shift in the movement and thrown himself into it with full fervour.

Now though, with a temporary lull in the protests and strikes, the mood had shifted wildly again, and resignation prevailed once more – especially in Joe. Often, in those days, momentary retreats felt like defeats, and victory an impossibility. Yet the country was about to erupt in a cacophonous frenzy of revolt, rage and long-suppressed life.

When Gary O'Brian spoke after Arnold's gushing ebullience, he solemnly and wearily explained to the meeting that they needed, following Lenin's dictum, to prepare themselves for a long, slow struggle, and the need to 'patiently explain'. Gary was an old member of the group – whose aged wisdom was both tiresome and frequently correct.

Joe was furious. "I'm fed up with patience. How long have we been patient? I bet that if we assembled all the years that we have been patient we would have a whole life of concentrated, but totally unproductive patience. Perhaps then, Gary, you will be satisfied. Once you have my life! I serve notice on patience. So, what do we do now? Wait another fifteen years? We are fanatical planners and organisers; constantly planning to live. And now you want my patience? I thought this meeting was about revolution – for me revolution can only be made by the impatient. Sometimes history needs to be given a push – a powerful KICK." The last word he shouted and at the same time thrust out his foot.

Sarah was also at the meeting, having been urged to attend by Arnold. The group had given their support to her campaign against the deportation of her Nigerian partner. The immigration squad – the "Nazis," Arnold called them – had broken into her flat three years before, dragged Godfrey Ujobolo from their bed to the deportation centre and on to a flight before a single call could be made. Fucking fascists.

The solidarity she had experienced – 'solidarity' in those days was really another word for love – had been instigated, organised, and managed by Arnold. He was absolutist in his politics and commitment, and he committed the group to Sarah's campaign. Yet he always had a contingency plan: "Sarah, this campaign will win, there is no question about that. Godfrey *will be* returned, and the British state, and its bureaucratic, snivelling, proto-fascist minions, *will be* humiliated. This certainty is the only way to fight. However, if they try to snivel, cheat, and legalese their way out of reversing Godfrey's deportation, I will personally go to Lagos, fetch him, and bring him back myself." Arnold meant every word – he always did.

In response, Sarah – while she respected and admired Arnold for his unwavering tenacity – had laughed at him, and said, without missing a beat, "What, like an 18th century slave catcher? A white Tarzan to the rescue... what is it with you male revolutionary heroes?"

She had campaigned like a woman possessed and discovered a capacity to organise and encourage others to confront the authorities. And confront the authorities they did. Her posters, badges and stickers, *No Borders, No Nations, Refugees Welcome Here, Cruel Britannia,* were posted, carried, and worn across the UK. The campaign won, and Godfrey was allowed to return – but Sarah had decided, in the second year of the campaign, that she no longer wanted him back. She had fought for Godfrey like a sister, but realised that she had changed, and grown – she was no longer the same person after the campaign – and that their relationship had tethered her, held her in a single place, whereas she now felt free for the first time in her life.

Richard made a few announcements, and the meeting came to an end. Then he remembered something and stood on a chair and announced, "Please, friends, I have good news, the cycle-couriers and climate activists are holding a protest tomorrow. It's going to be a big action, and they need us, our solidarity."

Richard's news had a remarkable effect on the room – a gust of cleansing wind. It blew away the remnants of inertia and despair that lurked here, in the lowly HQ of the revolution, cowering in the corner always waiting for an opportunity to rise up. As they tried to organise themselves for the next day, even Joe, for a time, forgot himself – the surge of hope that rushed into the room forced out the mass of his despondency as if it had been no more than a momentary shadow. Angry, confused, uncertain, Joe wavered, raged, and then seemed to embrace life once more with his arms out, his heart open, in a great grip. Such were his contradictions, and all of ours.

3

For some time, Joe had thought he was going mad, had been in deep despair – he wasn't sure what it was, emotional volatility, depression (he had already spent a lifetime, it seemed, on anti-depressants, first prescribed for his increasing physical rage at the unjust world around him), ADHD, HD, bi-polar, schizophrenia... It didn't really matter, it all led to despair.

The great genius of capitalism was its ability to personalise social injustice – how else could we tolerate a world of endless suffering, planetary destruction, and terrible distortions to our humanity, unless we saw emotional volatility as a symptom of our private psychology? We might know today that there is no such a thing as private psychology – a fact as straightforward to us as the law of gravity – but remember, readers, this was a heretical belief in those days.

Remember too that these were the days when every manner of human condition, generated by social circumstances (the almighty, inhuman pressures of a diabolically unjust society that fell on all of us, albeit in different ways and to different degrees), were given physiological explanations. A tremendous pharmaceutical industry grew up to diagnose our depressive disorders and despair as genetic and biological, generated by hereditary traits. Academics and researchers wrote, without a shred of irony, of our complex individual pathologies shorn of history, human society, and context.

As a child, Joe had been described as hyperactive, excitable, disobedient, a fidget, adjectives he now knew describe all children and should not be pathologized. By the time he was 15 he had become a lonely, solitary figure. Constantly trying to curtail his impulsiveness – his disobedience, and his loneliness.

Joe – I remember him telling me – was arrested for vandalism when he was seven. When the police arrived, they looked aghast at him and asked, "Did you see the boys who did this?"

"Fuck you," Joe replied.

In a world busying itself with its own obliteration, Joe despaired – the wars, climate breakdown, the nuclear roulette played by our rulers demanded action but seemed, for decades, to yield only lethargy and defeat. Joe's impatience to act, to get going at last, to call out to the world's injustices, *"Come on, let us fight!"*, led to an aching and acute sense of loneliness.

4 – From Joe's notebooks, April 2024

I don't know who I am anymore. I don't know how to feel or whether what I'm feeling is correct. I was haunted by these ravings all day. However fast I ran they followed me. I became convinced that they were a real, physical presence and I hoped that if I dropped suddenly to the ground, I could disorient them enough to escape. But I was wrong.

I spoke to Arnold who repeated himself, "We have 20 years to fascism, at the most – perhaps only ten. But it will be worse this time, as Hitler was worse than Mussolini, this will be a fascism armed with nuclear weapons. We would be well-advised to remember Einstein's words, 'I do not know what weapons World War III will be fought with, but World War IV will be fought with sticks and stones.'"

I am now too scared to sleep – I have no refuge. Where can I go if there is no escape even in sleep? Fuck me.

5 – From Joe's notebooks, April 12, 2024

I am a tormented man. Nothing is sacred here. Fuck this house. I cannot rule out that these words will be read. I think they are being read. So fuck you too, you nosey sneaking sons of bitches.

At work today I was struck by the dull, grey boredom of life, the emptiness of everything. I woke in the night to stillness in the flat – the lifeless, dim dawn light seeped through the shutters, outlined the bed, the table, the wardrobe. I felt an intense hatred for the world, and an overwhelming dread and gloom. At that moment, I wanted to kill myself.

Pressing down on me – like the walls were coming in – was a desperation that if I cried, or shouted aloud, no one would hear me, no one would care. I was utterly alone. Unreachable. And it was this

I knew that was circling me, it had smelt my fear, and was ready to pull me under.

I had spent the evening with Arnold on political work – 'contact visiting' we call it, meeting names on a petition, knocking on doors in housing estates, and leafletting for meetings. We found Debbie on a council estate. We waded across a flooded courtyard to find her. I recognised her from a meeting several weeks ago when she had shouted at the speaker. I mentioned that I had seen her at the meeting and embarrassed she said, "I am a little crazy, you see."

We talked, shivering on her doorstep, and at one point she said, "I feel so angry that I could shout." At this she let out a shrill, sharp cry that reverberated across the estate – when she had finished, I could hear her echoing through the flats.

Soon afterwards I returned home, Debbie's voice still in my head. I wrote an *Ode to Debbie*:

I met an angry woman today.
'I am so angry I could scream,' she said
And she did, she screamed.
Answering the cold with her freed shout.
Come to me sister, so I can feel your shoulder next to mine.
And let us cry together.

Coming back to earth, I read the news on my phone... one item after another, one horror after the other. What the fuck is wrong with us? The birds were singing outside the window, chirping obsessively, joyously, oblivious to the world. I read on, the first airplanes of asylum seekers had left the UK, trafficked by the government to an Atlantic island, where they would be held indefinitely in judicial limbo; the largest habitat for migratory birds in West Africa had been destroyed by a French oil company; and nuclear war now threatened Europe, *and* the world.

The fight back, the effort to reclaim the planet seems so vast, the task almost impossible for our puny agency, I do not know what to do. I stand up from the sofa, drop my phone, the bright white light from the news illuminating the room, and I feel, not even angry anymore, but just fucking lonely.

For the past month, every morning when I return from my nightshift at the bar and before going to sleep, I stand in the middle of my room, raise two fingers to my temple and shoot. Each day I wish I was holding a gun.

6 – From Joe's notebooks, April 25, 2024

I saw Sarah today.

There is a mood, a stirring – I can feel it. I need to feel it. I see people speaking in the street, muttering, comparing notes, and I can overhear the names of detested politicians. The lines of Brecht's poem come to mind:

> What times are these, when
> A talk about trees is almost a crime
> As it silently shrouds so many evils!
> S/he who walks calmly crossing the road
> Can surely no longer be reached by friends
> Who are in need?

And I thought how quickly this world of horrors can change, and we can reach each other after all. How simple it all is when we finally start moving forward. Rosa L. told us years ago, "Those who do not move, do not notice their chains." Well Rosa, the chains are rattling now; I can hear them, I can feel them.

I was in the post office and there she was, speaking loudly to a small group, jabbing a finger to the ceiling, "...those who run our hospitals, and throw good people out of work, I don't want a riot, I want to see something bigger, better than that. A riot they can deal with, a revolution they can't." There were cries of "bloody right" and "you tell them."

I then climbed on a chair and said, "You say you don't want a riot – well I do. And know this my friends, that a riot can be a prelude to a rebellion, and what historical rebellion did not have as its key component a riot? Riots are how our side builds confidence."

Sarah was quick to respond, "Yes, we need riots, okay, I get that, but we also need something more permanent that will only be possible when riots become political and revolutionary. How do we sustain a revolt, make it more than temporarily seizing a post office, or a parliament? How do we create a whole new system – a complex, beautiful body of distribution, production, equality, and harmony? Your riots might feel cathartic for a moment, but victory does not lie that way."

I knew I had lost the argument, and she was right, completely, utterly; what good was rhetoric now – we had already moved beyond that. Still, I continued: "Maybe not, but they would certainly make me feel better. It is those you indicated who deserve to feel our rage," I added – I mimicked her, and pointed to the ceiling – "that thin layer of privilege in society who when we are out of work tell us that we are scroungers, and when we are working that we must work harder and more flexibly, as the politicians enrich themselves, close our hospitals, run down our schools, privatise our world and destroy OUR planet. Let's face it, the rich – these people – that you were pointing at, are simply better organised than us and to tear away their privilege we need both riots and the riot of riots, a revolution. In fact, we need one, two, three revolutions simultaneously, to force the rich to scatter their forces as they are attacked by the rising hatred of all working people in the world!"

I saw the others in the post office, their heads turning from Sarah to me, and back again, eager to hear how this dispute, one of thousands taking place in every high street across the country, would be resolved. Others spoke, disagreed, and the arguments continued – Sarah and I finally agreeing, encouraging, and cajoling others, in a joint act of subversive radicalisation.

We now concurred on the need for both riot *and* revolution, for a new and radical re-organisation of society run by the poor and working class. I conceded to Sarah's complex new system of production, and she to my insistence on the need for a permanent, multitude of self-conscious riot-revolutions. We convinced each other; the post office was our loud hailer.

Eventually, we were both escorted out of the building and told not to return – then, at long last, I asked her for a drink, summoning up a bravado I usually only have for politics. She looked at me severely and then agreed.

7 – May 8, 2024

This was the second time that Sarah and Joe had arranged to meet. The first time they met – he had reneged on a 'drink' – was at a political rally, and he had spent the meeting whispering a running commentary into her ear, "Don't believe a word he says. He's all mouth and says the same thing every time he speaks. An armchair revolutionary."

This time, Joe went up to Sarah too quickly and his foot caught on a table leg, dragging it noisily across the floor. He fell into the chair opposite her and smiled awkwardly. He called to the counter for two coffees.

"How are you getting on with the book Arnold gave you?" Joe asked.

"Oh, you mean Lenin's *What is to be Done?* It's getting on wonderfully with the pile of other unread books Arnold gave me. I read very slowly. How does he do it?"

"Because he has time. Denying the capitalists his labour, he says."

Sarah laughed, loudly, freely, her head thrown back, "Well, Arnold doesn't have a Ricky."

Sarah was abused as a child. Her stepfather came into her life stamping and shouting, and then into her room. She fought him tooth and nail, as he put his hand into her mouth and pushed himself against her. Her mother would drown out her daughters' screams by singing to herself. Sarah could hear her mother, in between her stepfather's grunts, humming half-remembered Christmas carols.

"It always seemed to me that they were both at it – my mum with her fingers in her ears and my stepfather masturbating on top of me."

Sarah punched and elbowed him for two years, bit him, spat into his food, broke his DVDs and scratched him down to his veins – the skin would bunch up in thin bloody layers under her nails. He liked being hurt, she said. Then, suddenly, he left – finally bored by Sarah and her mother.

Even in 2024, years after the abuse, Sarah was still sick every morning. She ran to the bathroom and vomited – trying to expel the smell of his breath, the taste of him in her mouth, the invisible mark of his hands on her body.

Yet my mother didn't *need* the revolution like most of us – I mean the rest of us needed it to clear out the muck of ages, but Sarah, like so many women I knew, had already begun to clear away the filth, the chattering, hetero-patriarchal, capitalist monkey that resided in most of our hearts and minds.

So, in a sense, Sarah was already 'post-revolutionary' when I was born in 2016. She was also a 'socialist' long before she had read any of its history – it lay even in our darkest days as the word people associated with resistance; no one could quite knock the hope out of it, and boy did the powers that be try. Sarah lost her morning sickness when I was eight. The next day we began to build a basis for friendliness.

Joe was speaking above the noise of the coffee machine. "We patronise children and old people. The old because they can be controlled again like children, and the young because they are under the care of our broken, addled minds. I meant it when I said that Ricky should come to our meetings."

"If you need something smashed in the revolution, I'm sure Ricky will be more than pleased to help, but otherwise leave him out of your plans."

Joe laughed, like Sarah, loudly, abundantly: "Do you think he could smash the state? We have been trying for years!"

From the inside pocket of his denim jacket Joe removed a rolled-up pile of posters and placed them on the table in front of them; out of his grasp they sprang to life, unravelling, the banner headline in red ink read: *Make the Rich Pay.*

The couple left the café holding hands and kept holding them for four beautiful, devastating months.

Yet Joe's troubled state of mind could not be entirely silenced. The bitter truth back then was that not even new love was always strong enough to beautify the downward spiral. Amidst the tumult of their burgeoning love, Joe still felt alone, and the loneliness was more acute for being present in the company of others, even loving comrades – even with a lover.

8 – May 20, 2024

Ricky had been put to bed, but he could still be overheard through the bedroom wall, talking to himself. He too caught the whispers and stifled laughter of his mother and Joe through the wall, and worried for a moment if Sarah was safe.

On Sarah's bed, Joe traced her breasts, moving his hands slowly down her back. He then ran his tongue along the inside of her thighs – he tightened his hands around her waist.

"Joe, I want to see you."

"Are you alright? What is it?"

"Nothing, I just want to kiss you." She pushed him over and kissed him. Sarah was surprised how close she felt to Joe and when she came, she put her hands over her face and cried.

"Let the big tears fall," Joe said, holding her.

Joe felt equally close to Sarah then and knew her in the despair she was feeling. Maybe this is how we can be connected, he thought, along the lines of our fractured souls.

Ricky knocked on the door and Sarah pushed Joe's arm away, "I'm coming, Ricky." She sniffed in deeply and rubbed her eyes quickly with the palms of her hands.

Joe sat at the side of the bed and started to put on his clothes, searching blindly with his foot for his shoes.

"What are you doing?" Sarah asked sharply, standing by the door.

"I just thought it probably doesn't help having me around if Ricky's upset."

"So, it's got too heavy for you already? A woman and a little boy crying in one night. Can't cope, Joe?" Sarah let the hand that was holding her dressing gown together fall. The gown opened; she snatched it closed again.

"It's not that, I don't want to leave, but Ricky..."

"You need to ask Ricky's permission to fuck his mother? Ricky gets scared and when he does, I let him come into bed with me."

Ricky lay between them and insisted that Joe tell him a story. "Joe's going to tell you a goodnight story and then we are all going to sleep."

"Does Joey tell good stories?" the boy asked.

Ricky turned to face Joe, lying on his side.

When the story was finished, Ricky was asleep. The story Joe had told was adapted from the history of the Paris Commune in 1871, like all his references, even his children's stories, which were snatches of revolutionary history – a city forced to eat cats and dogs and zoo animals to survive, as they tried to build a new society against the rich.

Joe let his head drop onto the pillow. Ricky's mouth was open, and his eyelids moved as he dreamt. Sarah sat up in bed, "I'll take him back to his room." She started to slide her arms under her son.

"Don't, leave him... let him sleep here." Sarah leant across her son and kissed Joe's shoulder.

Joe spoke in a deep whisper, "I've missed you so much."

"So have I. I really have."

"I'm making myself sick missing you," Joe said.

"I think you are great, Joe. I feel so very close to you, sometimes," Sarah answered.

Joe jerked himself up, "What do you mean, sometimes?"

"Well yeah, sometimes, I don't know, sometimes you behave a little oddly."

"Jesus Christ," Joe exclaimed, sitting up, knocking Ricky. He got out of bed and walked between the bed and door in his underwear and an old t-shirt with a faded red fist and a broken chain and the words *The Weak Shall Inherit Nothing*.

"Please Joe, I should have just said that I miss you."

"Listen, Sarah, I don't do anything lightly; I don't live lightly and I sure as hell don't fuck easily or lightly. I can't stand meaningless shit. Alright?"

"Come here, Joe, forget it."

Joe lay down beside Sarah, she held him, and they rocked together in each other's arms. Joe breathed through her hair, wondering where this missing her was coming from after only one month of the relationship. How long, he wondered, could he hang on, could he bluff his way through their connection before he came apart again? Would his despair surface first, drive him back into the clutches of his depression, or would it be the crushing weight of loneliness – deeper even than before, now that he had Sarah?

What space was there for love anyway, in the overall seemingly impossible fucked-up-ness of the world? What even was love in this world? A fraud, a cruel oasis shimmering in the shipwreck of our collective failures, always out of reach – a gimmick sold to keep us desperate, insecure, and hungry for the endless 'more' of capitalism.

Ricky slept that night with his arms around Joe; Sarah listened to the birds that were pestering her sleep as they heralded a grey morning. As the dawn crept under the curtains and the closed door, Sarah wondered if Joe reminded her a little of Godfrey – the jealousy, the quickness to anger.

Joe liked Ricky's closeness and the slight twitching of his small body. He thought he could comprehend how he felt for Sarah only in the quantity of suffering he would envisage if they separated. And so, as Sarah silently cursed the morning, Joe thought that if they separated today, Friday, he would feel sick and not sleep for a week, until next Friday. Then, over the following week he would still feel nauseous whenever he thought of her, but he would be able to sleep a little better. In the following weeks, memories, images, and the smell of her would slowly – very slowly – fade, as his life became cluttered again by other anxieties. Until eventually she was forgotten, though he would still be struck, occasionally, during a meal, or as he got into bed, by an acute, devastating sadness. Yet even this would fade, he thought. He hoped.

This was the only way he could understand love, as the suffering it would cause, and this was exactly how he now realised that he loved Sarah.

9 – 2084 (Midsummer, Waning Gibbous – approximately July 28 in the old calendar)

Remembering is a battle for survival, a declaration of significance. After a lifetime dedicated to revolutionary struggle, I am working very hard to hold on to my memories and our history, especially the most important ones. I suppose as a child I had a better idea of what I touched and smelt and clung to. Today, when I try to remember what I saw, certain memories flash up like photographs, then fade. They slide out of my grasp – they melt into the air.

But I solidly recall Joe.

One day, Joey swore at me, "You're a shit, Ricky. You can be a little shit, Ricky." I cried and told Sarah. They argued and I heard it, as I heard most adults in those days, through a door.

"Fuck you, Joe," my mother yelled, "don't swear at my son."

"That is pure bourgeois moralism. I called him a shit, I admit it, because of the way he spoke to you. It would have been hypocritical not to. He was a shit." Joe's arguments, his very inhalations were political.

"Don't give me the bloody party line on child-rearing. The problem, apart from the 'shit,' is that a grown man and an eight-year-old are not equal – even on your fucking planet. Don't ever call my son a shit."

Joe didn't answer, instead he left the room and stumbled into me on my backward retreat from the door. He winked and mouthed, "shit."

Granted, I wasn't an instantly likable child. I made judgements and I didn't respond well to adults who bent over me, patted me on the head, or put on fake voices. What I liked specifically about Joe, however, was that he never did these things; on the contrary, he seemed incapable of being anything but Joe with me – he had one way of being, uncalibrated for me. No one had ever treated me like this, and I found it exhilarating.

For about two years between the ages of six and eight I carried handfuls of earth everywhere. When I was seven, I finally gave in to Sarah's protestations and began depositing the mud outside the front door.

I liked the sensation, the pressure of the mud pushing through my fingers, but I held on for two years mainly because I felt the mud would always be there. I knew that long after Godfrey, Sarah, and Joey, it would still be there, my dirty handfuls of loyal earth. I knew I could cope with everything because it was everywhere, under everything, fixing my feet to the ground, our flat to the planet, and my mother to me.

For two years, mud was the centre of my world.

Joey never questioned me about it and never asked what I was doing when we left the flat and I bent down to gather up a new allotment from my old deposits – occasionally, Joey would also take a handful himself and carry it around with me.

There was the mud and the stones.

Joey would launch into long soliloquies about the history of rebellions and stone throwing: "Get this right, Ricky, throwing stones is not an act of hopelessness and impotence. On the contrary, thrown correctly, in catapults stretched out by three people with one pulling or with thick elastic bands, a small stone the size of your fist can kill the enemy. The great, noble Palestinians have taught us this. No doubt, we will need stone throwers in our revolution."

Mud and stones. Perhaps I was clearing the earth to get to the stones, to one day throw them at the enemy, or perhaps I was burrowing into the earth to find the new world.

We left the flat together after Sarah had shouted at Joey. I sensed that something was happening in the country, but it was Joey who helped me understand.

"I can't believe this," he exclaimed. "Have you heard what the government did today?" speaking to me like a comrade.

Joe did this because it was the only way he could communicate. This is not to say he didn't simplify things for me. He gave me, in the few months that I knew him, the clearest explanations of how the world worked beyond our flat, my mother and the mud. He showed me that it throbbed and pulsated incomprehensively, not because I was a child but because that was how it appeared to everyone – until we could finally feel our part in it, through the changes we made.

I learnt this from Joey when I was eight.

Perhaps in another, quieter time I would have forgotten these lessons, as radical ideas were worn down by the sheer struggle of daily life, and the unremitting psychological and physical effort to keep standing, but then I felt Joe's words on the streets.

"You see, Ricky, it is women and children who make history, and who will make our revolution, not men, as Marx said. For men to change they must become children or women – it is as simple and as crude as that."

And I laughed and imagined men shrinking to the size of children (and immediately all fear of them vanished), and then I saw all the men I knew turn into women and I laughed again – relieved.

Nothing that Joey ever said to me jarred or struck hard against the limits of my understanding. He spoke directly, clearly and in neat unadorned sentences, without the habit among so many radicals of prefixing everything with, "this is complicated, comrades..." or, "before we can take action, we must understand the intricate and unimaginably complex dynamics of capital accumulation on a world scale." Yawn. Joey's Marxism, and revolution, came directly from his anguished heart. No need for opinion polls, tweets or statistics.

Shortly after these pavement lessons, just a few weeks later, Joey would be no more.

10 – From Joe's notebooks, July 25, 2024

The news is streaming on my computer and sometimes I look at it for a few minutes. I am distracted, there are too many things on my mind.

I am being disturbed by the same dream each night – the cry of a child that seems to be coming from next door. It is crying from loneliness. In the dream, in the fucking paralysis of my dream, I try to get up. I struggle to surface from my unconscious and inert body so I can reach the child whose cry has been unanswered for so long. Then I wake.

I have now lost control. I have fucking lost control. I don't leave the room anymore, instead I sit here alone.

My thoughts have become subjects – aching, punching, counter-revolutionary subjects.

I think Sarah has stopped calling. I can still see her arguing with one of my Joe Steins about the politics of hope.

I feel the weight of defeat, and failure, and it crushes me – I am thrashing around my room, searching my memories, and see only effort, exhausting endless effort. I think of the labour of Sisyphus forever condemned to the fruitless work of rolling an immense stone up a hill, only for it to crash again to the bottom.

Didn't Rosa say we needed the hammer blows of revolution, or else we would be condemned like Sisyphus to an eternity of thankless labour? But what if the real course of our political struggles was defeat upon defeat, a permanent and fatiguing climb with no summit, goal or end?

I turned, spun, and cried aloud in my room, and I could see no way out.

Yet I thought that the real tragedy of Sisyphus is not that he was condemned to roll the boulder up the hill, only to see it fall back down again, but that he was forced to do so *alone* for all eternity.

And now I count the pills I have collected, a mound of pills so high that it almost reaches the sky; and they say to me, "Reach up, up to the stars."

11 – July 30, 2024 (voice memo)

Joe,

Where the hell are you? You didn't say when we last spoke where you were going. "For a few weeks to think." I can't imagine a worse thing for you, for anyone, to do. Two weeks of pure thinking. Your hopeless thinking! Anyway, Ricky is missing you and he is bothering me as I record this message. [Ricky's voice can be heard in the background asking, "When is Joey coming back?"]

Actually, I think Richard is missing you most of all – he said to me yesterday, "I can't stand it without Joe. We lose our sense of urgency when he is not there. What did he say to you?" I told him and he replied laughing that he had received exactly the same message.

I am pleased you treat us all equally.

Now I must tell you how I am feeling, though I am not sure I have much time for feelings at the moment, between delivering and collecting Ricky from school, and organising the Solidarity Committees. Why would you go at such a time?

I've lost my sense of balance – I am so confused, and I only have a patchwork of thinking. I do not think in lines or sentences.

Sometimes, I remember your words and they cling to me; I can't brush them off.

For example, I recall you saying at the end of an argument that you lost, "I believe that we can change the world so much for the better that it's almost absurd and that future generations will find our pessimism, our depression and loneliness incomprehensible." You turned to Ricky – who was watching us – and said, "Ricky, or any child, could run this world with more humanity than all our so-called leaders. What child would tolerate hunger when there is food, misery when there can be justice? What child would calmly cross the street when there are so many people in need of her solidarity?"

Frankly, I wasn't seduced by those words but then, when you took Ricky to bed, I thought I could love you.

Four months ago, you seemed to be offering me your life, and now you have disappeared. Believe me, Joe, I know your fight, we *all* do – every one of us, each human being we want to free, knows the anguish and loneliness that seeps into our every unguarded thought.

And yet you are the great *acceptor*. "Change," you shout and, "don't accept," but you can't seem to see how you yourself are accepting that portion of despair and loneliness that society hands out to each of us to keep us in our place. Why are you not fighting back?

I see so clearly now that we will only make a new world, which is ruled as you said by Ricky's humanity, if we accept each other's solidarity – if not we will all be crushed by our despair. Yet right now I am not sure whether you are ready to accept anyone's solidarity any longer, and the thing I hate most of all is that I do not know how to reach you anymore.

Joe, I want you to hear this: I think we are nearing a period of great change, or at least an opportunity to make it great. The Solidarity Committees are up and running again and not like they were before. It seems we have learnt our lessons? – perhaps I am exaggerating, but I don't think I am.

I miss you Joe and want to see you when you return from this mysterious trip. What a ridiculous time to go.

12 – From Joe's notebooks, August 12, 2024

I had another dream yesterday, that I had climbed on to the roof. I had bathed and I was wearing a suit that was bought for a family wedding years before. I noticed that, as I pushed myself free of the building, I was wearing the suede boots I had acquired ages ago and as I jumped, I glimpsed the blue sky unfolding endlessly into the distance. I could breathe the air freely like the first breath ever taken. As I fell, the tangled noise of cars and voices faded, so I could hear as I passed the cries of birds in the sky. A triangle of swallows sang to me as they flew across my path, flying upwards, using the currents of air like stairs, to move on, and as I continued to fall, I could see their journey across the thousands and thousands of colours in the sky. Then before I hit the road, and as they soared up again, I knew I didn't want to die.

13 – Late November 2024

Sarah doesn't rush to the front of the room when her name is called to speak. Slowly, she passes groups of delegates huddled in circles, around laptops and phones, discussing the resolution – a resolution to dissolve most of the Solidarity Committees, and hand power to a small, provisional group headed by nominally socialist members of parliament. She weaves in and out of banners placed across the aisles, and as she climbs the steps to the stage, she passes a young man who looks up at her and smiles.

Sarah walks directly to the microphone and says, without hesitation, "We must be clear about one question, friends – what are we? Are we a department of the government? When we first organised ourselves two years ago, we didn't ask the government, or our bosses, for permission. And this year, as we spread our solidarity, did we ask parliament to sanction a democracy we had created for ourselves? No, we did not. Now the question before us is simply do we continue to do what we want and what we think needs to be done, or do we hand our committees, our everyday solidarity, back to the parliamentary left and their sham democracy of the rich?

"Comrades, if we submit to the proposal, we will be finished" – her voice fills with heavy irony, there are yells of delight from the room – "and suffer yet another defeat. Do you notice a pattern? If we allow them to claim our work, to take over our solidarity, then what?" Arnold and Richard shouted in agreement after each of her sentences.

"Well, let me tell you. Can you remember the old ways, friends? When they constantly tried to divide us and turn us against each other? And how successful they were at doing so? For now, they are merely trying to persuade us to hand back our power and everything that we have built." She pauses and opens her arms out and looks around. "But let us be clear that this is their nice way of asking us to step aside or... when push comes to shove, the wealth and interests they defend will stop at nothing, unless we match their determination, and finally say to them, 'The game is up, and we will now be the ruling power. We are here to take back control of the earth, with its immense beauty and life ... and we will never yield.'

"The choice before us is clear: we can either procrastinate," she is speaking now with fresh conviction, "doubt ourselves and allow this..." – her arms are still open, the hall is silent – "to be taken away from us. Or we can say that it's now finally our turn and act decisively." She is interrupted by the chair, who tells her to sum up.

"Enough is enough, comrades. I have an eight-year-old son who could run this world more humanely than any of our leaders..." She stumbles over the words. "What child would tolerate this misery and suffering? How many more decades and centuries of hardship do we need to endure before we can finally live as equal, just human beings? Our fight – this one, in this hall today, right now – is at its core the struggle of hope against despair. Is this not what it has always been? To see all that has been ruined, the planet a dry, dying husk, and the endless great sea of needless death, and to finally create some-thing infinitely better, and for this not to be a utopian dream, but a real world revolutionised in the hard, beautiful practice of our politics and solidarity. The chance is before us. Let them not take it away from us again."

Sarah walks slowly back to her place as the hall erupts in applause – computers closed, phones lowered. She feels the hands of delegates on her back as she moves along the aisle.

Joe is standing in front of her, his black hair dishevelled. She sees behind his eyes, that are watching her, a thousand fears.

She continues to move back to her place, around scattered chairs, and delegates. Joe, her Joe, *and* mine, undone on the eve of our beginning – just as we were building the foundations for friendliness, a new world that still required such care to be born and to keep on living. Suddenly, Sarah sees his loneliness, and death, for what they were: it was all of ours in those days, and she feels the loss of a lover and a comrade who was still desperately needed.

It is three months since Joe's suicide. Sarah had received a message from Richard.

The chair is speaking again, "Okay, friends, we are going to vote on the proposal."

Ricky was told to stay in the car.

Sarah steps over outstretched legs, cables – the hall is awash in noise and lit again with a sharp screen brightness.

Joe had said he would be back in a few weeks' time.

Someone in the hall raises an objection and stands waving her phone aloft. "Get on with the vote – we need to vote," another delegate shouts.

She broke a small panel of glass and hooked her arm through to the latch and pushed the door open. It was 28 August, in the middle of the day, that Sarah and Richard had found Joe dead. He had died on the floor of his flat in his underwear and a pair of suede boots, his face resting in a pool of bloody vomit, his mouth and eyes open as if he was shouting. When he saw Joe, Richard screamed and froze. Sarah's instincts were more practical, and she rushed to Joe in the hope that there might be a particle of life that she could revive. In vain. Richard placed a blanket over Joe's body, which Sarah snatched away.

"Delegates can now vote on the app," the chair announces.

Joe Stein was buried on 4 September, the day when millions protested against an attempt to shut down the Solidarity Committees, and to end the factory occupations and worker-led self-management of factories, supermarkets, restaurants and call centres. These were the days when everyone wanted to speak, so the crowd who gathered around Joe's death talked for nearly four hours. Friends stepped forward with stories, comrades offered anecdotes, powerful lessons that Joey had left them, but Sarah didn't speak. The newfound liberty did not help the dead. It seemed to Sarah that Joe's body was weighed down by the recent freedom and that his death was harder to carry amid the jubilation of the present.

Sarah was being prodded by Arnold, "Have you voted, comrade?"

The chair announced, "The motion is defeated."

Arnold turned to Sarah and assumed she was crying for their small victory.

14 – Postscript

I don't celebrate my birthday any more but I'm always being asked by younger comrades to resurrect the past. I'm busier today than I've ever been, and we still have an incredible amount of work to do – I suppose we couldn't know before that the major task of any great, popular and global rebellion is to keep nourishing the revolution. My job – as I now see it – is to help sustain the popular energy that was unleashed around the world after 2024, writing, visiting places, and when necessary, organising resistance. Even as an older man I am still capable and ready for action! I haven't yet reached the serenity of old age, which we falsely believe to be an entitlement, a privilege of the old. On the contrary, one of the disadvantages of the world we are creating is that death becomes harder. Leaving a world that has cursed us and cast us into despair and loneliness is one thing, but in a world where we are increasingly filled with love for each other, death becomes so much more difficult to bear.

We must remember that at the time they only had what in hindsight were but vague impressions and flimsy analyses. Sometimes I try to forget the last sixty years and when I do this, I think I've got the partial view that Joe, Sarah and the others had to manage on. I mean it didn't have to happen, our revolution didn't have to happen, and neither did Joe have to die. But then again history isn't a jigsaw puzzle for us to complete.

If you look around, like me, with one eye closed, you can see the past more clearly, more generously.

Never forget that day-in-day-out they organised, they unionised, they collected money for asylum-seekers, they fought against racist violence and the destruction of the earth, and they chose not to accept. Against all odds.

Speaking of defying the odds, I can still see Sarah laughing with her head thrown back and her arms in the air.

We were arguing, thirty years ago, about how quickly everything had changed, and I said, "But it didn't come out of the blue!"

"Nothing comes out of the blue except fish, Ricky," she shouted exultantly, then said, "Behind us there were years of patience and misery."

They had to manage on both the sombre gradualism of the world, and their inspiration to want to change it. Hard to believe today, but they were a constantly beleaguered majority *in potentia*. Maybe this is what Joey could never do – perhaps he never understood that his passion to transform the world came precisely from the loneliness he felt at having to live in it, the oppression of that reality and the exhausting struggle to remake it.

Little was ever said about revolutionary exhaustion, but generations of us were broken by Sisyphean labour. Time and again we were shattered into a thousand isolated pieces, forced to find our way out alone. Yet there was never a path that could be taken solely by one person.

I can still remember how we lived, so often in a haze of depression, solitude, and madness. The corners of the world where we resided – in our families and relationships but not, understand this, as you see them today – were often places of terrible isolation. It was in these places, with our lovers, comrades, and families, that we acquired the real battle scars that marked us out as the damned. They cushioned us of course, but only like a boxer who returns bleeding to his corner at the end of a round, seeking solace and advice, only to be pushed back into the ring when the bell sounds, to be beaten and bruised again and again. The truth is that we returned to our families, comrades and lovers because these were the *only* places to go, the only places that existed, the only places from which, despite all, we could lick our wounds and re-start the struggle to survive, over and over again.

Yet the haze cleared from time to time and allowed us a proper glimpse of our true revolutionary selves, of who we could become. I know that this is what Joe was fighting for, to clear the haze, to finally see again, to become human and in the process support others to come into existence as well.

Joe Stein was unique, but so were all the others who went down in the flood – who didn't survive the great turn of our world, and in our lives. Those who, like Joe, were on the cusp of the change, and fell, just as we began to win, but also the countless, mighty tide of people, so many of them, who fought before Joe and were defeated, their struggles and lives broken, so that others – like you and I – could finally rise and inherit the world.

Rest in Power, Joe!

Ricky Ujobolo
(Lower River Valley – formerly London, 2084)

Artist: Sula Gordon

Bloom[2]

Lena Grace Anyuolo

Kanyoni kaja...[3]
Kanyoni kaja...
Kanyoni kaja...
Chal nade Baba[4]
The village slowly comes to life
The bees on the way to collect pollen
A sweetening for the day
I kissed your hand on the way to Kikuyu
Wiathera, Akinyi, Aleyo and Mumbi climb in and out of fences
A nourishment for the day
Earth our mother holds us softly
pillowing where we step
Mrogi fare[5] takes a bath in the water tank's overflow
While grey flycatcher birds
As rare as white rings around their eyes,
Shelter us

We are preparing to sing our song of ujasiri,[6]
Jabali and Sulwe
archive our memory in pictures
and emwolo,
The humility of great warriors

---

2 This poem was originally published in Lena Grace Anyuolo (2022), *Rage and Bloom*, Kampala: Editor House
  Facility Ltd, pp. 62-63.
3 A Kikuyu singing game.
4 A Dholuo greeting.
5 A bird that doesn't get easily trapped in a slingshot.
6 Bravery in Kiswahili.

This is the world we built
Through struggle and arms,
we bore love
and surrender from old ways of unsatisfied consumption

Using the ballot and the pen
We colour in the black and white of race,
and sexual exploitation.

We bloom a colourful field of musical song

These are my comrades,
My sisters and brothers
Come,
Let us gather,
To lay the structures for a joyous existence

In Praise of Really Existing Comradeship: Gratitudes

> Compañerx,
> you know
> that you can count on me,
> not up to two nor up to ten
> but count on me.
> (Mario Benedetti)[1]

Isn't being able to count on someone, and being a someone for somebody else – not once, or twice, but counting on someone, and being a someone for somebody else – one of the most beautiful expressions of what it means to be a friend, a relative, a companion or a comrade? Isn't being able to say to someone, "I've got your back," and hear the same words spoken to you when you are in crisis, one of the most caring, reassuring, restorative, enheartening and empowering ways of being together and relating to one another socially and politically, that is humanly, especially in times of seemingly never-diminishing existential hardship and adversity, everyday war and structural violence, increasing breathlessness and exhaustion, widening despair and depression and yes, the occasional and at times threateningly permanent presence of left solitude and loneliness in our lives?

Apologies for finishing the paragraph on such a sobering note, because, truth be told, despite the frankly disgusting capitalist, colonial and heteropatriarchal status quo, there is clearly all kinds of amazing, revolutionary stuff being pulled off, against all odds, day-in-day-out by countless very, very good people and their/our collectives across the planet, and there can thus be no doubt that individual hopelessness, resignation, isolation and related left downers can (= ideally should) only ever be temporary states of (aching) mind and (breaking) heart, before we eventually recompose ourselves and literally regroup with others to continue the struggle. Then again, why not say out loud that in today's "great and terrible and complicated world" as *Compagno* Gramsci[2] once called it, a comrade in need continues to be a comrade

---

1 For an English-language selection of Uruguayan writer Mario Benedetti's poetry, see Mario Benedetti (2012), *Witness. The Selected Poetry of Mario Benedetti*. (Translated by Louise B. Popkin. With an Introduction by Margaret Randall). Buffalo: White Pine Press.
2 From a letter to Giulia Schucht, May 18, 1931, *in* Antonio Gramsci (1965), *Lettere dal Carcere*. Turin: Einaudi, p. 437.

indeed, and that looking out for someone and being looked out for by others is not only a basic ingredient in Rosa Luxemburg's elusive recipe of how to be human,[3] but also a fucking privilege-cum-treat, because, really, without us, we were, are and will be nothing, although – let's not kid ourselves – being there for and with each other is definitely hard reproductive, material labour and (finally) deserves to be recognised as such. No rest for the weary.

In sum, left comrade-, friend- and/or kinship is not a metaphor. It is not an ideological abstraction; it is not rhetorical hot air (fingers crossed). It is, first and foremost, a repertoire of life-giving actions – and presences – in time and space, and as such constitutes, following Jodi Dean in her reading of Soviet writer Andrey Platonov's soul-shaking novel *Chevengur*: "the zero point of possibility, what is left when everything else is gone, remainders existing in ruins, at the negative place of beginning."[4] Says Dean elsewhere, this time picking up from Mark Fisher after the latter's 2017 suicide (Rest in Power!): "We have to teach and encourage each other, be patient, encouraging, maybe even forgiving – especially of those who are on our side. If we aren't comrades, we can't fight the long fight."[5] Amen. Or rather, Hallelujah, because the negative place of beginning, the zero point of possibility for the composition and production of this book about and written from inside Left Loneliness(es) has been the unwavering patience, encouragement and support of a great many people – among individuals, communities and ancestors – true masters of the arithmetic of comradeship and therefore more than worthy of our collective praise and gratitude.[6] THANK YOU and let the celebrations begin.

hjje

---

3 From a letter to Mathilde Wurm (December 28, 1916), *in* Rosa Luxemburg (2011), *The Letters of Rosa Luxemburg* (Edited by Georg Adler, Peter Hudis, and Annelies Laschitza. Translated by George Shriver). London and New York: Verso Books, p. 363.

4 Jodi Dean (2019), *Comrade. An Essay on Political Belonging*. London and New York: Verso Books, p. 54.

5 Jodi Dean (2020), "Capitalism is the End of the World," *Mediations*, 33.1-2 (Fall 2019-Spring 2020), pp. 149-158. Available at: www.mediationsjournal.org/articles/end-of-world.

6 The decision to use the word 'gratitude' was inspired by Catherine E. Walsh's beautiful gratitude section in her 2023 *Rising Up, Living On. Re-Existences, Sowings and De-Colonial Cracks*. Durham and London: Duke University Press, p. ix.

alejandra ciriza: All *mi gratitud* to my brave feminist friends; my fellow women militants, kidnapped by the Armed Forces and murdered in La Perla, Córdoba; to my father for his insubordination and his courage; to my ancestors because from their torn flesh comes the duty of my memory; to my children for their lives, who have given me so much.

Derefe Kimarley Chevannes: Gratitude to the fearless women in my family: Winsome Chevannes, Kerry-Ann Chevannes, Sandra Walters, Althea Lewis, Gabrielle Graham, Elieth Murray and Veronica Lewis. You all have given me the courage and the support to find my voice and claim my stake in this world.

Richard Gilman-Opalsky expresses gratitude for the friendship and love of Robyn who walks with him through sadness and despair, side by side, looking for hope in hopeless times.

Sevgi Doğan: I convey my *minnetarlik* to Ismail Beşikçi, Ibrahim Gürbüz, Erkan Doğan and, in particular, HJJE – without him it could not have been realised.

Patrick Anderson: My gratitude to Schnuffel & Puff – without them, nothing.

Jane Anna Gordon: Profound thanks to Lewis Ricardo Gordon and John Comaroff, who meditated with me on this book's challenging theme, and to Sula Ruth Gordon, whose distinctive eye clarifies so much.

Giulia Longoni: *Gratitudine per "todas las compas marchando en reforma,"* who teach me the real meaning of sisterhood every day and contributed to make me who I am. To my comrade-sister Sevgi Doğan, who showed me that passion and commitment to the cause are amazing and can be proudly shared. To my grandmother, mother, sister and father (the only man in a family of independent women), because I love them, and they love me. To Marcello Sessa who knows me so well by now, he has been able to perfectly represent what I was trying to express with his beautiful drawing. To comrade Hjalmar for involving me in this project and for so much more.

Lena Grace Anyuolo: I'm grateful to everybody. Let's keep going! Amandla.

Kimberly Chiimba would like to express her gratitude to her cousin Unathi Chiimba who is the model in the painting in the book, and her mother for inspiring her to create and feel the precious companionship of art.

Meghan Markin: I am grateful for the work of Derefe Chevannes, lending his words to the silenced voices of others and amplifying the community around him. I am grateful to have my name attached to a project that promotes equity and action. And I can only hope that my small contribution to this work, with my art, will reflect that gratitude.

Hjalmar Jorge Joffre-Eichhorn: It's been a mighty rough ride in recent years, neither pretty for myself nor for those around me, so my special *gratitud/Dankbarkeit* goes out to all those who have stayed the course and supported me in myriad of ways to somehow hang on to the red downward spiral, especially Lars, Pat, Jo, Saleem, Sabrina, Tracy, Tina, Jana, my parents and Sevgi. GRAZIE. I owe you a drink and a hug. Or two.

Leo Zeilig would like to express gratitude to those who have held and supported him during the great, recent (lonely) vicissitudes of life: Maurice Caplan, Gillian Zeilig, Tanaka Chiimba, Benjamin Joseph and Ray Bush.

Lena Stoehrfaktor: I'm always on the lookout for people who understand me, and whom I can understand. Through our contact, we find out what is important to each of us. We don't have to see eye to eye; what is important is that we try to do what is best for ourselves and others, and that we work in whatever form we can to create a better society. A better society means one that seeks to accommodate everyone. I am grateful to everyone who resists the apparently easy option of going it alone in neoliberal society. Rest in Power, Sandro!

Georgy Mamedov: My gratitude goes to Hjalmar. Without him being a pushy and demanding yet open and sensitive editor this piece would probably have never been written. I'm also grateful to A. for evoking aspects of myself I was not aware of until we met.

Marcello Sessa is deeply grateful to Giulia Longoni, because every time he meets her he feels like the fairy in Perrault's *conte*: a flower blossoms in his mouth instead of words, and he speaks spitting red roses; she blows him what is called *"le baiser de la fée."*

Sula Gordon: I would like to thank my husband Simeon Mark Cofie, my siblings Mathieu Gordon, Jennifer Gordon, and Elijah. As well as my parents. I am forever grateful for your love and support.

James Martel: I am grateful for all of my anarchist friends and comrades, for my wonderful, beautiful family and for the larger community that I feel a kinship with on the left. You all sustain me and I hope that I play a part in sustaining you as well.

Tate Quesada: When I think of *gratitud*, all the people who helped me along the way come to mind, those who saw my light and supported me. Trusting in the work of others is sometimes not easy and the trust they have given me replenishes me day after day. The path of art is full of instability and uncertainties, but also bright and hope inspiring.

Daria Davitti: I am grateful to the warmth of the sun and the cold sea water, for swallowing me whole when I wanted to disappear and helping me resurface although bones and soul were broken. And to the warm embrace of my friends, you all know who you are.

Nina Bagdasarova: I am grateful to my partner/husband, who is radically left in his political position but always right by my side. I also would not survive without my dear leftist friends: Georgy, Mohira, Anara and Charlie. My gratitude cannot be truly expressed, so let me simply say, with warm affection, take care, comrades, because I need you! And I care for you very much...

Artist: M. Lukyanov, CCCP, 1985

The Left Loneliness Collective

Patrick Anderson is a lifelong student of language and people, conflict and harmony, relationship and solitude. He has an admiration bordering on reverence for words, written and spoken, and the profound, at times circuitous yet always unbroken, lines of revelation and meaning they preserve. Cryptic crosswords and etymological databases unsurprisingly number among his chief sources of pleasure. Having lived, worked and studied in five continents, and with an MA in Conflict Resolution, his professional life largely consists in supporting individuals, organisations and diverse communities to navigate the world with courage, purpose and levity.

Lena Grace Anyuolo is a writer and a poet. She is the author of the poetry collection *Rage and Bloom*. Her work regularly appears in *Jalada Magazine, Writers' Space Africa, Ukombozi Review, Review of African Political Economy, Africa is a Country,* and *Gemini Spice Magazine.*

Nina Bagdasarova has a PhD in Educational Psychology and works as a professor at the Psychological Department of the American University of Central Asia in Bishkek, Kyrgyzstan. Her areas of research are education, equality and inclusion while her political position and activism take place from within a leftist spectrum close to the approach of queer communism. She has authored a number of academic papers and recently published a book dedicated to exploring the idea of left happiness (together with Mohira Suyarkulova and Georgy Mamedov).

Ismail Beşikçi is a Turkish sociologist, philosopher, revolutionary, and writer. He graduated from the Faculty of Political Sciences at Ankara University in 1962. In 1964 he began to work at Atatürk University's Faculty of Science and Literature as a research assistant. In 1968, he was dismissed from the same university after the publication of his book *Eastern Anatolian Order: Socio-Economic Fundamentals (Doğu Anadolu'nun Düzeni: Sosyo-Ekonomik Temeller)*. In 1971, he was arrested by the Diyarbakır Martial Law Court on the allegation of being Kurdish and separatist. He was subsequently sentenced to eight years and four months in prison for the book *Eastern Anatolian Order* and eight months for lectures he had given. Amnestied on 14 July

1974, he was imprisoned again several times in the following years, for instance in March 1991 due to a message he sent to the Night of Solidarity with the Kurds held in Germany in October 1990. Beşikçi has written dozens of books, most of which were banned, and has been imprisoned eight times, so far spending 17 years in incarceration.

Derefe Kimarley Chevannes is a native from Jamaica. He holds a PhD in Political Science. Chevannes primarily specialises in political theory and is also trained in the field of public law. His research focuses, broadly, on Africana political theory, with an emphasis on Black liberatory politics. His research project lies at the intersection of Africana Studies, Deaf Studies, and Modernity Studies.

Kimberly Chiimba is a young black British-Zimbabwean portrait painter based in London UK. Best known for her bright, natural and hyperrealistic paintings of contemporary Black subjects, she enjoys capturing and drawing inspiration directly from her family and external surroundings.

alejandra ciriza is a feisty feminist activist and human rights defender. She is the mother of Andrés, Valentín and Martina and the *abuela* of Amparo and Emiliano. She looks after plants and enjoys dancing. She is a researcher at CONICET and a professor of philosophy and feminist theories in the Faculty of Political and Social Sciences at UNCuyo in Mendoza, Argentina. Her research is situated at the intersection of feminist political philosophy and the history of women and feminist ideas, based on a perspective that recognises class, racialisation and *corporalidad*. ale has written, edited and published scientific articles, book chapters and books in her realm of expertise. She currently leads the master's program in feminist studies at UNCuyo, supporting the emergence of new researchers in this field.

Sevgi Doğan gained her doctorate degree from Scuola Normale Superiore di Pisa. She is currently a precarious post-doctoral researcher at the same university, where she also collaborates with the Scholars at Risk Network (SAR) – Italy. Her doctoral thesis, *Marx and Hegel: On the Dialectic of the Individual and the Social*, was published by Lexington Books (2018). Her fields of research are modern and contemporary political philosophy, (Italian) Marxism, Hegelianism, German and Italian idealism, Rosa Luxemburg, authoritarianism and totalitarianism, gender and feminist studies, the social and political modernisation of Turkey, and academic freedom. She has translated Gramsci's *Letters from Prison* from Italian into Turkish and submitted it to Alfa publishing house. Her most recent book *La grande malattia dell'Europa,* about HR violations in contemporary Turkey and with texts by Gustaw Herling, will be published by Rubbettino in 2023.

Richard Gilman-Opalsky is Professor of political theory and philosophy in the School of Politics and International Affairs at the University of Illinois at Springfield. He is the author of many articles and book chapters, and six books, including *The Communism of Love, Specters of Revolt, Precarious Communism* and *Spectacular Capitalism.* He has lectured widely throughout the world and his work has been translated and published in Greek, Spanish, French, and German editions. In 2018-2019, Dr. Gilman-Opalsky was named University Scholar, the highest award for scholarship granted at all three campuses of University of Illinois. Dr. Gilman-Opalsky's work explores the powers of everyday people, particularly those typically regarded as powerless. He challenges the idea that politics is the private property of the ruling political class, and aims to highlight how impoverished and marginalised people participate in the radical transformation of the world.

Jane Anna Gordon is Professor of Political Science with affiliations in American Studies, El Instituto, Global Affairs, Philosophy, and Women's, Gender, and Sexuality Studies at the University of Connecticut. She is, most recently, author of *Statelessness and Contemporary Enslavement* (Routledge 2020) and *Creolizing Political Theory: Reading Rousseau through Frantz Fanon* (Fordham University Press 2014) and co-editor (with Drucilla Cornell) of *Creolizing Rosa Luxemburg* (Rowman and Littlefield 2021). President of the Caribbean Philosophical Association (CPA) from 2014-2016, she continues to direct the CPA Summer School and to co-edit the *Creolizing the Canon and Global Critical Caribbean Thought* book series. With Lewis R. Gordon, she edits the new, open-access journal, *Philosophy and Global Affairs.*

Sula Gordon is a multimedia artist. Through her art she creates the world she sees and the world she wants to see. Gordon focuses on healing rather than pain, since it seems like the only time Black people are depicted it must be surrounded by suffering. It would give the impression that being Black is nothing but turmoil when she loves being Black. Through her paints, prints, and whatever else she can get her hands on, Gordon writes love letters to herself, her family, and her community, telling them their beauty is not unseen.

Hjalmar Jorge Joffre-Eichhorn is a German-Bolivian Theatre of the Oppressed practitioner, compulsive reader – printed books only – and reluctant writer. In recent years, he has dedicated himself to publishing a couple of activist books and in spite of his ever-deepening Left Loneliness he is still toying with the idea/desire of opening a leftist bookstore-cum-dancehall in the not too distant future. As a result, he has been obsessively hunting red kitsch, aka Communist memorabilia, to eventually be exhibited and worshipped in the store. So, if anyone wants to get rid of their Lenin busts, Angela Davis posters or Che Guevara beret, please do get in touch.

Giulia Longoni is a Ph.D. student in Philosophy at the University of Pisa. Her research interests focus on the concepts of gender, class and 'race' as theorised by the philosophical current of Marxist feminism, with particular attention to Rosa Luxemburg's work. Giulia's research aims to identify some of Luxemburg's main concepts and use them as critical lenses in order to critique the connections between mainstream feminism and the capitalistic system. Her interests include feminist philosophy, social justice, postcolonial and decolonial studies and class struggle. She is a feminist activist and co-founder of CONTRA/DIZIONI, a group which aims to introduce feminist philosophies to the Academic world.

Georgy Mamedov is a curator, artist and activist based in Bishkek, Kyrgyzstan. Georgy has co-authored and co-edited several publications including *A Book on Happiness for Young (and not so) and LGBT (and not only) People* (Bishkek 2020), the pioneering Russian language collection of feminist and queer science fiction, *Utterly Other* (Bishkek 2018); *Queer Communism is Ethics* (Moscow 2016); and *Bishkek Utopian* (Bishkek 2015). His most recent artistic projects include the experimental montage *TikTok: A Blue Blouse Edit* (2020); a collaboration with Werker Collective on the project *A Gestural History of the Young Worker* (2019); and the lecture-performance *Delirious Blues: A Philosophy Letter from the Low Life during the Parliament of Bodies* *at the Bergen Assembly* (2019). Georgy teaches history and theory of modern and contemporary art at the American University of Central Asia in Bishkek. In 2015, Georgy became a chevalier of the French Order of Arts and Letters.

James Martel teaches political theory in the department of political science at San Francisco State University. He works on anarchist politics, political theology, comparative literature, post-colonial theory and legal theory. He is the author, most recently, of *Anarchist Prophets: Disappointment and the Power of Collective Sight* (Duke 2022). He is currently working on a new book entitled *Material Rights: a New Law For the Living*. Previous books include *Unburied Bodies: Subversive Corpses and the Authority of the Dead* (Amherst 2017), *The Misinterpellated Subject* (Duke 2017), *Divine Violence: Walter Benjamin and the Eschatology of Sovereignty* (Routledge 2011), *Textual Conspiracies: Walter Benjamin, Idolatry and Political Theory* (Michigan 2011), and *Subverting the Leviathan: Reading Thomas Hobbes as a Radical Democrat* (Columbia 2007).

I am **Tate Quesada**, a visual artist born in Mendoza, Argentina. I studied in private painting workshops from a very early age. In 2005 I entered the Universidad Nacional de Cuyo, where I completed a Bachelor's in Visual Arts and Teaching and specialised in engraving. After experimenting with painting, my work turned towards the graphic arts, through which characters and stories emerge that allow me to express my way of seeing the world. Since 2014 I have been giving screen printing workshops in my private studio. I also work as a teacher at the Escuela Provincial de Bellas Artes, as a member of a group of artist-teachers. I am in constant search of creative expression.

Lena Stoehrfaktor is a Berlin-based rap and hip hop artist. Some of her most recent releases include "Die Angst vor den Gedanken verlieren" (2012), "Blei" (2018) and "Essenz" (2022). Lena not only walks through the streets of Berlin, she literally scratches its surface to reveal the dirt. In this sense, she doesn't just talk about the underground, she is the underground. DIY-mentality instead of economic interest, skills and flow instead of interchangeable blah blah. Lena is ready to confront anyone unwilling to act in solidarity with others. Compromise on this is out of the question.

Mohira Suyarkulova is a queer communist and feminist activist scholar living and working in Bishkek, Kyrgyzstan. She holds a PhD in International Relations from St Andrews University. Mohira is an "undisciplined scholar," who has been hosted by departments of political science, social anthropology, sociology and, now, psychology. Her research interests lie at the intersection of politics, art and activism. Most recently she led a participatory action study of the sexual lives of LGBTQ people in Bishkek with the aim of creating a queer sex education curriculum. Currently she is working on a Leftist manual on happiness alongside her colleagues and comrades Nina Bagdasarova and Georgy Mamedov.

Leo Zeilig is a writer and researcher. He has written extensively on African politics and history, including books on the working-class struggle and the development of revolutionary movements, and biographies of some of Africa's most important political thinkers and activists. Leo is an editor of the *Review of African Political Economy* – the radical African-studies journal founded by activists and scholars in 1974 – and an Honorary Research Associate at the Society, Work and Development Institute (SWOP) at the University of the Witwatersrand in Johannesburg, South Africa. Leo's critically acclaimed novel *Eddie the Kid* was published by Zero Books in 2013. It was praised in The Guardian: "This passionate, sad and well-told book offers a compelling portrait of a flawed young radical." *Eddie the Kid* won the 2014 Creative Work prize at the University of the Western Cape in South Africa. In 2017 Leo's second novel, *An Ounce of Practice*, was published by Hoperoad, praised in *The Conversation* as "a brilliant work of literary imagination that takes the reader to new realities in an engaging, moving read, hilariously humorous at times." Leo has recently published *The World Turned Upside Down* through Nigerian publisher Books Farm House & Publishers.

Index

Index

Index